PITCHING UP!

Romps from one camping catastrophe to another

Deborah Aubrey

This is for Steve, my lovely Yorkshireman, and for the nicest, kindest, most generous woman, Aunty Jean xx

ISBN-13: 9798756400403
ISBN-10: 1477123456

April 2023
Cover design by: Art Painter
Library of Congress Control Number: 2018675309
Printed in the United States of America

CHAPTER 1

Day 1 – Friday

It suddenly occurred to Faye that she wasn't sure where they were headed. Brian had, of course, told her at some point but she hadn't paid much attention.

"Where is it we're going again?" she asked, as they hit the M40 motorway.

"Somewhere in't Cotswolds." He paused. "I think it's the Cotswolds."

"Might be a tiny flaw in the whole caravan trip if neither of us actually know where we're going."

"Worry not, I put the postcode into satnav woman on my phone, she'll guide us there."

"Will she? Hopefully not onto a gypsy caravan site like last time. My god, that was embarrassing, all those people and their pets staring at us like we'd just landed from outer space and what the hell were we doing there."

"She'll do fine."

"Or that time it suddenly declared, 'Prepare to go off-road' when we had to take that detour. Or – " she said, really warming to the subject now, " – all those times it took us down ridiculously narrow lanes where oncoming tractor drivers swore at us and you could feel the hatred from the queue of cars behind us. Or when it took us through tiny villages where we couldn't turn on the hairpin bends and the caravan got wedged between – "

"She'll get us there, you'll see."

Faye huffed. Jane, he called her, the satnav woman on his phone. She sounded very haughty and arrogant, more like a Camilla or a Princess Anne, the sort of voice that sips champagne at Ascot and has a high-pitched laugh that could crack crystal. Faye knew she shouldn't be jealous of it, but Brian always said, "Thank you, lass," every time Jane gave directions, which was, after all, her *actual job*. He flirted with Alexa in the house, too, "Thank you, lass," he'd say, when she gave him the music he'd asked for. Faye usually told him to stop flirting with the robots.

The journey through what did turn out to be the Cotswolds was scenic and, thankfully, uneventful; apart from a sharp turn in the road where they were unexpectedly confronted with a traffic island. Brian slammed on the brakes and, after everything had stopped rocking, said, "Well, if everything wasn't at the front of the van before it is now. All I can see," he said, looking in the rear-view mirror, "is a mountain of cushions piled up against the front window. Do we have to have so many cushions? It's like an Arabian harem in there."

There then followed a protracted bicker about cushions and overpacking, which only ended when they turned left into a pub car park and the satnav trilled, "You have reached your destination."

"Thank you, lass."

Faye huffed. "Hang on," she said, looking at the pub on their right, "Are you sure this is the place?"

"Satnav lady says so."

"And she's never wrong, is she! Wait, I'll check on Google. What's the pub called?" She glanced through the windscreen and tapped in 'The Woodsman'. The website came up and she shoved her phone into Brian's face, so close he had to push it away to focus. "Look!" she said. It was a photograph of a lovely-looking country pub surrounded by flowerpots and hanging baskets and people sitting outside at wooden tables, all smiling and happy in the sunshine. Faye lowered the picture and they both observed the run-down pub with its tubs and baskets full of long-dead plants. Two aged wooden benches stood outside, decidedly bereft of people.

"So, it's an old picture," Brian said.

"Doesn't bode well for the campsite though, does it."

Brian started singing, "Always look on the bright side of life," and whistling. He put the car into gear and drove slowly passed the pub on their right, through the car park, to a closed wooden gate at the end. In front of the gate to the left was a large shed with a RECEPTION sign above the door. Beyond the gate on the right, attached to the side of the pub, was a large concrete structure with TOILETS & SHOWERS printed on its whitewashed walls.

It was always exciting to arrive at a new place to pitch. Worrying too, in case it turned out to be a run-down bog of a field swarming with rabbits/midges/wild boar (like that one time in France). Beyond the Reception shed and the gate was a huge grass field bordered by trees and hedges.

Brian heaved himself with some effort out of the car and entered the shed. Seconds later he was out again carrying sheets of paper. He threw himself back into the car, making the car rock, and gave the sheets to Faye.

"There's a little shop in there but no one in it," he said, "They left these on't counter with our name on. Looks like there's a few other arrivals expected today as well. There's an X on't map where we're to set up camp, you guide us there."

"Jane not up to the job then, eh? This has to be handled by a *real* woman, does it?"

Brian stared out of the windscreen, waiting for Faye to 'do her thing'. When she didn't, because she was reading through the Local Area page, he said, "You can either open the gate or I can plough through it, your choice."

"Oh, right." Faye leapt out and scuttled to the gate, fumbled about for a bit trying to find the latch, fumbled a bit more trying to open the latch, and then, with a huge smile back at Brian, she proudly dragged it across the gravel driveway. He drove through and waited for Faye to get back in, her eyes eagerly scanning the field ahead. He followed the driveway round to the left.

It was a big field, recently mowed, with the grass left on top to dry. It was almost completely surrounded by trees. The driveway curved left again into a small hardstanding site for caravans that was bordered by bushes, long dead. Brian turned into it. There were six rectangular pitches, three on each side, with a grass area between them, the gravel driveway running down the middle. A forest of trees started a couple of feet away at the back and right-hand side

Faye got all excited with the site map. She had six pitches to navigate, one already occupied by an old caravan in the corner that looked like it had been there for a long time, so only five to choose from. Brian waited as her head bobbed up and down, looking at the map, looking at the five pitches, trying to figure out which one was theirs.

"Number?" he asked.

"Three, but I can't seem to – "

Brian turned the car to the right, having spotted Pitch Number 3 in the middle on the left. Faye looked a little confused, then realised Brian was reversing the caravan in and leapt out, ran to the back of the van and started waving her arms around. "Back," she cried, "Back. Back a bit more."

"I CAN'T HEAR YOU!"

"BACK! BACK!" Faye screeched, "IT'S A BIT CROOKED, CAN YOU MOVE IT THAT WAY A BIT?"

"I WOULD IF I COULD SEE WHICH WAY YOU'RE POINTING."

"LEFT, I'M POINTING LEFT!"

"YOUR LEFT OR MY LEFT?"

"YOURS! NO, MINE. OH WAIT!"

Brian still couldn't see her, had no idea where she was or which direction she was pointing. "FOR GOD'S SAKE, WOMAN, STAND WHERE I CAN SEE YOU!"

Faye suddenly popped into view in the driver's side mirror. She was waving. Was that backwards? Left? Right? All three? Brian turned the steering wheel and checked in the passenger mirror to make sure he wasn't reversing into a wall/

car/person/wife. By the time he looked back in the driver's mirror again Faye was gone. A tiny voice filtered through his open window, "Back! Back! Left a bit. Left a bit more. Now right. RIGHT!"

Brian sighed. They must have done this 30 times. More. And still Faye couldn't grasp the basic principles of guiding a 'long vehicle' backwards. He caught fleeting glimpses of her sidestepping left, sidestepping right out of view again, perpetually waving her arms like she was trying to take off. She suddenly stopped flapping and glared into the driver's mirror with slumped shoulders, her palms up, as if to say, 'Why aren't you listening to me?'

Brian did what he always did in these situations, for the sake of his sanity, for the preservation of his marriage and the avoidance of a bloody big row, he reversed the caravan by sight alone – God knows he barely caught a glimpse of his wife. He drove forward onto the pitch opposite, then manoeuvred the caravan expertly onto their allocated space, an expertise gained from lots and lots of practice. When he'd placed it perfectly on the edge of the gravel and turned off the engine, Faye came rushing up to the driver's window, all smiles, and cried "Team work!"

After 23 years of marital compromise, Brian simply smiled and nodded. He got out of the car, stretched his back and looked around.

The big field had a bell tent tucked away in the far left-hand corner and half a dozen family tents further up on the right. He turned and raised a hand at the man sitting outside the caravan in the corner, under a gazebo with a mug of tea and a book. "Hi there," he boomed.

"Hi," the man called back.

"Nice day for it."

"Yes."

Brian unhitched the car and drove it sideways onto the hardstanding in front of the caravan – it was a nice big pitch. Faye was already inside the van, despite the stabilising legs not being down yet, flittering round like a little bird, opening cupboards and flinging cushions around with wild abandonment. He picked up his battery drill from inside the caravan door and went around the outside, setting down the legs, while Faye started bringing out chairs and tables and piling them up at the back, where the electric hook-up was. Together they hauled the two long and heavy canvas bags out of the back of the car and set them down on the grass area next to their pitch.

"Ready, lass?"

Faye took a deep breath, rolled her shoulders and her head, and said, "Yes, I'm ready."

They emptied the poles out of one bag and strategically lay them on the gravel at the side of their van. They didn't bicker much, just about where each pole should go. Brian thought his wife had some sort of impediment that prevented her from actually visualising how the poles held up the awning. Faye thought Brian was very pedantic about placement.

A spark was briefly ignited as they rolled the awning out of its bag, with Faye convinced that the wrong side was the right side.

"Be different to have the curtain pole hangers on the outside for a change," Brian commented dryly, "Shake things up a little.

Faye looked at it and said, "Oh, this is the wrong way round, Bri."

"Which I think I mentioned about 10 minutes ago."

They hauled the canvas round and began securing it onto the side of the caravan. All Faye had to do was 'thread' the canvas edge into the metal slot that ran across the top, while he pulled the whole awning across. He either pulled it too fast, "Slow down, I can't thread it in that quick!" or too slow, "Hurry up, my arms are killing me!" He imagined himself on a boat, hauling the sail up the mast. He thought about maybe buying a blow-up awning, or maybe a little one-man sailing dinghy.

Faye thought about how nice it was all going to look once it was up.

Once the awning was securely attached to the caravan they glanced briefly at each other, knowing what was coming next. This was the most volatile part of 'setting up camp', the Erecting of the Poles and the Lifting of the Canvas. They'd almost come to blows once in France, and in Devon Faye had just stormed off, leaving him to do it on his own; luckily a fellow camper took pity on him and wandered over to help.

In Wales, during a storm equalling the force of their arguing, Faye had almost been carried off inside the awning by strong winds. He could still see her face now, smooshed against the plastic window, screaming out his name. He felt he had hesitated a millisecond too long and still felt a thump of guilt that he had, at the time, hoped she would be carried far, far away. Thankfully the wind blew her and the awning up against their big car and not over the cliff edge.

Erecting and Lifting never failed to set off an argument as they both sweated and manoeuvred themselves underneath the heavy canvas, but today might, just might, be the first time they did it without swearing or threatening each other with divorce or death.

Maybe.

Faye disappeared underneath the canvas and strained to lift the middle pole, holding it in position so at least the canvas was raised and not smothering them. The still saggy roof messed up her hair as she stood there, stoically holding the pole, waiting for Brian to attach the roof poles onto the caravan. She hated this bit, feeling claustrophobic and ever so slightly panicky. Why didn't he get a move on? She was bloody boiling in here.

"You can let go of it now," Brian finally said, "It should stand on its own."

Faye let go with a sigh of relief and went to help raise the other poles. Except the middle pole didn't stand on its own at all and tilted over, crashing down on her head and causing the roof to cave in. She yelped in pain.

"Bloody hell, lass!"

"It's not my fault, you said it would stand on its own!"

"Did I say it was your fault?"

"No, but the tone of your voice says I'm entirely to blame."

"Just hold it up again."

Faye huffed and forced her way through the fallen canvas back to the pole, heaving it up again and holding it firmly with one hand. She brushed her hair away from her face with the other, wishing she'd tied it back, wondering if she could do it now. She pulled a hairband from her jeans pocket and supported the pole with her shoulder, struggling to lift her arms up against the weight of the limp awning. The pole immediately dropped, whacking her sharply across the head again. She cried out in pain and heard Brian huff, which annoyed her even more. She quickly tied back her hair, hauled the pole up again, gripping onto it with both hands, pretending it was Brian's neck, as Brian raised the front and back poles. Faye's hairband fell out and her hair dropped again, sticking to her sweaty face. She growled in frustration. Brian yelled, "Just hold the bloody thing, woman!"

"I *am* holding it!"

"Hold it properly!"

"How many ways are there to hold a pole?"

"You seem to find new ways each time, none of them particularly effective."

Faye was about to snarl some equally sarcastic answer when she sensed they weren't alone inside the awning. There was someone in there with them but she couldn't see through the great swathes of canvas all around her. She heard Brian talking to someone in a surprisingly low voice. Suddenly a man, a total stranger, appeared out of nowhere. She started for a moment, flinching as the man reached out a hand, but he smiled as his hand curled around the pole she was holding. "I can take it from here, if you like?" he said.

"Oh. Yes. That's very kind of you. Thank you."

"Exact words your husband used," he laughed.

She moved away with a swell of relief, lifting the canvas in front of her until she met up with Brian and helped him clip and extend the side poles to the caravan. When that was done and she was finally outside in the fresh air again, hair awry, the two men wordlessly rolled up the doorways. Funny, she thought, watching them, how men could do that, just seemed to know what needed doing without saying anything. Faye flittered about, throwing down the groundsheet, positioning tables and chairs and hooking up the electricity. This was the bit she liked most, setting up home.

"Thanks for the help," Brian said to the man. "Usually takes us a lot longer than that, what with all't bickering and death threats."

"No problem. I'm Mark, by the way."

He held out a hand and Brian shook it. "Brian, and this is my wife, Faye."

Faye popped her head out of the caravan door and gave a little wave.

"You couldn't give me a hand with the coolbox, could you, lad?"

"Sure."

They went to the back of Brian's black Kia and he lifted up the boot. Inside sat an enormous coolbox. Mark gave an appreciative whistle and Brian nodded proudly. "40 litre capacity, mains, 12 and 24 volts."

"Impressive."

"Best thing I ever bought," Brian boomed, patting it. "Here, grab a handle."

They lifted it down onto the gravel.

"Blimey, what have you got in here?" Mark asked.

Both men looked at each other and laughed.

"Dehydration is a serious risk at this time of year."

"Absolutely."

"Holds 56 standard cans of lager."

"Wow."

"I know."

Brian pulled out the handle on the side and dragged it under the plastic table Faye had set up beneath the caravan window. Right on cue, she opened the window and popped out an extension cable. Brian plugged it in and fell back with a gasp of satisfaction into a camping chair.

"I think we deserve some cold refreshment after all that hard work," he said. He opened up the coolbox and Mark noticed that it contained a carton of milk, a small tub of margarine, a bottle of fizz and about 30 cans of lager. Brian pulled out two and offered one up to him. Mark was about to sit down and take it when his mobile started ringing.

"Sorry," he said, glancing at his screen, "I have to take this," and walked away.

Faye, who was now diligently hammering in awning pegs because Brian's back had been playing up lately, heard him say, "There's nothing to talk about," quite irately, before he disappeared into his caravan. She was instantly intrigued.

"Woman trouble," she said to Brian, "Bet you anything he's got woman trouble."

Brian didn't care, it was none of his business, and also, he didn't care. He was about to pull back the tab on his cool lager when Faye put her lips next to his ear and said, "Water before beer, Bri."

He hauled himself out of the chair, barely rested from the Raising of the Awning. Faye had already hooked up the electric, filled the toilet cistern with water and 'blue', and set up the greywater container for the sinks. His job was water supply.

He attached the handle to the Aquaroll and looked around for a tap. He spotted one at the end of the caravan area, right next to Mark's van, and headed towards it. Except, when he got there, Mark came out of the caravan and started pacing up and down, talking animatedly into his phone. When he heard the approaching sound of hollow plastic rolling on gravel he turned and looked awkward. Brian threw up a hand and said, "No problem," turning left through some dried up bushes that bordered the caravan area and heading off across the grass towards the toilet block, where he assumed there'd be another tap.

There was. He hauled it back, connected the pump, and flopped into the chair under the awning.

"Cup of tea?" Faye asked.

"Tea?" he roared, "It's beer time." He picked his abandoned can up off the table and pulled back the tab. It gave a satisfying click, followed by a gratifying hiss.

"Brian!" Faye cried, "It's only quarter-past three!"

"It's five o'clock somewhere."

"Not in the Cotswolds, it's not."

"Close enough." He took a long swig from the can. It cooled and refreshed his parched throat. Faye tutted her disapproval but he didn't care, he was on holiday, he could do what he liked on holiday.

Even so, when he'd finished it he quietly slipped it under the caravan, behind the wheel, and opened another.

* * *

Mark sat outside the caravan on that Friday afternoon. It had been a hot day so far, too hot to actually do anything, he decided, so he hadn't, he just lounged around, tinkering with a few things in the caravan and making endless cups of tea to pass the time. Truthfully, he was bored. It had seemed like a good idea to take a break from work, to sit and think for a while, he had a lot to think about, but he discovered self-exile wasn't really his bag at all and solitude didn't make thinking any easier.

He'd actually popped into work twice this week to see how they were getting on without him, but his small team were well on top of things and coping perfectly fine, which made him feel a bit redundant. Now he sat around the caravan, his mate's caravan on his mate's campsite, and tried to ponder the meaning of his life. He'd been pondering for almost three weeks now.

At least Friday afternoons gave him something to look forward to, a distraction from the chaos going on inside his head. The 'newbies' usually arrived on Friday and he had a ringside seat. You could learn a lot about people and the state of their relationships from observing them set up camp. If only insight into his own relationship was so easy, he mused. He pushed the thought away and dunked a chocolate digestive into his mug of tea.

The first one came mid-afternoon. A small caravan, two-berth, old and ever so slightly shabby, so not a wealthy couple. And here they were, Mr and Mrs Couple, Mrs Couple getting out of the black Kia to 'assist' Mr Couple reverse the caravan onto the gravel pitch and doing a very poor job of it. They were one pitch away from him on the right-hand side, which gave him a good view, and within earshot too. Mark snuggled deeper into his chair and dipped another chocolate biscuit into his brew.

Mark didn't have to struggle to hear Mr Couple as he reversed the caravan onto the pitch, the man had a bellowing voice. "FAYE! STAND WHERE I CAN SEE YOU, WOMAN! WHERE IN'T HELL ARE YOU NOW?" There was no doubting his accent, Yorkshire through and through. When they'd parked up Mr Couple got out, looked around, spotted Mark and gave a wave of a giant hand, so a friendly bloke.

They looked to be in their early 50s. Mr Couple was tall and heavily built, not fat but wide in all directions, a huge bear of a man in a giant t-shirt and shorts. He had thick salt and pepper hair, neatly cut, and a huge but well-trimmed beard. The woman was medium height, shoulder-length brown hair, quite a nice face from what he could see from this distance. She was a flitterer, he noticed, jumping from one job to the next, never quite finishing what she was doing before starting on another; unfolding chairs on the grass, getting distracted by pulling down the legs of a camping table, one leg down before hurrying to drag the groundsheet out of the caravan boot.

The husband was a plodderer, just got on with it, pulling heavy green bags from the back of the car and emptying them onto the grass. Mark dubbed them The Divorce Bags after watching several erections and several fights over the last three weeks. He watched as Mr and Mrs Couple threaded the awning onto the caravan, a critical pressure point in any relationship. There was some frustrated hissing but no actual fisticuffs, he'd seen worse; one couple last week had given up entirely, pushed the whole awning into the caravan with some considerable fury and driven off, still screaming at each other.

With the awning attached to the caravan they disappeared underneath and began erecting the poles. There was a lot of metal clanging, a bit of muted hissing. When the awning collapsed and the woman cried out in pain for the second time Mark decided he couldn't just sit and watch and wandered over.

"Need a hand?" he said, approaching the large bulge under the canvas which he assumed to be the man.

"Oh. Yes. That's very kind of you. Thank you."

Mark ducked under the fallen awning and made his way inside. The woman seemed a bit startled to see him, but smiled quick enough when he took the pole from her. He stood and held it while they clipped poles together and soon the awning was up. "Team work!" cried the woman.

The bearded man introduced himself and his wife, Brian and Faye, and asked for a hand with the coolbox. It was a pretty impressive coolbox, the biggest he'd ever seen. Brian offered him a cold beer from it and he was just about to take it when his mobile went off.

"Sorry," he said, glancing at the screen and walking away, "I've got to take this."

He didn't want to take it. Janis called him at least 10 times a day, asking where he was, begging him to come home, but he wasn't ready yet, wasn't sure if he'd ever be ready. She cried a bit, got angry, cried again, the same old routine.

Halfway through the call Brian suddenly appeared at the water tap next to his van, but the big man just threw up a hand, turned his head, and quickly plodded off towards the shower block. Shortly after that Janis hung up.

Even 20 minutes later he still felt guilty and annoyed and, yes, more than a little angry. This wasn't his doing, she'd caused this, not him. He felt his anger again, but then a large motorhome pulled up at the gate by Reception. Mark welcomed the distraction, briefly wondering if he had time to brew another cuppa before they arrived at the pitches. He watched a tall man leap out of the driver's seat and enter the Reception shed. He quickly reappeared and started up the motorhome before Mark could raise himself to put the kettle on. He sat back to watch, tealess and nibbling on dry chocolate biscuits.

The windscreen of the motorhome was so huge as it trundled towards him that he could clearly see the occupants within; a long-faced man with tight lips, and a woman who was smiling but looked quite tense in the passenger seat. The grey beast pulled onto the pitch in front of him but neither turned their heads to acknowledge him, or perhaps they were too high up and didn't see him sitting beneath the gazebo. He watched the driver haul on the steering wheel and reverse onto the pitch opposite at a slight angle. It drove forward again, then reversed and stopped half-way on.

The woman jumped down from the passenger side and hurried to the back, standing on the driver's side and guiding it silently with her arms. Mark could see the man's expression tighten as he navigated the huge grey beast into position. The woman, quite small, black curly hair pinned to the top of her head, raced up to the driver's side. Mark couldn't hear clearly but words were exchanged, the man's fierce and abrupt, the woman's gently high-pitched and placatory. She bowed her head before scuttling to the back of the motorhome again. It took three more forwards and backwards before it finally parked.

The man clambered behind his seat into the motorhome, disappearing for a few minutes as the woman waited patiently outside the door. The man leapt out wearing a backpack, glanced at his watch and said, "I'll be back around 7.30 for dinner."

"Okay, darling. Have you got your directions?"

"Of course. I've left twenty pounds and seventy-six pence."

"Yes, darling."

The man bent and brushed a brief kiss across her cheek, then strode off through the dead bushes around the caravan area towards the gate and disappeared.

The woman watched him until he was out of sight, then brought a hand up to her mouth, chewing absently on a nail. Her eyes rolled towards him, sitting under his gazebo, and her face instantly broke into a huge smile. She had a lovely smile, with a slight but cute overbite.

"Hello," she waved, "We're not in your way here or anything, are we?" She had quite a posh voice, very high and soft. "Only I'd hate to be in your way."

"No, no," he smiled back, "Absolutely fine."

"Lovely." A final beaming smile, and then she jumped up into the motorhome and hauled out a metal bistro set, laying them neatly on the gravel area, then disappeared inside again. He heard a vacuum cleaner being turned on, cutlery clattering, saw through the large windows as the woman rushed to and fro, apparently cleaning. After a while the delicious smell of cooking wafted towards him, definitely something with garlic, and his stomach grumbled. He went and made another cup of tea, then sat and waited for his next distraction.

It came about an hour later.

* * *

A flash of light caught the corner of his eye. When he looked over at the Reception shed he was totally blinded by a glare emanating from behind a white van. Mark reached out for the sunglasses on the table next to him and put them on. The van pulled away from Reception and headed towards the hardstanding pitches. It towed the smallest and shiniest bullet thing Mark had ever seen, the sun shining so brilliantly off its chrome surface that it was hard to look at directly, like the sunlight itself had been captured and magnified.

The van and its glowing bullet pulled slowly onto the pitch in front of his. It had a black wraparound window like the Mask of Zorro. Mark shielded his eyes and managed to read 'AIRSTREAM EVENT HIRE, BECKFORD' printed on the side. Two men jumped out wearing matching shorts and t-shirts. Without a word they promptly detached the gleaming tin can and manoeuvred it into position in the far corner, afterwards wiping their handprints from the chrome surface with dusters, one man saying, "Keep it clean, they've paid a lot of money for this." It looked very tiny on its pitch. The side door faced Mark, which was the wrong way but the right way for the shiny cannister as the Airstream was an American brand.

One man pulled open a small canopy above the door, like the peak of a baseball cap, securing it on two poles. The other pulled a table and two metal chairs from the back of the van and unfolded them, then went inside the shiny thing and opened tiny windows and vents in the roof. The electricity was plugged in, then they pulled what looked like industrial wind breakers out of the back of the van and started enclosing the area. When they ventured onto the grass area between him and them, which technically was Mark's pitch, he yelled out, "Oi, that's my grass." They pulled them off and fenced off the hardstanding, almost shielding the shiny can from view except for the reflective roof.

Was the Queen coming? A celebrity? Please, Mark thought, don't let it be Katie Price or, worse, Kerry 'nobody knows how hard it is to be me' Katona. Whoever it was it must have cost them a pretty penny, delivering shiny objects onto campsites didn't come cheap. Maybe it was Angelina Jolie and Brad Pitt, come to soak up the British countryside for a bit. Hadn't they broken up? Okay, maybe Harrison Ford and his skinny girlfriend, Flock-something, he'd read they liked to holiday on canal boats in the UK, maybe this was their next adventure, holidaying in a tin can on a slightly run-down campsite in the Cotswolds.

One of the men wandered over towards him with the Aquaroll and started filling it from the tap. Mark raised his voice against the sound of gushing water and asked, "What's all this in aid of then?"

The man shrugged.

"Someone famous, is it?"

He shrugged again.

"Anyone I might know?"

"Depends who you know," said the man, screwing on the top and hauling the Aquaroll back to the shiny object.

"Rude," muttered Mark.

When it was all done the men climbed back into the van and drove off, leaving the Airstream alone within the confines of the massive wind breakers.

Whoever was coming to stay they'd have to be bloody small to fit in that thing.

"Oompa Loompas," Mark laughed to himself. He stopped laughing when *Oompa, Loompa, doom-pa-dee-do* started playing on a loop in his head.

But at least he wasn't thinking about Janis.

* * *

Faye noticed it too. You'd have to be blind and have your head in a bucket not to.

"Bloody hell!" she cried, "Look at that! Brian, look at that! BRIAN!"

Brian snuffled awake in his camping chair, still clutching his can of lager. "WHAT?"

"Look at that!"

Brian turned his head to look where Faye was pointing, right opposite them, and cried, "OH MY EYES! WHAT THE

HELL IS IT?"

"Aliens have landed," Faye said, "It's a spaceship."

"Is it?"

"No, of course not."

"Where's the rest of it? It's only half a caravan!"

"Never seen nothing like it before. My sunglasses need sunglasses to look at it."

"Airstream," Brian declared, "Very expensive, very pretentious. Ignore it, it might go away."

"The people who brought it drove off and left it there. There's nobody in it now."

"Fascinating." Brian's head rolled back and his eyes started closing again. "Bloody thing's blinding me through my eyelids."

"It's intriguing," Faye insisted. "Why are you asleep anyway? You should be relaxing."

"I *am* relaxing."

"But you had a sleep before we left."

Brian straightened himself up in the chair, knowing any chance of sleep now was long gone. "I was up at four this morning," he said, "I was at work by five. When I came home I tried to catch some much needed zeds but it wasn't entirely restful because somebody, whose name I won't mention, kept screaming up the stairs, where's this and where's that and have you packed this, have you packed that? Which is why I'm now trying to counter sleep deprivation, and guess what, that same person keeps nudging me and telling me to look at bright, shiny objects!"

Faye humphed as Brian settled back in his chair again. He was just dreaming of sailing dinghies and perfect blue water when he heard the glug of escaping water coming from the back of the van. He half opened his eyes to see Faye racing towards the water tap with a now empty bottle.

"Hi again," she said to Mark, sitting under his gazebo with a cup of tea. "Saw you talking to one of the men who brought the shiny thing."

Mark nodded and smiled.

"Any idea what it's for?"

"None at all."

"Did they say who it belonged to, who was coming?"

"No."

"Didn't give any clues?"

Mark shook his head, still smiling. "Nothing at all."

"Oh."

Faye wandered back to the caravan with the now half full bottle of water.

Before the mystery of the shiny bullet thing could be suitably discussed, she noticed a small white van roar up to the Reception shed. It skidded noisily to a halt and a man dashed inside and dashed out again. He opened the gate, sped through it and left it open. The van raced down the gravel driveway and slewed left into the caravan area, despite it not actually towing a caravan. Faye couldn't see it now, it was behind them. After checking Brian still had his eyes closed, she jumped into the caravan to peer through the window.

The tiny Transit parked on the end pitch next to theirs. A man and a woman leapt out of the car, both young; the girl early 20s, the man early 30s. She was bleached blonde with her hair up in a clip, slim, wearing a very tiny dress that plunged at the front, not leaving a great deal to the imagination. She tottered unsteadily across the gravel pitch in high heeled shoes to the back of the van.

The man threw open the back doors and produced a roll of blue plastic and a large yellow hand pump, which he immediately used to blow up the air bed, both of them giggling and looking around furtively. When it was fully inflated he threw it into the back of the van and grinned at the woman. The woman giggled again as the man grabbed her round the waist and fell backwards, pulling her with him into the van. The back doors slammed shut. Inside, the woman shrieked, the man laughed, and the van rocked and shivered. Faye reluctantly tore herself away before Brian caught her and called her a 'curtain twitcher'.

There was, she thought, filling up the kettle, only one more pitch left, and then they would have a full contingent. She felt a bit excited about meeting new people, she liked people.

"Cup of tea, Bri?" she yelled.

A pause, and then, "WHAT?"

"CUP OF TEA?"

"You've already asked me once."

"I'm trying to steer you onto the straight and narrow."

"Too late, I'm already wavering down the bent and wide."

She heard the click and hiss of a can, followed by a very satisfied sigh.

She left the kettle and took a bottle of wine out of the fridge instead.

CHAPTER 2

"Where are we going?" Sophie laughed, as Tel's red sports car sped down country lanes, far, far away from the hustle and heat of London.

"Surprise," he grinned.

"What kind of surprise?"

"You'll see."

"Will I like it?"

"Of course." Tel gave a wry smile. She stared at his face, glowing like warm coffee in the sunlight. He was very handsome, incredibly intelligent and enormously attentive. He could be arrogant and sometimes Sophie liked that about him, that he was so confident, knew what he wanted and how to get it, sometimes it annoyed her, but not today, today she was just excited, she liked surprises.

A small pink suitcase and a smaller Briggs & Riley case sat on the back seat. The roof was down, the sun was out, and the breeze cooled her face as they raced down narrow lanes lined with lush foliage. A canopy of tree branches speckled the sun across their faces. It was so wonderful to be free at last, no more stuffy offices or dark courtrooms. Finally it was all *over* – they'd won, all their hard work had paid off.

She had to admit, it had been thrilling when Tel grabbed her hand in the middle of the company celebration and whispered, "Come on, let's get out of here and have some fun." Sophie wasn't a spontaneous person, never did things on the spur of the moment, always liked to plan things well in advance, not missing a single detail. It was how she worked too. But she had allowed Tel to drag her away from the office, to the amusement of their colleagues, who all jeered and whistled as they grabbed their coats and raced to the lifts. It added to the excitement of the win.

He took her back to her flat first and waited outside while she quickly packed a bag.

"What should I bring?" she'd asked.

"Enough clothes for a long weekend."

"But what type of clothes? Where are we going?"

"Pack whatever clothes are *comfortable*," he smirked, enjoying her excitement and her frustration. "All will be revealed. Now hurry up before rush hour engulfs the whole of London."

"Just give me a clue?" she begged him now in the car.

"No, you'll just have to wait and see."

"Oh please, Tel, just a little clue?"

He was silent for a long while and Sophie thought he wasn't going to answer, but then, as he navigated a particularly tight bend in the road, he suddenly said, very seriously, "It's something I know you've never done before. It's unique. Different. You're going to be wowed, Sophie, trust me."

Did she trust him? She still wasn't sure. Technically she'd known him less than a year, was that long enough to really know someone? She stared at him behind the steering wheel, his face glowing in the dappled sunlight, a cheeky smile playing on his full lips. He really was very good looking, and she liked it when he reached out a hand and rested it on her leg, rubbing gently with his thumb; it sent chills up and down her spine.

Sophie rested her head back on the seat and watched the tree tops whizz by overhead. It would be good to have a break, a proper break from the gamut of work, and it would be good to maybe get to know Tel a little better too.

"We're nearly there," he said, in his low, husky voice.

"Where?" she asked. "Just tell me, the suspense is killing me! A clue, one clue?"

"A clue?" Tel grinned, liking her frustration and impatience. "Okay, the man assured me that it was the top of the range, the very best on the market."

"What man? The hotelier? What's top of the line? The room? Is it a newly refurbished penthouse suite?" She could hardly contain herself. It was nice to be spoiled.

"I'm saying no more," he said.

"Oh, go on!"

"No."

"Cruel man." She pouted unashamedly and Tel laughed.

Miles of beautiful countryside passed by. Sophie had almost forgotten what countryside looked like, smelt like. She sighed deliriously.

"And," Tel said, turning left into the car park of a slightly run-down pub, "we're here!"

Sophie sat up straight in her seat, almost giddy with anticipation. She looked around. Good grounds, she thought, a rugged field surrounded by trees. She searched for sight of a great, majestic hotel; she was certain he hadn't brought her to a country pub surrounded by pots of dead plants. She hoped the hotel had a swimming pool, and maybe a spa with massage facilities, she could really do with a good ...

Sophie's excitement dimmed a little when the sports car came to a stop by a gate and Tel clambered out, smiling back at her mischievously. She could see no great mansion, only a very large shed with 'RECEPTION' printed above the door. Reception to what?

Sophie viewed her surroundings, hoping to spot tranquil and luxurious lodges, perhaps one of those amazing 'escape it all' tree houses she'd read about in *Cosmopolitan* that offered champagne and fine foods at the tinkle of a room service telephone. Of course she wouldn't spot them, they'd be hidden away, that was the whole point.

Tel bounced out of Reception and leapt back into the car. "Ready?" he said, flashing his perfect white teeth.

"Ready for what?"

"For your surprise?"

"Yes. Yes, of course."

Tel pulled away, drove through the open gate and into a

large, mostly empty field with some tents scattered on it. He followed the driveway round to the left, and then left again into an area that had rectangular patches of gravel on each side. Two caravans, a huge motorhome, a white van and the top of something very small and shiny were parked there. It looked like ... no, it couldn't be, but it looked suspiciously like a campsite.

Not here, she thought, horrified, surely not here.

The car stopped. Tel went "Ta da!" motioning towards a shiny object on their right that was surrounded by what looked like a plastic fence. He jumped out and rushed around to the passenger door, opening it for her. "Madam, your abode awaits."

Sophie couldn't bring herself to speak as she gingerly exited the car. She couldn't think, couldn't comprehend. He wouldn't have, would he? He hadn't, surely?

Tel pointed to a circle of barriers encompassing what she thought must be a spotlight it was so bright. The sense of anticipation dissipated. This was not what she'd been expecting at all. Top of the range? Top of the range *what*, exactly? A caravan? Good god, surely not a tent, he wasn't expecting her to sleep in a tent, was he? Did he not know her at all?

"You said you'd never been camping," he said, the smile hanging anxiously on his face as he looked at the disappointment on hers.

"No, and there's a perfectly good reason for that."

"I thought you'd like it?"

"Like *what*, exactly?"

Tel hurried to one of the three-foot barriers and pulled it aside, beckoning her inside. Sophie thought, 'If there isn't a bloody fairy bridge leading to a magical castle on the other side I'm off.' She stepped through the barricades and immediately had to shield her eyes from the bright, all-encompassing glow.

"Do you like it?" Tel asked.

"I'm not sure, I don't know what 'it' is, I can't see

anything. What is it?"

"It's a top of the range Airstream adapted for the UK market, at least according to the man I made the booking with this afternoon."

"What's an Airstream?"

"It's an American, aluminium travel trailer."

"A what?"

"A caravan."

Oh God, Sophie thought, kill me now.

"It's the best on the market. Although, I must admit," he said, peering at it through squinting eyes, "I was expecting something a little ... bigger."

Sophie laughed. "It looks like a metal bucket and it's burning my retinas."

"You said it was cute when we saw one in that *Thor* movie the other night."

"Chris Hemsworth was cute, I don't remember a caravan."

"Oh."

"Does it actually have a bed in it or is it just for show, like an ornament to put in your garden or something?" Maybe it was a water feature, or one of those Transformer things that turned into something else, like a country hotel.

"It has a pull-out bed, I think."

"You want me to sleep in a metal bucket on a *pull-out* bed?"

"It'll be cosy."

"It'll be claustrophobic."

"You don't like it."

He stood in front of her, between her and the gleaming brightness, and his smile slowly faded. Sophie felt bad. She was being a brat, a snob, one of those spoiled rich kids she so despised. She didn't like that about herself, that she could be such a cow. "I didn't say I didn't like it," she said softly, "I'm just ... surprised."

"You certainly look surprised, verging on horrified."

He reached out, taking a gentle hold of her hand, "You said you'd never been camping before, and I've never been camping before either, and I thought it would be nice to share the whole 'back to nature' experience together."

"I have been camping, once," she said softly, "with the Scouts when I was 10. Mom and dad made me go, they said it would be 'character building'. It was awful. I hated it, all those kids, all those stupid team games they expected you to play, the rain and the cold, the whole *outdoors* of it all. I called a taxi and was home the same day. Dad was furious."

He stared at her with his beautiful brown eyes, still in his office suit, as she stood there, still in her office suit, both spotlighted by the glare of whatever that shiny thing was behind him. "I'm sorry, Soph, I think I misinterpreted. This isn't your thing at all, is it."

She knew she should say something but didn't know what, exactly. 'Take me home, *immediately*?' or 'What the hell were you *thinking*?' perhaps, or maybe 'Are you completely out of your mind? I live in an apartment in Mayfair!' Instead, she said, "No, it's fine," and forced a smile to accentuate her lie. "It's lovely. Really."

"Are you sure?" He recovered from his slump and looked for all the world like a small child who'd been given a reprieve for some misdemeanour. "We can go home if you really hate it, or find a hotel nearby, or... something."

"No," she replied, feeling magnanimous, and ever so slightly resentful, "Let's give it a go, it might be quite fun." She didn't feel the conviction of her words at all, but Tel's smile reappeared and she was glad.

"I've brought champagne," he said.

* * *

"Ooh," said Faye, "Someone's come to the shiny spaceship. Two of them, a man and a woman."

"Outstanding," Brian muttered, not bothering to open his eyes.

"They look very posh. They're both wearing suits. Who

comes on a caravan holiday wearing suits? The man is drop-dead gorgeous though." She adjusted her sunglasses for a better look, trying to shield some of the glare with a hand. "And the woman is really quite stunning. But suits?"

"CIA," Brian said.

"Really? Do you think so?"

"Absolutely. Why else would they be wearing suits?"

"Yes," Faye breathed, excited. She turned her chair slightly in order to get a better view. "They're just standing there and talking. Neither of them looks very happy. No, wait, the woman's smiling. Now the man's smiling. Gosh, they're both so young and beautiful."

"So are you," Brian said, automatically.

"Thanks, Bri." She unconsciously flicked back her hair.

'Not young, obviously," he added.

"Thanks."

"Welcome."

Brian went back to sleep, totally disinterested. Faye couldn't tear her eyes away from the young couple, they were so beautiful and elegant, like supermodels. The man pulled a bottle from the back seat of the sports car. She heard the pop of a cork, probably champagne. How fabulous, she thought, it must be nice to be treated like that, made to feel special. She glanced at Brian, lying limp on the camping chair, his mouth wide, his snoring not yet fully revved up. She sighed and smiled. Good bloke but a bit lacking in the whole romance department. They had a good life though, they were happy, and she felt grateful for that, but the odd bunch of flowers or bottle of champagne wouldn't go amiss once in a while.

* * *

Tel popped the cork and they both gave a little cry of surprise as it flew off into the trees next to them. He went to open the caravan door to fetch some glasses but it was locked and he couldn't for the life of him remember where they said they were going to leave the key. He doubled up and briefly glanced underneath. There was a lot of gravel but nothing particularly shiny or key-like. He straightened up and smiled at Sophie, who was waiting in anticipation for the glasses, the bottle of champagne warming gently on the table outside.

Where would someone hide a key?

He bent slightly and felt across the top of the tyre next to the smallest door he'd ever seen. Keyless. Trying to look as casual as possible, he hitched up the trouser legs on his very expensive suit and fell to his knees, reached underneath, behind the wheel, and began tapping the ground. Nothing. He rested his head on the gravel and surveyed the length of the caravan, up and down – its footprint wasn't much bigger than his car. Still nothing. He stood up, brushing the dust from his knees, the dust from his hands adding to the growing patches of white. He strode as casually as he could to the back, where there was another door, quite high up actually, but that was locked too. He checked the top of the other tyre before falling to his knees once more to check behind it and under it.

Nothing.

Sophie was standing next to him when he stood up again. "Problem?"

"Can't seem to locate the key," he laughed.

"Where did they say they'd leave it?"

"I can't remember."

"Oh. Well, there's a blobby plastic thing at the front, have you checked in that?"

They both moved to the blobby bit at the front and looked at it. "Is there a button to open it or something?" Sophie asked. "Maybe we need a degree in mechanical engineering to figure it out, or maybe," she said, looking at the shining cannister again, "A degree in microdynamics."

Tel lifted the lid. There was a shelf inside. On the shelf were some cables and a few tools. Sophie leaned over and nudged at them with the tip of a manicured finger. A key revealed itself. Tel exhaled silently. "Shall we look inside?"

"Why not?"

"Prepare to be amazed".

"Already there."

They went back round to the side door. Tel fiddled to get the key in properly, then pulled it open with a flourish and went, "Ta da!" There was a gap between the floor and the door and he quickly pulled out the hanging step. Sophie gingerly stepped inside in her high heels. Tel followed. They stood closely together in the confines, looking at the innards of the Airstream, which looked exactly like the innards of a tin can, everything was aluminium.

"That is amazing," Sophie gasped, and Tel smiled with relief, "It actually looks *smaller* on the inside than it does on the outside." Tel's smile went down a notch.

There was a minuscule kitchen area on their right; above the tiniest sink and two hob rings were some storage hammocks, below was some shelving, what she hoped was a dishwasher and a microwave. In front of them was what looked like a high steel cabinet. She reached out and pulled the handle, thinking it might be a wardrobe, but it was worse than that, it was a tiny aluminium cupboard with a showerhead and a plastic toilet in it. She would *not* be using either

"I have a broom cupboard in my kitchen that's bigger than that," she said, closing the door. "In fact, my bathroom at home is three times bigger than this whole caravan."

"It's compact and bijou." Tel shrugged as best he could in the tiny space, adding, "Nice and cosy."

"I have a suitcase," said Sophie.

"Yes, I'll go and get it."

"Why? There's nowhere to put it."

"No, look, it's got loads of storage." He indicated the hanging hammocks and waved uncertainly at whatever cupboard space there might be underneath.

Sophie looked. She didn't like what she was seeing but she looked anyway. She bit her tongue, thinking, 'Don't be ungrateful, don't be a brat, don't throw a hissy fit, smile, SMILE!' She smiled. "Cute," she said.

"Oh, come on, Sophie, help me out here. It was very

much a last-minute thing, I did the best I could under the circumstances. This could be the best break away from it all you've ever had."

A break away from it all, she thought, or a Ray Mears survival course?

"We'll be lovely and comfortable - "

Cramped and tripping over each other.

" – cuddled up together - "

Fighting for space and air.

" – very romantic."

Nightmare come true.

"Glasses?" she said, remembering the champagne losing its bubbles in the heat outside, a bit like she was losing her fizz of excitement.

Tel checked the shelving under the sink. Empty. He checked the hammocks. Empty. There was nowhere else to search.

Sophie rolled her eyes and, feeling quite hot and sweaty in her suit, went back outside. Tel followed, wondering what the hell to do, this wasn't turning out how he'd imagined at all.

"I need a drink," Sophie said, picking up the champagne and considering just necking it straight from the bottle.

"Wait," said Tel, "I can fix this, just give me a sec."

His mind was buzzing. He had to save the situation, but what to do, what to do? He spied the caravan on the other side of the gravel driveway right opposite them. Two middle-aged people were sitting underneath an open awning on camping chairs, one a hairy giant, fast asleep, but the other was staring straight back at him and waving with quite some enthusiasm. He marched towards them, leaving Sophie standing there, still eyeing the neck of the bottle.

* * *

"He's coming over!" she gasped, shaking Brian awake.

"WHAT?"

"He's coming over!"

"Who's coming over?"

"The man from the spaceship! He's coming over here!" He walked, Faye thought, like a lithe panther, the tiniest of swagger in his shoulders. In her mind he moved in slow motion, with powerful music playing in the background and Morgan Freeman's voiceover saying, 'He was young, handsome, *magnificent*.' She suddenly felt a bit faint and forced herself to breathe.

Brian sat up. The man stood outside their awning and said, in a deeply husky voice, "Excuse me, I'm sorry to bother you, but you don't happen to have a couple of glasses we could borrow, do you?"

"Glasses!" Faye cried, leaping out of her chair and disappearing into their caravan, "We have glasses, lots of glasses. What type? Champagne flutes, I imagine, how fabulous. Here," she said, hurrying down the caravan steps, "Will these do?"

She held out two champagne flutes. Brian wondered why they had champagne flutes in the caravan, then remembered the bottle of Prosecco in the coolbox.

The man took them from her with a huge smile, displaying perfectly straight, perfectly white teeth. He exhaled, *breathing on her*. She suddenly felt faint again. "Thank you so much," he husked, "Really appreciate it. I'll bring them back when we've - "

"No, no, that's fine," Faye gushed, "Keep them, it's not like we need them or anything, this is a champagne free zone." And she laughed, and Brian rolled his eyes, and the man nodded with a smile and went back to the shiny object.

Faye fell back into her chair, fanning herself with a hand.

"Interesting display of fawning adulation from a woman of your age," Brian said with a grin. "We don't happen to have any sick bags in the caravan, do we?"

"Shut up, Brian, I'm having a flush. Does my face look red? How's my hair look?"

"You *do* remember you're married to a handsome

Yorkshireman?"

"I may be married, Brian, but I'm not dead, I can admire youthful gorgeousness if I want to."

"Far too young for you, lass."

"I can dream, can't I?"

Bored now, and marginally refreshed from his power nap, Brian glanced at his watch. "Right," he bawled, extricating himself from the chair, "Pub time!"

* * *

They sauntered down the gravel driveway, passed the white van next to theirs that rocked and emitted high-pitched shrieks of laughter behind closed back doors. They quickened their pace.

Faye popped her head into the toilets; three showers and three toilet cubicles, pretty basic but clean enough. The Reception shed still had its door open and they both wandered in. There was nobody behind the counter. Shelves were filled with random items of grocery, some small camping equipment, and essentials like can openers and candles, all covered in a fine layer of dust. A tall and full display fridge hummed noisily in the corner, next to a buzzing chest freezer with a glass top. The bread and buns were fresh though, as were some fruit and vegetables near the counter.

"PUB!" Brian bawled.

The Woodsman was quite old looking but not in an historic way, more a weathered, left to its own devices kind of way. There were various pots and hanging baskets outside full of long-dead plants, with a chalkboard beside the flaking paint doorway that just said 'Food'. Brian hoped it was better inside than it looked outside.

It was, but only marginally. As he opened the door for Faye he took a deep breath, expecting the delicious aroma of cooking but getting instead the stale smell of beer. The décor reminded him of when his grandad used to take him to the working men's club when he was little. It was dark and quiet, with a few people sitting at tables looking morose. Faye went off to pick a table, a big one to accommodate all the food they'd be ordering, she was famished. Brian approached the bar.

"What beers do you have, my good man?"

The barman – short and chubby, with a mop of unruly, mousy-coloured hair, somewhere in his 30s – replied, "Lager and stout."

Brian surveyed the taps lined up along the bar.

"We've just got Heineken," the barman said.

"The others for show, are they?"

"Barrels are empty."

"Have you considered buying full ones? I hear it's all the rage in pubs now." The barman looked at him blankly. "A pint of Heineken it is then, and what wines do you have?"

The barman glanced behind him at the bottles behind a glass-doored fridge. "White," he said.

"Chardonnay?"

"No."

"Sauvignon Blanc?"

"No."

"What, then?"

The barman sighed as he bent down, opened the fridge, pulled out a bottle from a bunch of similar bottles, and read the label. "Zin ... Zinfan ... "

"Yes, a glass of that, please."

The barman spent an inordinate amount of time looking for a corkscrew under the counter, located one, looked at the bottle, saw that it was a screw top, and struggled to unscrew it with a lot of huffing and puffing.

Brian fished out his wallet while he waited. "What do you recommend from the menu?" he asked.

"Menu?"

"You do meals here, don't you?

"No."

"There's a sign outside that says 'Meals'."

"Sez 'Food'." He offered no other information.

"What *food* do you do then?"

The barman took a deep breath. "Cheese toastie, baked bean toastie, ham and baked bean toastie, crisps, nuts and scratchings. There's snacks in the Reception shop, just leave the money in the honesty box on the counter. Or these," he said, slapping shiny pamphlets down on the bar, "are the menus for the Chinese and Indian takeaways in the village. They'll charge an arm and a leg for delivery and take about 90 minutes to turn up, if at all. Don't take the menus away, I've only got those two and other people might want to use them. If you want anything else use your Uber app, there's a MacDonald's, Burger King and Kentucky Fried Chicken a few miles down the road."

Brian considered the vast array of options. "Do the toasties come with chips and salad?"

"No."

"So, just toasties then?"

"Yep. There might be a couple of pies left in the freezer, I could throw one of them in the microwave if you want?"

"What kind of pie?"

"Meat."

"Any particular type of meat?"

"Just says 'meat' on the label."

"I see, and do the pies come with – ?"

"No."

"Not even oven chips?"

"Dunno how to work the oven, mate."

"Oh, you've not been here long then?"

"Ten years."

"And you've not figured out how to – ?"

"Kitchen is the girlfriend's department."

"And the girlfriend is ... ?"

"Not here."

"Estimated time of arrival of said girlfriend?" Brian asked, hopefully, as his stomach rumbled.

"Went to her mom's about a month ago, ain't been back since."

All Brian's hopes and dreams crashed into a cavern of hunger. "I'm sorry to hear that. What about instant mash and peas to accompany the microwave pies?"

"Don't know how to make instant mash, even if I had any, and I gotta keep an eye on the bar in case it gets busy, ain't got time to be faffing about in the kitchen."

Brian glanced around at the few people currently in the pub.

"Are you expecting a rush then?"

"No, not really."

He tried a different tack. "Have you considered hiring someone to cook meals while the girlfriend's away?"

"No."

"Okay then." Brian picked up the glasses. "Good chat."

The barman sat back on his stool behind the bar and shook out a newspaper.

He carried the glasses back to Faye at a table. "I can't find a menu," she said.

"And there's a very good reason for that. There's no meals at the inn."

"But it says 'Meals' on the board outside."

Brian glanced out of the window next to them, at the offending sign standing forlornly outside. "It says 'Food', not 'Meals'. 'Food' apparently consists of cheese toastie, bean toastie, or ham and cheese toastie."

"Does it come with – ?"

"No."

"Just toasties?"

"Apparently so. Oh," he said brightly, "The barman informs me there may be some pies lurking in the back of their freezer. Meat, he thinks."

"Does that come with – ?"

"No."

Faye looked aghast. "No pub grub?"

"No."

"But we always eat out when we're away."

"We did pass a Sainsbury's 10 miles down the road on our way in, maybe they have a cafe."

"I'm not eating meals at *Sainsbury's* all week!"

"Home-cooked meals it is then."

"But I'm on holiday, I don't cook on holiday, I never cook on – "

"I'll do it then."

Faye's eyes widened. Brian didn't cook, *couldn't* cook. The height of his culinary skills was a cheese omelet, and that was dodgy at best. She huffed and sipped her wine. It was warm. She grimaced and put it down. "What made you book this site?" she asked, a bit miffed now.

"You did."

"I did?"

"Yes, don't you remember? You saw it on Facebook and said it would be great to camp near Woodstock, where all the hippy gatherings happened in the 60s. Took me days to stop laughing."

Faye tutted. They sat in silence for a while, both contemplating this terrible blow to their holiday plans. She remembered now that one of the reasons she'd been drawn to this campsite in the first place was that it had a pub close enough to eat in every night if they wanted.

"Oh look," she said, looking up and suddenly brightening, "There's Mark."

Brian raised a giant hand as Mark strolled up to the bar. He nodded back with a smile. The barman actually seemed quite happy to see him and immediately pulled a pump into a glass.

"Come and join us," Faye called out to him.

"Unless you prefer to drink alone," Brian quickly added.

Mark picked up his pint and approached their table, still smiling. He seemed a cheerful chap, Brian liked that.

"They don't do meals here," Faye told him as soon as he sat down, her eyes still aghast.

"I know. I keep telling him to bring a cook in, he'd make

a roaring trade with the camping at this time of year, but he's a mean bugger, hates putting his hand in his pocket. Lazy, too."

"You know him well, then, the barman?"

"Yeah, Ant's an old mate of mine from school. I only live down the road. Well," he looked down at his pint, "I *used* to live down the road."

"Used to?" said Faye, but Brian gave her a look before any further questions could manifest themselves. She was dying to interrogate him until she knew every detail of his life, Faye loved getting to know new people.

"This used to be his parents' pub," Mark said, "But they had a health scare last year and went off to live in Spain, left Ant to run things. Not the best decision they've ever made. Nice couple. Then Ant's girlfriend left him about a month back and it's been downhill since then really, she did all the cleaning and the cooking. Guess she just got fed up of it in the end. No kids though, thankfully. Sorry." He looked at them both and gave a little laugh. "I haven't spoken to anyone for a while."

"Speak away," said Faye, sipping gingerly at her warm wine.

"So, as a local man," boomed Brian, "Do you have any recommendations for us?"

"Yeah, don't eat the pub grub." They all laughed, Faye a little wanly.

The doors to the pub opened and the couple from the white van sauntered in. Faye thought the woman was a 'type', the type you didn't take home to meet your parents, all makeup and bleached hair and barely-there clothes. She admonished herself for being so quick to make a judgement. To repent, she waved over at them with a smile. The woman hurried straight over and Faye's smile faded. It was the universe's way of telling her to stop being so mean-minded. She stoically accepted her punishment.

"Hello," the woman breathed, slipping onto the seat next to Mark. "I'm Julie, and that's Jim."

"Lovely to meet you," Brian boomed. "I'm Brian, and

this is Faye, my wife."

"And I'm Mark," said Mark, "I'm an old mate of Jim's."

"Oh, are you?" She was playing with one of many necklaces hanging around her neck and brushing against Mark in an overly intimate way.

"He's gorgeous, isn't he," Julie sighed, casually rubbing Mark's leg as she stared at Jim at the bar.

"Oh, he's something alright."

"So manly, so virile, so – "

"Married?" Mark suggested, sipping at his pint.

"I know he's married." Julie sat up straight and pouted a little. "He said he's leaving her for me, we want to be together."

"Don't think Bethany's got that memo yet. That's her name, Jim's wife, Bethany. Lovely girl. Saw her yesterday at the garden centre, she didn't mention anything about Jim leaving her. Strange, that."

Julie made a big display of waving at Jim as he turned away from the bar with two pints of lager in his hands. He sat down and Julie immediately draped herself around him, kissing his neck and stroking his chest. Jim seemed not to notice.

"How's it going, Mark?"

"Not bad, Jim. I've left Janis. Hear you're about to do the same with Bethany?"

"What?"

"Yes, Julie's just been telling us you 'want to be together'."

Jim extricated himself from Julie's embrace. "What you telling people that for? I never said that."

"You said you loved me."

"I never said that either." He glanced briefly at Mark. "I never said I was leaving Bethany."

"Yes, you did." She was back nibbling his neck again, whispering loud enough for them all to hear, "You remember, this afternoon, in the van?"

"I'm Brian," Brian boomed awkwardly, "And this is Faye,

my wife."

"Pleased to meet you."

Julie said, "We're the young, star-crossed lovers, kept apart by a cruel, cruel world."

"Leave it out, Jules, you know I don't like it when you talk like that." Jim sucked on his beer and turned to Mark. "So, you've left Janis? How come?"

"Clash of personality, morals, values, the usual."

"Eh? I saw her in Sainsbury's the other day, she said you'd gone, kept asking me if I knew where you were. Didn't, not then. Do now though," he snorted.

Faye was about to let rip an explosion of questions when the pub door opened and a tall, thin man peered inside. He glanced at them around the big table and then strode in. He was wearing a black hoodie that obscured most of his face. His boots were big and heavy. He looked ever so slightly scruffy and a bit dirty, and he wore black, wraparound sunglasses. He went straight to the corner of the bar.

"Who's that?" Faye gasped, as they all watched him raise a finger at the barman, who hauled himself off his stool and started pouring a pint.

"Nobody knows," said Mark. "He turned up about three weeks ago, and set up a tent at the far corner of the field."

"Oh, I saw that," Brian said, "Big bell tent."

"Even Ant doesn't know who he is, his name, where he comes from, anything. Pitch was booked online and he paid for a full month. A real mystery, never talks to anyone, just has two pints and leaves."

"A spy," declared Brian.

"Do you think so?" Faye gasped.

"Definitely. Undercover. Incognito."

"How exciting. I wonder why he's here?"

"Have you been stealing sticking plasters from your care home again, Faye? They're onto you, lass."

Faye tutted.

"He's tracking down the Cotswolds' branch of the

Mafia," Mark laughed.

"There's a Cotswolds' Mafia?" Faye gasped.

"Oh yeah," he said, catching Brian's amused eye, "Extortion and corruption in black market sheep."

The man in the hoodie turned his head and caught them all staring at him. They instantly averted their gaze in different directions.

"Mark!" shouted Ant from behind the bar, "Got summat for ya."

Mark struggled up from behind the table, squeezing tentatively past Julie, who casually reached out a hand and stroked the top of his leg.

Ant handed him an Amazon parcel. "What's in it?" he asked.

"None of your actual business." He grinned. "It's that new thriller book I was telling you about." The hoodie man snapped his head towards them but they didn't notice. "I've been looking forward to this, it's the second part of – "

"Bored," said Ant.

"Okay, another round of whatever they're drinking."

"How am I supposed to know what they're drinking?"

"You *just* served them, can't you remember?"

"What am I, a computer?"

Mark turned back to the table. "Shout out your orders," he said, and they all cried out for lager, Faye pushing her glass of warm wine away. Ant slowly lined them all up on the counter and Mark returned to the table with a tray of glasses to find them all discussing pub grub, except Julie, who was too busy fawning over Jim and looking to see if anyone was noticing. She looked up at Mark as he squeezed past, winking and blowing him a kiss.

"Book, is it?" Brian asked, nodding at the parcel.

"Yeah, I pre-ordered it, been waiting ages."

"So not a consignment of illegal substances then."

"Nah, not from Amazon, that comes via UPS."

"'We attempted to deliver your parcel but you weren't

in'," Jim laughed.

"'Here's a random picture of a parcel on someone else's doorstep to prove we attempted to deliver your parcel somewhere'," Brian boomed.

"'We left your parcel with a neighbour, who's now too stoned to open the door'," Faye shrieked.

As the hooded man at the bar slowly sipped his pint and looked on.

CHAPTER 3

"It's no good," Brian declared, standing up unsteadily after finishing his second pint, "Drinking on an empty stomach is making me even more hungry. To the van, woman, and cook me some food!"

"There is no food," Faye said, gathering her things together.

"No food?"

"You said," she told him peevishly, "I always bring too much food and waste most of it, and that we'd go shopping tomorrow, so there's no food in the van."

"Ye gods!" he boomed, "What kind of woman let's her man *starve*?"

"The kind of woman who does what her husband tells her against her better judgement!"

"I'm a bit peckish myself," said Mark, standing up. "I have bread for toast if you're interested?"

"Very kind of you, lad, but I was hoping for something a bit more substantial."

"We'll walk back with you," said Julie, jumping up and pulling Jim to his feet, "We have some unfinished business to take care of, don't we, Jim."

"Throw a bucket of water over the wench," Brian cried, as Faye helped him navigate the table and the short walk to the door.

"He's only had two pints," Mark laughed.

"Lightweight," said Jim.

"Two pints, plus the three cans he's hidden behind the caravan wheel thinking I won't notice," said Faye.

Outside, a now quite drunk Brian sucked in air. "Oh my God!" he cried, "What is that delicious smell?"

They all sniffed. "Definitely garlic," said Mark.

"Beef," said Jim, "A nice, rich, beefy aroma with some herbs and just a hint of – "

"STOP!" Brian boomed, "JUST STOP!"

They crunched their way to the gate. The field beyond was awash with rabbits. "Faye!" Brian cried, "Grab a bunny and throw it in a pot!"

"I will not."

"Mark, you're a local lad, do you know how to skin a rabbit?"

"Brian!"

"Oh, that smell, that fantastic smell! I'm weak with hunger. Faye, you're not looking after your man properly, I need to be fed on a regular basis!"

"We might have some pasta packets from the last trip in the cupboard."

"Pasta! Bloody pasta! I need *meat*, woman!"

They'd just reached the entrance to the caravan area when Tel, the man from the silver bullet, raised a hand towards them and they all staggered over as one.

"Really sorry to bother you again," he said, looking flustered, "It's just ... well ... "

"Spit it out, man, I'm about to die from neglectful starvation."

"Do you know anything about caravans?"

Brian leaned forward conspiratorially. Faye leaned with him to stop him falling over, not that she'd be able to do anything about it if he did. "It's funny you should ask that," he said, "Because, I don't know if you've noticed, but we appear to be surrounded by them. And bunnies. Do you know how to skin a rabbit?"

"Er, no."

"What's the problem?" Mark asked.

"Well." Tel laughed, scratching his head. "We can't seem to locate the bed."

"The bed?"

"We can't find it anywhere."

Brian laughed uproariously. "Good grief, no food and now no bed, what is the world coming to?"

"It's probably a pull-out thing," said Mark.

"We've pulled everything."

"Have you indeed," Julie breathed, clinging on to Jim but giving Tel a lingering look-over.

Brian made his way unsteadily through the windbreaker barriers to the open camper door. They all stood and watched as the pull-down step bent a little and squeaked a bit, straining to take his weight. Sophie watched from inside as Brian tried to step up but got his enormous shoulders stuck in the doorway.

"Turn sideways a bit," said Mark.

Brian wriggled until he was sideways enough for his shoulders to go through. Once inside he took a quick look round; sink, hob, tall steel cabinet, probably the loo, and then two small benches at the back, all of it encased in shiny metal. "It's like being inside a tin of baked beans," he bawled.

"That's what I said," said Sophie.

Mark appeared behind him. "Blimey, it looks smaller on the inside than it does on the outside."

"Thank you!" said Sophie.

"Okay," came Tel's voice from outside, "I know it's small, you don't have to keep going on about it!"

Mark tried to get past Brian to the benches at the back and failed, there simply wasn't enough room. "You'd be better off outside I think," he said, and Brian struggled to turn in the confines and force his shoulders through the door again. Outside he cried, "Will someone find the source of that delicious smell and bring it to me, *bring it to me now*!"

"Hi there, I'm Olivia." The woman from the motorhome stood meekly behind the barriers, watching the crowd around the shiny object. "I'm not being nosy, but is everything okay? Nobody's ill or anything, are they?"

"No, no," said Faye, hauling a windbreaker aside so she

could join them. "We're just helping them find the bed."

Olivia laughed, a pleasant, high, tinkling sound. "Oh, thank goodness. I was worried, watching you all gather around, I thought something had happened."

"Have you found it yet?" Jim shouted.

"No."

Julie was wandering around the silver object. "Hey," she said, "Would you believe there's a second door at the back? I mean, something this size and it's got two doors!"

"We've established that it's small," sighed Tel, "I'd be grateful if everyone could stop mentioning it now."

They all moved to the back. Mark opened it from the inside. They stood there, looking at the benches on either side, at Sophie, standing at the back of the benches, and Mark on his knees between them, tapping things and pulling things, trying to find the bed. They started pointing and saying, "Have you tried that? What about that in the corner? Is there a button or something? Is it hidden in the walls?"

Mark held up two round objects. "I think these are tabletops," he said.

"Oh!" cried Faye, startling them all, "Look under the benches."

"I've tried that, there's nothing ... oh, there's some poles stuck under the lids."

Everyone got really excited then. "The poles!" Brian cried, "It must be something to do with the poles!"

Mark was now holding four of them, two long ones and two small. He shuffled back on his knees to expose two round indentations on the floor. The crowd went wild, shouting instructions, yelling for him to 'stick them in' and 'twiddle them round a bit'.

"Have you tried looking it up on YouTube or something?" asked Olivia, and they all looked at her. She flinched at the attention and stepped back.

"Lass," Brian boomed, making her take another step back, "You're a genius."

Everyone pulled out their phones. “What make is it?” asked Jim.

“Airstream,” Tel said.

“What brand of Airstream?”

Tel just shrugged.

“Found it,” cried Julie, standing at the front of the tin can and pointing at an orange badge, “Basecamp.”

Everyone tapped it into their phones.

“Got it!” Faye declared. They all stood around her, watching the video play of a man doing a ‘walk through’ of the Airstream Basecamp. There were minutes of silence except for the voice on the phone.

“Right,” Jim yelled to Mark, “This is what you do.” He played the video again and talked him through the Construction of the Bed. Mark followed instructions, fitting poles to the floor and screwing on the table tops and, ingeniously, opening the flaps from inside both benches to rest on the table tops, which formed a bed base. Everyone cheered as he pulled the bench cushions on top.

“Voila!” he said smugly.

“A bed!” Sophie cried, “There’s an actual bed. Well, an approximation of one anyway.”

Faye climbed into the side door. “Right, where’s your sheets?”

“Sheets?”

“You’ve brought sheets, haven’t you? We’ll have that bed made up in no time.”

Sophie looked at Tel, outside the back door. He said, “I just assumed it came with everything required for caravanning.”

They were all looking at Tel now. “That’s not how it works,” said Brian, “You have to bring your own stuff.”

“Oh,” said Tel.

“Oh,” said Sophie.

“Have you brought *anything*?” Faye asked.

“Some clothes,” Sophie told her, “Not that there’s

anywhere to put them, or any need to wear what I've brought really."

"Cooking equipment? Food? Towels?"

Tel shook his head.

"Right," said Faye, getting out again, "I've got a spare set of sheets, newly washed and ironed. Might have a couple of extra towels too."

"We have extra sheets and towels, for some unfathomable reason," Brian called after her, "And yet you forgot to bring actual food?"

"I didn't forget," she snapped back, "I was *told* not to shop by my stingy husband."

"I've got tea, sugar and a tin of evaporated milk," said Mark, heading off.

"Oh," said Olivia, getting caught up in the excitement, "I've got some beef bourguignon, if you're hungry." Brian's eyes fell upon her and stayed there. "It's Richard's favourite, so I made a big casserole so that he can have it for lunch tomorrow with some nice crusty bread and some – " She stopped. They were all staring at her. She stepped back until she was now outside the windbreaker barrier.

"Don't let her escape!" Brian said, "She has food."

Olivia made a little sound of alarm and half turned to run back to her motorhome.

"Stop scaring people with your gob," Faye said, walking back across the driveway with her arms full of linen, towels and cushions. "Take no notice of him, love, he's just loud and hungry."

"How big is the casserole?" Brian asked, licking his lips.

Olivia indicated with her hands.

He made a surprisingly high-pitched sound at the back of his throat for a man of his size. "Do you think that you could spare a morsel for a starving Yorkshireman?"

Olivia gave a tentative smile. "Well, I suppose, if I did a big pot of rice, there might be enough for ... well, everyone."

Brian clapped his hands together in glee. "You are an

angel! Thank you, thank you so much, you are literally a life saver."

Olivia hurried off. Mark came back with a plastic bag of items, including two metal mugs and a teaspoon, a packet of chocolate digestives, two bottles of water and a saucepan. Jim and Julie suddenly appeared at the top of the driveway, struggling to carry a wooden bench they'd taken from outside the pub. They manoeuvred it inside the barriers, then spotted the fold-up table and metal chairs. "Was that there before?" Julie asked.

"Perfect," Brian said, helping them for the last few steps, "Put them together. We're having a meal, an actual meal." He was almost jumping from one foot to the other with joy.

"I wish you got that excited when I cook you a meal," Faye shouted from inside the Airstream, where she was busy putting the sheets on the newly discovered bed and cushions inside the pillow covers.

There was a sound. They all turned back towards the tin can. Sophie was standing in the doorway, crying. Tel raced up to her. "Are you okay, Soph? What's wrong? If you hate it so much we can go home, it's not a problem."

"Oh, I'm so sorry," Faye said, coming up behind her, "We've just all turned up and taken over. We were just trying to help but I can see how - "

"No," Sophie said, sniffing and quickly wiping tears from her eyes, "It's not that. It's just ... I can't believe how *kind* you all are. I'm so overwhelmed by your generosity. You don't even know us and you've ... you've – " She turned and hugged Faye, who seemed a bit surprised, then stepped out and went up to each of them, hugging them and saying, "Thank you. Thank you."

"You're going to me make me cry in a minute," Faye sniffed.

"Me too," said Mark.

Brian stared off into the distance and took a deep, wavering breath.

* * *

20 minutes later the eight of them were sat at two tables that were strewn with paper plates and plastic knives and forks, courtesy of Faye, eagerly anticipating the arrival of actual food. Tel had opened up another bottle of champagne and was pouring it into plastic pint glasses that Faye had found at the back of a cupboard. Brian had rolled his coolbox over and was doling out cold cans of lager. Jim and Julie shared the warm, fizzless champagne that had been opened earlier, drinking it straight from the bottle, Julie making rather a lascivious show of it.

Oliva came out of the motorhome holding a large casserole dish between two oven gloves, and they all gave a cheer. Mark jumped up to help her, but she said, "If you could just bring the pan of rice out, and the crusty bread and butter on the side."

"Crusty bread and butter," Brian repeated in an extraordinarily high voice.

The casserole was placed on the wooden table. When Olivia took off the lid they all sniffed and gasped. Olivia produced two serving spoons from her apron pocket and gave it a stir. Brian looked like he was about to expire with happiness. Mark hurried over, struggling with a heavy pan in one hand and a giant plate piled high with buttered bread in the other. Jim leapt up to take the bread from him, quickly pushing a piece into his mouth.

Dinner was served amidst much talking and a great deal of laughter.

"Your name," Tel said, "We don't even know the name of our fine cook!"

"Olivia," she said, with a tinkle of laughter, "And my husband's called – "

"Richard," said Richard, standing outside the windbreakers and staring at them all. "What the bloody hell is going on?"

"Oh darling," Olivia laughed, "Isn't it marvelous, we're

all eating together. I've left yours in the oven, but I can bring it over and you can – "

"A word," he said firmly, turning on his heels and marching away. Olivia's smile vanished. The group fell silent. She got up quickly and followed him back to the motorhome.

Mark stood up.

"Best not," said Brian.

Mark hesitated, looking at the motorhome. It rocked slightly, and the sound of a deep and very angry voice wafted across the driveway.

"Do you think she's okay? He seemed a bit of a brute."

"If you really want to find out what's going on," said Brian, "You send in the professionals. Faye, go do your thing."

Faye leapt up and threw the serving spoons into the now empty casserole dish, grabbed the lid and picked them all up. She hurried beyond the windbreakers straight towards Mark's caravan, then did a sharp left and slinked across the gravel driveway to the back of the motorhome. She approached the closed door, making a big show of staring at her feet as she passed the window so, hopefully, they wouldn't see her head go past. She heard voices from within and stood still, casserole dish at the ready.

"Just what do you think you're playing at?" she heard the man hiss. "I leave you for a few hours and return to find you cavorting with the bloody natives!"

"It was just a meal, darling."

"MY meal! Is there any left or did you forget me entirely?"

"Yes, yes, I put it in the oven to say warm, I knew you wouldn't be long."

"I don't want it now."

"Don't you, darling? But it's your favourite."

"Not now I've seen the hungry hoards shoveling it into their mouths like animals. I'm very displeased, Olivia."

"I'm sorry, darling."

"Did you find the money?"

"Yes, all of it."

"I want it back. You don't deserve to keep it."

"Oh, it's here. Here, darling."

"I'm very annoyed with you, Olivia, this is not the behaviour I expect from you. Remember, you nearly lost me once but, perhaps against my better judgement, I gave you a second chance. Don't make me regret that decision."

"Yes, darling. I mean, no, darling."

Faye realised her teeth were clenched and her jaw was aching. Before she could fully acknowledge her rising anger the motorhome door flew open, making her jump. Richard looked down at her, surprised to find her standing there.

"Yes?" he barked, "What do you want, more of *my* food?"

"I've just brought back the casserole dish, thought I might have a word with Olivia?"

"Olivia is tired. You will not bother her again, is that understood?"

"But I just thought – "

"Don't think, just stay away." Richard started to reach out to take the casserole dish, then thought better of it and pulled his hands away. "Olivia," he said, "Take the dish."

Olivia moved forward as Richard moved back and took the casserole from Faye. "Sorry about this," she said, forcing a smile.

"Why are you apologizing?" Richard snapped. "I hope you're not apologizing for *my* behaviour when it's *your* behaviour that caused this!"

"No, darling. Sorry, darling."

Olivia and the casserole disappeared into the motorhome. Richard reached out for the door. "You will not take advantage of my wife's kind nature again," he snapped, and slammed the door shut.

As Faye turned, she saw Olivia sitting inside on the far sofa, facing the window. She raised a hand and mouthed, 'You okay?' Olivia forced a smile and nodded. The blinds came crashing down, and Faye hurried back to the now quiet group around the table.

"Is she okay?" Mark and Sophie both asked at once.

"Man's an arsehole," she said, and began clearing off the table.

* * *

None of them slept very well that night. Mark tossed and turned, thinking of the poor woman across the driveway. Tel and Sophie couldn't get comfortable on the thin mattress of their new-found bed. Brian and Faye lay awake, staring at the caravan ceiling, listening to the sound of screaming laughter and heavy grunting coming from the tiny Transit next door. Eventually, Brian could stand it no longer and sat up, threw up the blind and opened the side window.

"YOU PAIR!" he hollered, so loud Faye had to cover her ears against the echo in the van. "STOP FORNICATING, SOME OF US ARE TRYING TO SLEEP!"

"Jealous?" Jim laughed.

Julie giggled.

"WE ARE OLD PEOPLE – "

"Speak for yourself," said Faye.

"We're not," Tel shouted from inside his tin can, "But we *are* very, very tired."

"WILL YOU STOP THAT INFERNAL YELLING," yelled Richard.

"IT'S NOT ME, IT'S THEM!"

"I DON'T CARE WHO IT IS, STOP IT AT ONCE!"

"The arsehole speaketh," Faye said, grimacing in his direction.

"I'M WARNING YOU," Brian blasted at the van, "OLD PEOPLE RISE EARLY. WE WILL GET OUR REVENGE!"

"We'd quite like a lie-in," Tel yelled, "Could you make it a quiet revenge?"

"WILL YOU PEOPLE BE QUIET!" Richard screamed.

"Night, granddad," Jim laughed.

Brian slammed the window shut and threw himself back onto the bed. The slats beneath it creaked unnervingly.

"Feel better for that now, do you, Bri?"

"No." He stared at the ceiling, still fuming. When the grunts and groans echoed across the campsite again, even louder than before, he growled deep and low, like an irate lion. Faye placed a couple of small, brightly coloured objects on his hairy chest. "Whack these in," she said.

"Sweets?"

"Earplugs. I have a stash for when your snoring gets too loud."

Brian wriggled them in. The world fell unnaturally quiet. He could hear his own blood pumping, but inside his head he could still hear them.

Revenge, he thought, will be mine.

He fell asleep, dreaming of his revenge, but nobody else slept because of his rumbling, reverberating snoring.

Still awake, Tel turned to Sophie, lying like a goddess on the thin mattress. "Do you want to leave tomorrow?" he asked.

She didn't answer, just stared at the metallic ceiling.

"Imagine it as an adventure," he said. "Think of it as preparing yourself for the zombie apocalypse."

She laughed. "The zombie apocalypse?"

"When it happens you'll be fully prepared to mix with people, you'll know their lingo, you'll know how to inspire and lead them."

"Beef bourguignon is clearly the way to go."

"The success of humankind is down to you, Sophie, you need to prepare, like Sarah Connor."

She laughed again as he shushed the beat to *The Terminator*. She rolled over towards him, their heads close together on the cushion-cum-pillows. "Sarah Connor?"

"I can totally see you as Sarah Connor, fighting against the robots, a heroine, a saviour."

"Your analogies are getting mixed up, Tel, are we talking zombie apocalypse or war on the machines?"

"Whichever takes your fancy." They kissed. "Do you want to leave?" he asked again.

"I think," she said, wrapping her arms round him, "It might be quite interesting, and tactical, to stay."

"Good."

Day 2 – Saturday

"What are you doing?" Faye grunted.

"Getting up."

"Why are you getting up, it's only 6 o'clock? Oh Brian, get back into bed and leave the young people alone."

"I will not. They disturb my sleep, I disturb theirs."

"You'll wake everyone up again."

"I will not. I have a plan."

"Oh god."

Wearing only a pair of boxers, Brian stomped out of the caravan and round to the white van. He put his hands on roof and pushed, and pushed again and again until the van was violently rocking from side to side and he could feel bodies rolling around inside. A screechy voice cried, "What the bloody hell's going on?"

"Jim, Jim, is it an earthquake? What's happening, Jim?"

Brian carried on rocking until the back doors of the van flew open and a very naked Jim fell out.

Smiling, he turned on his heels and walked back to his caravan, flexing his arms in a Charles Atlas pose as he went and muttering, "Warehouse Manager, steel stockholders, gets his revenge."

As he entered the awning he could see Jim streaking across the grass to the toilet block with his arms in the arm, yelling, "Yee-haa!" and somehow managing to waggle his hips at the same time, making his manhood slap from side to side. Julie screamed with laughter.

"Never right in the head, that lad."

* * *

A short while later, just as Brian was clinking a spoon around two mugs of coffee, faces appeared at the front window of the awning. Jim and Julie stood there shivering in the early morning chill. "Spare a mug of tea?" Jim whimpered, as Julie clung to him for warmth.

Brian sighed and pulled up the zip to let them in. Julie immediately threw herself into his favourite chair. Faye popped her head out of the caravan door. "Waifs," Brian said, "Come to scrounge our meagre supplies."

"Tea or coffee?" Faye asked.

"Tea please, and a couple of bacon sandwich if there's any going spare?"

"Pah!" Brian bellowed, "You'll be lucky, we are apparently a meat free zone."

"Only because you told me not to buy anything!" Faye yelled.

* * *

Three hours later, with Jim and Julie firmly ensconced in their awning, Brian and Faye had a whispered conversation inside the caravan, then Faye went across to the shiny tin can and gently tapped on the door of the Airstream. She waited, hearing movement inside. The door opened and a very sleepy Tel stood there yawning and running a hand over his neat, curly hair. He was only wearing a pair of boxers and it took several moments for Faye to catch her breath again.

"What time is it?" he croaked.

Faye hauled her eyes off his magnificent body. "9 o'clock," she spluttered. "We're just off to Sainsbury's for supplies and wondered, since you literally have nothing, if you'd like to come?"

Tel turned his head. "Shopping, Sophie?"

"Really? Must we?"

"It's up to you. We'll need supplies for the uprising of the robots, or zombies, whichever comes first."

Sophie appeared next to Tel wearing only bra and knickers. The woman, Faye thought, was gorgeous from head to foot. "Just give me five minutes," she told Faye.

Brian got into his car.

"Where you off to then?" Jim asked, wandering out of the awning with his third mug of tea.

"I don't have to tell you," Brian replied, staring straight ahead.

"Sainsbury's," Faye said, walking back across the driveway. "Do you need anything?"

"Ooh," said Julie, "Can we come?"

Brian huffed and gave Faye 'a look'. Faye ignored the look and said, "Yeah, there's plenty of room." Brian groaned.

Tel and Sophie came over, still wearing their suits but without the jackets. Sophie nearly broke an ankle on the gravel driveway in her high heels.

"Do you have anything more – ?"

"Practical?" said Sophie. "No, just high heels and designer clothes suitable for a stay in a ridiculously expensive country hotel."

"Okay, okay," Tel sighed.

Mark came out of his caravan and waved. "Off somewhere nice?" he shouted over.

"Sainsbury's," Faye said, "Want anything?"

"Nah, but thanks anyway."

"I hate shopping," Jim said, "I think I'll stay here and chat with Mark. That okay with you, Mark?"

"Well actually," Mark said, tossing his book into the caravan and pushing the door shut, "I could do with some more chocolate biccies."

"Yeah, come one, come all," Brian muttered behind the wheel. "We can squeeze another 13 people in yet, bring your family, bring your friends, drag total strangers off the street and bundle them in!"

"What was that, Bri?"

"Nothing, my love."

The side door opened and Julie clambered in, brushing her hand slowly across Brian's broad shoulder and giving it a brief squeeze. "In the back," he bawled, "Make room for the

40,000 who appear to be coming to Sainsbury's with us."

Tel and Sophie sat with Julie on the back-back seat. Mark sat on the middle seat behind Brian. Julie, deciding she didn't like the back seat, scrambled between the middle seats to sit next to Mark, staring at him with a smile and gently stroking her lips with a finger. Jim noticed from outside and said, "I think I'll come after all." He nodded at Mark to sit in the back so that he could sit next to Julie, and Mark gratefully obliged.

Instead of getting in, Faye hurried off towards the big, grey motorhome, and Brian groaned. "Scott crossed the Antarctic in less time than it takes my wife to actually get in the car."

Richard opened the motorhome door when she knocked and looked down at her contemptuously. Before he could utter something derogatory, she said, "We're off to Sainsbury's."

"Splendid! Decided to eat your own food, have you?"

"I wondered if Olivia needed anything. We could replace the food we ate last night if she has a list?"

"We don't need anything," he said, and slammed the door shut.

"Bloody rude," she breathed.

As she was walking back to the car she heard a window opening and Olivia shouting, "Could you get me a dozen eggs, darling? I'll pay you when you get back."

Faye raised a thumb in response and heard Richard's really annoying voice yelling, "Olivia!"

"What? I need eggs!"

Faye finally jumped into the passenger seat, avoiding Brian's low-lidded eyes. "Are we quite ready?" he drawled. "You don't want to ask the man in black at the bottom of the field if he needs anything?"

"Oh, never thought to ask him, do you think I should?" She turned her best, biggest smile on him and he rolled his eyes. The woman was impossible.

"SEATBELTS!" he hollered, and they all faffed about finding the belts, swapping them with each other whilst Brian glared at them in the rear-view mirror, tutting wildly and saying, "It just goes in there. No, in there!" Finally, they all looked back at him in the rear-view mirror like a bunch of excited schoolkids going on a day trip.

"READY?" he bawled.

"Ready."

"Okay, and we're off."

It was to be a shopping expedition he would never forget.

CHAPTER 4

They entered the supermarket en masse, like the charge of the 300 Spartans, and piled straight into the café, chattering excitedly about food. Full English breakfasts were ordered, Julie had a coffee; "Got to keep an eye on the figure," she said to no one in particular, running her hands over herself. When no one said anything, not even Jim, who was more interested in ordering crispy bacon, she pouted and cat-walked off to a table.

"What is wrong with the girl?" Brian whispered to his wife.

"She's young, hormonal, desperate for attention."

"Aren't you worried?"

"About?"

"Well, you know, her coming on to me or something? She seems very highly ... charged. She brushed my shoulder as she got into the car, did you see that?"

"Oh, poor baby, do you want me to find a local counsellor you can speak to about sexual harassment?"

"Shut up, lass." He ordered extra fried bread, just to annoy Faye.

Afterwards, they charged towards the trolleys and, to Brian's horror, each grabbed a large one. "Space is limited," he yelled at their departing backs, "I have a car, not a truck. Restrain yourselves!"

"And don't run amok," Faye added.

Julie twirled past them singing, "Amok, amok, amok," and blowing a kiss at Brian.

"Still not worried?" he asked.

"Not in the slightest."

"Right, I'll wait in the car. Trying to control this lot will be like herding feral cats. Good luck." And off he lumbered.

Tel and Sophie stood next to the fruit and veg, looking around uncertainly. "First time in Sainsbury's?" Faye asked.

"First time in a supermarket," Sophie said, and Tel nodded.

Faye just looked at them for a moment, and then asked, "But how – ?"

"Ocado."

"We have everything delivered."

"We simply don't have the time to shop ourselves."

"We lead very busy lives."

"And we eat out a lot."

"A *lot*."

"I see." Faye was silent for long seconds, trying to imagine a life where you Never Had to Shop. It sounded wonderful. "What do you do for a living, if you don't mind me asking?"

"We're corporate lawyers."

"Ah." Faye nodded. "Well spoken, well dressed, I should have guessed. Come on, I'll show you how people shop in real life. Oh good, they've got a clothes section."

"Clothes?" Sophie gasped, "In a supermarket?"

"Your snobbery's showing," Tel breathed in her ear, "I'd cover that up if I were you."

Sophie pursed her lips but she knew he was right. Turning tight lips into an overbright smile, she followed Faye, who was now holding up what looked like a baggy sweatshirt with a glittery logo emblazoned on the front that looked suspiciously like a unicorn. "Nice," she said.

"Pick whatever you want," Tel said, "I'm paying."

"You're paying are you, Tel?" Jim bawled from further down the aisle, and raced off with their trolley like they were on Supermarket Sweep, so fast Tel didn't have a chance to respond. Sophie laughed. "I hope you brought your American Express card." The laughter died when Faye held up two pairs of monstrously ugly trainers and said, "Which ones do you like?" Now it was Tel's turn to laugh as he wandered off to the men's section.

Jim and Julie reappeared in the tinned food aisle, dragging a kettle barbecue on wheels behind them that was piled high with bags of charcoal. "Thought we could have a barbecue later," he said.

Sophie laughed behind her hand. To show stoicism in the face of adversity, and hoping it might earn him brownie points for later, Tel said, "Brilliant, let's get some meat."

They crowded round the meat section, randomly lobbing packages into their trolleys as Jim cried, "It's okay, Tel's paying." Julie raced off for bread rolls, returning with them piled high in her arms, just as Jim was throwing a vast array of barbecue sauces into his trolley. Faye, very practically, collected salad and disposable eating equipment.

She led Sophie and Tel down the aisles, giving a running commentary of camping requirements as she chose towels and bed sets and toiletries. Sophie became obsessed with the price of everything, "Look at this!" she kept saying, picking things up and thrusting them into Tel's face, "I normally pay ten times that much! And this, look how much this is!" Faye preened proudly.

They all met up again at the drinks section, where Sophie's eyes lit up as she stacked various bottles of spirits and mixers into their already full trolley.

"Steady," said Tel, as she pushed a litre bottle of whisky in next to a bottle of vodka. "You're not that much of a drinker."

"I'm a quick learner, I'm going to drink to kill the pain."

"You don't need that much, Soph."

She looked at the trolley. There did seem to be rather a lot, maybe she was going a bit overboard. She picked up a bottle of lemonade and put it back on the shelf, giving Tel a dare-to-question-me look.

It was chaos as they all crowded round the checkouts. "He's paying," cried Jim, loading up the conveyor belt first and dragging the barbecue and its bags of charcoal through.

The checkout operator had her work cut out as she rang everything up, the pinging almost non-stop. Tel's face became more and more anxious. As they walked away with their full trolleys they each cried, "Cheers, Tel!" Sophie laughed as she emptied theirs, and was still laughing as she packed everything at the other end of the conveyor belt, something she'd never actually done before - it was quite therapeutic, like a fast game of Tetra. Mark went through with a single box of lager, a box of tea, and a packet of chocolate digestives rolling precariously on top. "Cheers," he said to Tel.

"Is that all you've got?"

"S'all I need. Man of simple means, me."

The final bill was astronomical and Sophie couldn't stop laughing.

"I'm glad you find shopping so entertaining," he said, "We'll have to do it more often."

"Over my dead body. Anyway, think of it as cheaper than a weekend stay at a five star hotel." That actually cheered Tel up, and he nodded and followed them all out.

* * *

Brian was listening to Smooth Radio in the car when he saw them emerge from the supermarket with their trolleys piled high and Jim dragging something large behind him. He uttered a few choice expletives as he slowly clambered out, and was still spluttering them when they arrived at the car.

"And where," he boomed, glaring at them all with his hands on his hips, "Are you going to put all this stuff?"

"Oh, it'll go in," Jim said confidently, "It's a big car."

Brian slid open the side door and waved a hand towards the inside. "Be my guest."

It took a while.

The ride back to the campsite was very uncomfortable. Jim and Julie had a barbecue across both their laps with shopping bags and charcoal bags piled on top, to the side and at their feet. Mark was wedged into the back corner almost buried beneath bags, and Sophie and Tel couldn't even see each other in the middle seats. Faye desperately clung on to bag handles to stop them toppling over to Brian's side, who was still fuming and had loudly declared that he 'needed space to actually drive'.

They pulled up at the campsite and slowly extricated themselves. Bags were piled up on the grass in front of Brian and Faye's caravan. "And where are you going to put all this meat?" Brian enquired.

"We don't have a fridge," Jim said, "Can we put our stuff in yours? Oh, that's a nice, big coolbox."

"It's *my* coolbox, filled with *my* beer."

"But you don't need 56 cans in there all at the same time, do you, Brian." To his utter horror, Faye began taking cans out and putting them into carrier bags. "How many do you need for tonight?" she asked.

"All of them!"

"You can't drink 56 cans of lager in one night."

"I'll give it a bloody good go."

"Don't be silly. I'll leave you six, that should be enough."

"But … but … "

"Three each for us," said Jim.

"Excuse me?" Brian could hardly believe what he was hearing.

"You're right, make it four each for us, Faye. Four enough for you, Jules?"

"Yeah, sure."

Jim turned and yelled, "Hey, Tel, you drinking lager at the barbecue tonight?"

"WAIT! JUST WAIT!" Brian hollered. "THIS IS MY BEER AND MINE ALONE. IF YOU DIDN'T HAVE THE FORESIGHT TO BUY YOUR OWN REFRESHMENTS DURING YOUR RAMPGAGE THROUGH THE SUPERMARKET THEN THAT'S ENTIRELY YOUR FAULT. Put them back," he said to Faye.

Faye continued to take cans out, saying, "Okay, if I leave 25 in that should be enough for everyone."

"EVERYONE? I'M NOT A BLOODY FREE BAR!"

"Don't be selfish, Brian."

"Selfish?" He rushed over to his wife, who was now putting meat into the spaces where his cold beer had once been. "A man's beer is his own, Faye. You have no right to touch what is mine."

She lifted a can-filled bag up to him and said, "I think if you stow these under the caravan they should be alright. You'll have to move the empty cans behind the wheel first though."

Brian held the bag as his wife fussed over fitting packets of meat into the coolbox – *his* coolbox. Should he make a stand? Should he put his foot down and demand that she leave his cold cans alone? Should he say something deeply profound about an Englishman's cooler is his own private property?

He took the bag of cans and pushed them underneath the caravan, where he hoped they might stay cool and where he might get to keep them all for himself.

"Okay, pass your meat over," Faye was saying, packing it into the coolbox until it was full. "Sophie, you can probably fit these sausages and burgers in your fridge, can't you?"

"I don't know, we haven't located the fridge yet."

"Well, that will be a thrilling ten seconds of exploration," Mark laughed.

"Fridge space?" Faye asked him.

Mark shrugged, knowing that there was nothing in his fridge except a packet of chocolate digestives and a small carton of milk. Fay handed him four big packs of chicken pieces.

"We're never going to fit all this onto one barbecue," Brian muttered miserably.

"Oh, get our portable one from underneath the sofa, will you?" Faye said, and Brian lumbered off into the caravan, mumbling under his breath.

It was only when provisions had been safely stowed away, one way or another, that Faye finally stood outside the awning, brushing back her hair and surveying the campers on the field. During their shopping excursion several tents had arrived and set up camp down the right-hand side. Children ran around throwing things at each other and screaming, as their parents fought over poles and canvas.

"There goes the peace and quiet," Brian said, coming to stand next to her.

"I like the sound of children playing." A parent next to a particularly large tent screamed, "Get over here, you little sods, and fookin' help us put the bleedin' tent up."

"Ah, the joyous sound of family holidays."

"You don't really mind about the beer cans, do you, Bri?"

"No, love," he said, "Of course not. Whatever makes you happy. Happy wife, happy life."

She rested her head on his broad chest for a moment, and then said, "Right, I'll take these eggs over to Olivia, and then I'm going for a shower."

* * *

"Hello," Olivia trilled excitedly, "Come in, come in."

"Is Richard here?"

"No, he's gone out, won't be back until later."

Relieved, Faye stepped into the motorhome. Unlike the baked bean tin Sophie and Tel were in, this actually looked bigger on the inside than it did on the outside. It was like her living room at home, only longer, with a kitchenette in the middle and a ready-made bed at the back. "Oh, this is nice," she said.

Olivia fussed around. "Do sit down. Would you like a drink? Tea? Coffee? Something a little stronger?" She gave a high-pitched giggle and her hands flustered to her face and fiddled with her hair. Faye thought she didn't get many visitors.

"I'm okay, thanks. Just on my way to the showers, but brought your eggs over."

"Oh, lovely, lovely. How much do I owe you?"

"Nothing after that meal you provided last night. Brian nearly expired from famishment, so you basically saved his life."

Another high-tinkling laugh.

"Your beef bourguignon was delicious, by the way, you'll have to give me the recipe. Shame it ended so abruptly."

"Yes, sorry about that, Richard can be a bit ... fussy about the company I keep. He means well."

"Does he?"

"Oh yes, yes. He likes things a certain way, drives him mad when things don't go quite how he imagined. I was supposed to stay here to cook and clean, not galivant off across the campsite." More laughter. "Are you sure you wouldn't like something? Cappuccino?" She put her hand on a shiny machine on one of the counters. "Richard loves his cappuccino, I'm sure he wouldn't notice one capsule missing."

Faye thought, if I open my mouth things will fall out, so she stood up and said, "No, I must go before I start to smell like something that's died." Another high peel of not quite so frantic laughter. "I'm not quite sure how it happened, but we seem to be having a barbecue later if you want to come. How long is Richard out for?"

"Oh, he said he'd be back around eight o'clock. That's what the eggs are for, I'm making him a frittata for supper. I suspect he'll be back earlier though, just to check I'm behaving myself."

"We'll start it at five and have you safely home before seven, how does that sound?"

Olivia's eyes were bright with delight. "Lovely."

* * *

"How are the showers?" Brian asked when she got back.

"It's a very basic setup. You have to wash in the big sinks outside."

"You didn't."

"Yeah. Not very private, are they. You'd think they'd at least put some partitioning round them or something. Doing *down below* was a bit awkward."

"You didn't!"

"Bit of a struggle to get my foot up on the side of the sink and give *down there* a good scrub. I got a few strange looks from the other campers, I can tell you.

"Faye, tell me you didn't!"

"No, of course not!" she told his horrified face. She allowed a suitable pause before adding, "I just did my top half."

"Faye!"

"I'm joking, I'm joking! Showers are good."

She ran a brush through her hair while Brian sat on the sofa, scrolling through something on his phone. "I'm a bit worried about Olivia," she said.

"Leave it, Faye, it's none of our business."

"Bad things happen because good people let it."

"That's not an argument to interfere in other people's relationships."

"I know." She sat on the sofa opposite him, still brushing her hair. "She just seems very ... I don't know, lonely. She was really excited when I went over, almost like she'd never had visitors before."

"Nobody knows what goes on behind closed doors, Faye. Don't presume to know a man after meeting him for two minutes."

She sighed. "You're right, I know you're right. Is that the Men's Answer to Everything website you're on?"

He laughed. "No, but if you want something to worry about focus on the pair behind us." He threw a thumb over his shoulder, at Jim and Julie sitting on the grass outside with their backs against the wheel of his van. "I've never seen two less motivated people in my life. They're just sitting there, doing nothing."

"Perfect holiday for some people."

"They've already asked me where you are and if we're going anywhere today."

She looked at them through the window behind Brian. "They're just picking at the grass."

"And smoking it, by the smell."

"What, smoking the grass?"

"Smoking *grass*, Faye, or whatever they call it nowadays, skunk, ganga, bud."

"We used to call it whacky baccy," she said with a wry smile.

"Stinks to high hell."

"I can't smell it," she grinned.

"That's because you have no sense of smell, my love, but take it from me, it *pongs*."

A voice from outside cried, "You two going anywhere today?"

"Can we come with you?"

"We're not adopting them," Brian growled, "And we're definitely not taking them home with us."

* * *

When Jim and Julie wandered over to the toilet block arm in arm about an hour later, Brian whispered, "Now! Go! Go!"

Faye grabbed her bag and a jacket in case it rained, and they both scrambled out of the caravan, locked the door, zipped up the awning and raced to the car. Brian started up the engine, did the fastest three-point turn in history, and rammed his foot on the accelerator, making gravel spray out behind them. As they drove in a flurry of dust past the shower blocks, Jim and Julie came out and stared after them, looking for all the world like abandoned children.

"Maybe we should – ?"

"No!"

"But it wouldn't hurt to – ?"

"It would!"

They went to a nearby town and spent a pleasant afternoon wandering amongst the tourist shops, Faye picking up a nice bamboo wind chime with a dragon clinging to the top and Brian mostly buying cheese and fancy crackers.

When they got back mid-afternoon they drove straight between Jim and Julie having a massive argument with a woman in a bright yellow VW van that was now parked opposite them.

"Say nothing," Brian warned Faye as they parked up and looked back, "Do not, under any circumstances, get involved." He unzipped the awning, pulled out a camping chair, and positioned it in the middle of the gravel driveway facing the fight. Faye did the same.

"But you don't need a hardstanding pitch!" screeched a blonde woman with an extremely posh voice. "You've only got a van."

"So have you!" Jim returned.

"Just move it and let my friend park there." On the grass field stood another VW van, this one bright orange and adorned with flower stickers. Two small children ran around it, throwing pieces of gravel at each other. A dark-haired, surly looking woman with her arms crossed tightly over her flat chest shouted, "Just move the bladdy thing!"

"No! Why should I?"

"We've paid good money for a hardstanding pitch," yelled the blonde.

"So have we," Jim countered.

"We want to be together."

"Oh boo hoo, poor you."

"Just move your bladdy van!"

"I will not!"

"It's not even a proper camping van," cried the blonde. "We've got beds in ours."

Jim turned and quickly urged Julie up from the back ledge of the van. He pointed at the blow-up bed beyond with both hands.

"We've got an awning to erect," the woman cried, so furious her face had turned red.

Jim reached into his van and pulled out a golf umbrella, opened it up and balanced it between the roof and the open door. "Ta da!"

"We," she sneered, "have a kitchenette we have to plug into the electricity point."

"We," Jim countered, pulling the kettle barbecue out from beside his van, "Have a barbecue."

"Which doesn't need electricity!"

"It's ... it's an electric barbecue," he said, shrugging at a giggling Julie.

"WE HAVE CHILDREN!" the woman raged, indicating two small, bored children leaning against the VW staring blankly at their phones. "Jackie can't park in a *field*, on *grass*, if it rains the children will trail their muddy shoes into the van."

Jim sat on the back of his van, put one leg across the other and dramatically pulled at his trainer. He'd given them a double-tie this morning because he'd kept tripping over the laces in the supermarket. When it wouldn't come off his foot he used his eyeballs to call for assistance from Julie, who rushed over and quickly unpicked them. He stared over at the woman again and pulled off his trainer with a flourish. "They come off," he said.

The woman was beyond furious now, she was clearly used to getting her own way. "You've not even got any camping gear!" she shrieked.

"I have always depended on the kindness of strangers," Jim said.

"And the strangers aren't too bloody happy about it," Brian laughed.

The woman snapped her head towards Brian, sitting with Faye in the middle of the driveway. "Uh-oh," she whispered, "You're in for it now."

"What are you looking at?" snapped the woman.

"Lass, if you're prepared to put on a public display of outrage it would be impolite of us not to enjoy it."

The woman gave a quick scream of frustration. The woman in the field yelled "Will you just move your bladdy van!"

Mark appeared, dragging his chair behind him. "So what happened was, these two posh totties pulled up and wanted Jim to move his van so they could park up together.

Jim refused and got a bit mouthy. Then the fight started."

"How much have we missed?" Faye asked.

"Not much, about five minutes."

Olivia, dragging an ornate metal chair, came and sat with them. "It's all terribly exciting," she said, "I've been watching through the window since it started. I've never seen a fight before. It's a bit like a soap opera, isn't it, only better because it's real."

In front of them the two adversaries faced each other from their side of the gravel driveway, poking fingers at each other.

"I was here first!" Jim yelled.

"Yours isn't even a caravan or a motorhome, you don't belong in this section."

"I'm *not moving*!"

Julie sat on the back of the Transit, arms outstretched as if protecting it from invaders. "Don't let them intimidate you, Jim."

"I don't let shrieking harpies intimidate me," Jim laughed.

"We've paid good money for these two pitches."

"So have we!"

"You don't even need a hardstanding pitch, you could park anywhere."

"So could you!"

"Just park it somewhere else!"

"I won't! Look, your kids have got a massive field to play in over there."

"Over there?" the woman cried, horrified, "With the common people? Are you insane? We can't have our children mixing with the lower classes!"

"Did she just say 'lower clarses'?" Brian asked Mark.

"She did, and 'common people'."

"Blimey," said Faye, "They're going to fit right in here."

"Right," said the blonde woman, taking a mobile phone out of back pocket of her jeans, "You wait, just you wait."

"Waiting," Jim heckled, glancing at his watch, "Not seeing much happening."

The woman stabbed at the phone with a manicured finger. "Benjamin! Benjamin, we're having some trouble with the natives."

"Ooh, 'natives', good one," said Mark.

"They're parked in *our* spot, Benjamin, and positively refuse to move."

"It's *my* spot," Jim yelled.

"No, they won't let us have it, the man's a raving lunatic and his girlfriend looks like she has some kind of eating disorder."

Julie leapt to her feet. "The bloody cheek! Did you hear that, Jim? I do not have – "

"Yes, Benjamin, I will, I'll tell him." The blonde held the phone away from her ear and shouted, "My husband said if you don't move he's going to come down and punch you in the face."

"Where's he coming from then?"

"He's in Cornwall at the moment on a job."

"Which part of Cornwall?"

"The end bit, I think he said, near Penzance."

"Oh, it's nice there," Jim said, nodding.

"Sorry, Benjamin, what did you say? Of course, of course. My husband says he can be here within hours."

Jim laughed. "Long enough to build up a sense of anticipation, then. I mean, we're only booked until tomorrow morning, will he make it here by then, do you think?"

"No, Benjamin, it didn't help at all. The man's obviously a moron."

Jim threw up a very stiff middle finger.

"Reception?" said the woman. "Yes, there's a reception hut but there's nobody in it. The pub? Yes, yes, I'll go and speak to the landlord straight away."

"Good luck with that," Mark laughed.

"Okay, Benjamin, I'll call you back afterwards." With

a final look of contempt at Jim, the woman flounced off to the pub with her two small children in tow, who were crying, "We're hungry, mummy, when are we going to eat?"

"Soon, darling, just as soon as mummy's sorted out this horrid man."

The other woman and her children followed.

Jim threw himself down on the back of his van next to Julie and high-fived her.

"She said I had an eating disorder, Jim."

"Take no notice," he told her, giving her a sideways hug, "She's just jealous, the fat cow."

Mark stood up and picked up his chair.

"There might be more," Brian said.

"I doubt it. Ant won't do anything, he's allergic to confrontation and anything that involves him having to do something."

"Oh, is it over then?" said Olivia.

"Right," said Faye, "We'd better get this barbecue started."

"Can I help?" Olivia said, "I'm a marvelous cook, if I do say so myself, and I have a fantastic recipe for sticky barbecue chicken that I've been dying to do for ages."

"I'll get the chicken," Mark cried, racing back to his caravan, dragging his chair behind him.

It was going to be a barbecue to remember.

CHAPTER 5

Tel and Sophie had left the campsite shortly after Faye and Brian had gone on their cheese and windchime hunt. Far from 'taking in' the tourist areas, they drove straight to the nearest five-star hotel, had brunch in the very sumptuous restaurant, and were now lounging across a four poster bed in a room upstairs.

"Terribly embarrassing to hire a room for the afternoon," Sophie was saying, stroking Tel's chest. "The woman at reception gave me a really funny look."

"Thought you were a hooker, I expect."

"Really?" Sophie lifted her head, smiling. "How exciting."

"We can stay here if you want, I can ring the man to come and collect the tin can and I'll book us – "

"What, and miss the fun of the barbecue, after all we've been through to muster supplies?"

"You want to go back?"

"Yes." She rested her head on his chest again. "I think I'm actually quite liking it. The people are nice, friendly, kind. I like that. I like them."

"Well, there's a shocker."

"I'm not so much of a snob that I don't recognize decent people when I see them."

"You're giving up a room in a five-star hotel to go back to a campsite to eat burnt chicken?"

"Yeah, why not? You said to treat it like an adventure."

"Slumming it with the common people? Down and dirty with down to earth people."

"No, not at all! I told you, I like them. I think I'd quite like to spend more time with them and learn a bit of humility, god knows I need it."

Tel laughed. "Okay then. I must say, you've surprised me."

"I'm full of surprises," she grinned, and leaned up to kiss him.

* * *

They drove back to the campsite with the roof down on the car, Sophie's curly black hair blowing freely in the wind instead of bound tight at the nape of her neck. Tel was wearing a satisfied smile and kept looking at her, very pleased with himself, no doubt, and so he should be.

"Happy?" he asked.

"Very."

When they pulled into the caravan area the place was *buzzing*.

"Oh my god!" Sophie cried, jumping out of the car.

Tel was open mouthed.

Everyone and everything was on the hardstanding pitch next to their silver bullet.

"You don't mind, do you?" cried Mark, tending sausages on the kettle barbecue while Brian tended beefburgers on a smaller one. The giant coolbox of beer and meat stood between them, plugged into an extension cable that was attached to the outside of the Airstream. "You've got the most space."

"No, of course not," Tel replied, smiling. "This is amazing."

"Isn't it," Faye said, "It's all a matter of teamwork. Oh, Olivia, do you think the chicken will be done yet?"

"I'll just check," and she raced back to the motorhome.

"There's drinks on Mark's camping table over there," Faye said, pointing at it *laden* with a variety of bottles next to the Airstream. "Paper plates, napkins – "

"Ooh, napkins, bit posh," said Julie, snuggling up next to Jim on the wooden picnic table.

" – plastic knives and forks and glasses on Olivia's ornate

bistro table over there, and there's bread rolls and a knife on our table. Try not to kill yourselves with the knife, people, Brian likes to keep his kitchen implements sharp."

"Chicken!" Brian boomed, watching Olivia carry a very large serving plate across the gravel driveway, "Smells bloody delicious. There's cold lager here if anybody wants one."

"Yeah, I'll have another, Bri," said Jim.

"Did you bring anything to the party at all?" Brian enquired, handing him a can.

"My sparkling personality, and the *actual* barbecue."

"Which I paid for," Tel grinned, pouring himself a whisky and soda.

"And what are you going to do with a kettle barbecue in a third-floor apartment in the middle of London?" Sophie whispered, unlocking the door to the silver bullet and going inside.

"You can keep it," Tel shouted over to Jim, who shouted back, "Cheers, Tel."

Sophie reappeared at the door holding two spirit bottles, one of expensive whisky with a cork, another of coloured gin.

"Oh, what flavour is it?" Julie asked.

"Raspberry and elderflower."

"I'll try some of that."

Sophie poured two small, plastic glasses and handed one to Julie, before quickly sipping the other and jumping up into the bullet again, returning with two more bottles.

"How many did you buy?" Tel asked.

"Lots," Sophie laughed. "I've got cherry flavoured rum and Mediterranean orange gin if anyone's interested." She plonked them down on the table, next to several bottles of wine. The table wobbled precariously. She picked them up and put them underneath, in the shade, and jumped back into the van, returning with two more.

"Sophie!" Tel cried.

"What? I'm on holiday! Peach flavoured vodka," she

called out, reading the labels, "No idea why I bought that, it sounds appalling, and some fiery bourbon." She put them under the table, where they clanked against the others. Julie wandered over, closely followed by Jim. "Which one's the expensive whisky?" he asked. Tel snatched it up and held it tightly in his arms.

Olivia placed the giant plate of oven-cooked chicken covered in barbecue sauce on the wooden table and flushed red when they all 'oohed' over it. "There's more," she said, and raced back to the motorhome, returning with something in a large, round tin. "Ta da," she said, placing it next to the chicken, which was already half gone.

"What is it?" Julie asked.

"Is it an omelette?"

"It's a frittata," Olivia said, cutting into it. "It's an Italian dish, similar to a crustless quiche. I've used chorizo, cheese, mushrooms and fresh tarragon, with just a hint of mustard to boost the flavour, and asparagus on top. I made two, a big one for us and a smaller one for Richard."

"My god, woman," Brian said from his position at the barbecue, "Is there anything you can't cook?"

"Yorkshire puddings," she said with a giggle, "Just can't seem to get the hang of them at all."

"See me later," Brian winked.

They all held out their plates, Mark and Brian leaving their barbecues unattended for a moment. "Cooks first!" Brian cried, snatching the first plate and another for Mark. There was a moment's silence as they all started eating, followed by the hum of people murmuring their approval, like the low mooing of cows. Oliva flushed again.

"Burgers are done!" Brian boomed.

"And the sausages," Mark cried, "Get your fresh cooked sausages here!"

There was a mini scuffle and plates were piled high with cooked meat, piled even higher with Faye's enormous salad. Brian and Mark sat at the wooden bench to eat, adding the remainder of their cooked meats to the feast.

"This is amazing," they all kept saying, and then fell into silent appreciation, interspersed with the occasional nomming.

"So, how long you two been married then?" asked Mark.

"21 years," Brian said.

"23 years," Faye corrected.

"Oh, is it? My, how time flies when you're enjoying yourself. Murderers get less, you know."

"The old ones are the best," she sighed

"Wives, you mean?"

"Don't make me get up and beat you, Bri."

"How did you meet?" Mark reached over for another chicken piece, already deciding to ask Olivia for the recipe, the sauce was *amazing*.

"I was working at a steel stockholders in Bradford and they asked me to cover some staff shortages at their branch in Cradley. I thought, why not, didn't have anything else to do and they say a change is as good as a rest. I walked into Tesco Express one day to grab something for lunch when I spotted the most beautiful woman in the baked beans section."

Faye rolled her eyes but smiled.

"Big, brown eyes, face like an angel, voice straight out of Peaky Blinders."

"Hey, cheeky!"

"Went same time next day and there she was again."

"I worked in a care home just up the road," said Faye, "I used to go to Tesco's for stuff the residents wanted. Took him three weeks to ask me out, the residents were sick of baked beans by the time he got round to it."

"Two kids later and we're still happy," Brian said, and reached out to hold Faye's hand across the table. She dramatically brushed a tear from her eye. "Apart from the stabbings and the fights and the police being called to the house several times a week."

"And the dreadful sense of humour."

Everyone laughed.

"So," Mark said, now tucking into a slice of frittata, "What's the secret to a happy marriage then?"

"Sheer determination," said Brian, "Bloody-minded, teeth grinding, fist clenching, mind-blowing determination."

Faye dropped her plastic fork onto her paper plate and looked at him.

"What?" he asked.

"I didn't think I was that hard to live with," she said quietly.

"Don't be daft, woman, I'm not talking about *me*, I'm talking about *you*. Patience of a bloody saint, no idea how you've put up with me for so long!"

Faye stood up and quickly walked round to the other side of the table, wrapped her arms round his neck and planted a kiss on his hairy cheek. "Earplugs," she said, "I owe it all to earplugs. And alcohol."

The laughter echoed over the campsite. More drinks were poured, more food was eaten. Tel, noticing that Olivia didn't have a drink, went over with a plastic glass and a bottle of wine.

"Oh, not for me, thank you," she said, "I don't drink, Richard doesn't like it."

"Richard's not here," Tel winked, "Go a little mad, you are on holiday, after all."

"Oh," she laughed, "Go on then, just a little one."

Tel half-filled her glass with a rather nice Chianti before she raised her hand and stopped him.

Julie dripped some barbecue sauce on her chest and cried, "Oh Jim, look what I've done!"

"Fear not, my lovely," and he dipped his head and licked it off. Julie threw back her head and shrieked with laughter, quickly glancing round to make sure everybody was watching.

"So how long have you and Richard been together then?" Brian asked.

"Oh, we've been together for five years, married for

three. No children or pets, Richard is allergic, to pets I mean, not children, at least I don't think he's allergic to children." She laughed. "We didn't meet, daddy brought him home from his golf club one day and said he was good husband material, so we got married."

"Sounds so romantic," Julie said, twiddling her hair as she leaned against Jim.

"Well, maybe not romantic, but he looks after me and I look after him."

"Is he a good husband?" Faye couldn't resist asking.

"I think so, but then I've only had one," she laughed, "I have nothing to compare him to. We're not like you and Brian, you seem so happy together, it must be lovely, but Richard and I get along quite well."

"Even though he's a bully," Jim blurted, and they all glared at him. "What?" he said, "He is!"

Olivia's smile waned. "He can't help it," she said, "It's just the way he is. He's very particular about everything, likes things done in a certain way, a bit like daddy. Mummy said if you keep the men happy they won't cause you too much trouble. And Richard has a germ phobia and OCD, which makes life very difficult for him, I have to keep everything scrupulously clean and tidy."

"Sounds like *your* life is difficult, not his," Faye dared to say, and Brian gave her a look, she could almost hear him saying, 'Not your business, woman, don't interfere', but he was the one who started it.

"I don't mind," Olivia said, lowering her head, "It's my job as his wife to look after him and do what he asks."

"Have we time-warped back to the 1950s?" Mark whispered to Brian. Brian shrugged, thinking that women seemed to have enormous stamina when dealing with their menfolk.

"Where does he go all day?" Tel asked.

"Oh, he's researching old Cotswold churches. He wants to become the leading expert on the subject, so he digs up all the old history and writes it down. He's going to publish a book, he says it will make him very rich and famous and that people will finally realise what a genius he is."

"How interesting," Sophie said, "How long has he been doing research?"

"Since we got the motorhome, so about three months now."

"And I think that tells us all we need to know about the man," Brian whispered to Mark, who nodded.

"Anyway," Olivia brightened, eager to change the subject, "Does anyone want more chicken?"

Everyone groaned and rubbed their stomachs "Couldn't eat another thing," Brian boomed.

"Me neither."

"I'm so stuffed."

"I may never eat again."

"I've made some cheese biscuits, with a fresh tomato relish to go with some stilton, if anybody's interested?"

"Oh, go on then."

"Would be rude not to."

Olivia picked up the now empty serving plate covered in barbecue sauce and the empty frittata tin and hurried back to her motorhome. Mark suddenly said, "I know what we need." He hurried to his caravan, emerging moments later with a CD player. He put it on a table, plugged it into the extension cable running Brian's coolbox, and pressed the play button. Barbara Streisand starting singing about some wayward man with Celine Dion. Mark pressed another button and Whitney Houston belted out *I Will Always Love You*, followed by Dolly Parton, standing in a stream.

"What's this CD called?" Brian asked, as Mark flicked through it, trying to find some decent barbecue music, "Wailing Women?"

"How to Make You Feel Worse About Your Broken Heart," Julie laughed.

"Think You're Depressed Now? Then Listen to This,"

Faye cackled.

"Kill Me Now!" Sophie added.

"It's all there is," Mark shrugged, "It was already in the CD player when I got here."

"Was it?" Tel questioned with a sideways look, "Or don't you want to admit to owning such a disc of despair?"

"Disc of Despair," Faye cried, "That's it, bestseller in the Mangled Heart section on Amazon."

Jim fell off the bench laughing, dragging Julie down on top of him, where they stayed snogging for a bit.

"We need proper music!" Brian boomed, stomping off across the driveway.

"I bet it's Frank Sinatra," Jim laughed.

"Buddy Holly," said Mark.

"Vera Lynn," Sophie suggested.

"He's not *that* old!" Faye said.

"Oh, sorry. He has a timeless look about him. Indeterminate."

"It's the beard," said Faye, "Covers up a multitude of sins."

Brian returned with a CD and slotted it into the player, pressed a button and moved the volume up a tadge so they could all hear it. Turning, he held out a hand to Faye and she took it and stood up, just as Alan Jackson began singing *Chattahoochee*. He led her onto the gravel driveway, where there was more room, and then, looking straight ahead with their hands on their hips, they started dancing. Line dancing.

Sophie cried out with delight, nearly making Tel and his whisky topple off his seat. "I know this one!" she said, jumping up and joining Brian and Faye on the driveway. All three side-stepped and jumped, spun and swung their feet around in time to the music, Sophie almost perfectly in step with Brian and Faye. "Dance classes," she laughed at Tel's confused and amused face, "It's good for stress."

Julie jumped up and joined them. "I didn't know you could line dance, Jules?" Jim called after her.

"She can't," Mark said, watching her rub her hands over her body as she pouted provocatively at Jim, "But top marks for turning line dancing into pole dancing without a pole."

"That's my girl," said Jim.

"Ooh," cried Olivia, and got up, rather unsteadily, walked unsteadily to the driveway, and unsteadily tried to follow the steps, almost tripping over her own feet. "I think I'm a bit squiffy," she giggled.

"Get up there, Mark," jeered Tel. "Go on, you know you want to, you can barely restrain your country-tapping feet."

So he did, slapping Tel on the shoulder as he passed and saying, "You too, mate, you too."

So now everyone except Jim was on the driveway, line dancing, some better than others, as Alan Jackson started singing about tall, tall trees. Jim lounged across the wooden table, watching and laughing and lighting up a spliff. A couple of campers in the field opposite started barn dancing along to the music, and someone hollered, "Yee-haa!"

Suddenly, the posh blonde woman from next door appeared, standing at the edge of their pitch with a face more horse-like than before and much more thunderous. "What's all this noise?" she cried.

"It be music, love," Jim said, "You may have heard of it?"

"My *children* are trying to *sleep*!"

Jim looked at his watch, his spliff hanging from the side of his mouth. "It's 5.45! What are your children doing in bed at 5.45?"

"They're preparing for sleep, relaxing and unwinding. They can't be excited or they'll never get off."

Two children appeared from behind the Airstream, idly wandering over the way small children do, running their hands along the shiny surface and kind of staggering nonchalantly onto the scene. "Mummy," said the little girl, "I'm hungry, when are we going to eat?"

The boy, a couple of years older than his sister, came up to the wooden picnic bench and began picking at the sausages, biting one before moving onto the next.

"Tarquin, don't eat that!" snapped the woman, "It's not plant-based."

The boy continued to chomp on the sausage, and now his sister started picking at the remaining beefburgers. They'd all stopped dancing now. Brian came over and turned off the music, taking a plastic glass of beer that the girl was about to upend into her mouth. The others stood there on the driveway, a bit surprised that everything had suddenly stopped.

"Sorry to disturb," Brian said, "The music's not actually that loud."

"What's happening?" Faye asked.

"Your music is disturbing my children!"

"Oh. Sorry." Faye looked at Brian, who shrugged.

The woman's attention remained firmly on Jim. "Are you ...?" She feigned horror and outrage as she raised both her hands to her face. "Are you smoking *drugs*?"

Jim quickly spat the nub onto the gravel.

"Are you smoking drugs *right next to my children*?"

"No, it's just – "

"Are you just going to leave it there to burn down the entire campsite?"

Jim picked the nub up, didn't quite know what to do with it, and quickly pushed it into an empty beer can.

Several campers were now standing outside their tents on the field, looking over and watching the scene unfold.

"JACKIE!" the woman cried, "JACKIE, COME AND HAVE A LOOK AT THIS!"

The woman from the other VW van, which was now parked next to the other woman's VW on the grass, not the gravel, came scurrying over. "What is it, Candice-Marie?" Her two children followed her and immediately rushed to the food on the picnic table, where all four now stood merrily munching away at the barbecue leftovers.

"This man," Candice-Marie declared, pointing a waggling finger at Jim, "is smoking drugs!"

"Why are you smoking drugs?" the second woman cried, overly horrified, "Don't you know there's children round here!"

"We do," said Tel, "and most of them appear to be stuffing their faces at our table."

"You shouldn't leave food lying around like that in the countryside," said Jackie, "It encourages vermin."

Tel opened his mouth to say something about hungry pests, but Sophie dug him in the ribs with her elbow and he just *oophed* instead.

"Why have you got a picnic table anyway?" shrieked Candice-Marie, "We haven't got a picnic table." Jackie firmly shook her head. "Did you take our table before we got here?"

"No, we stole it from the pub," Mark laughed.

"Stole it? Right, that's it," Candice-Marie declared, "The music, the drinking, the lewd dancing – "

'Lewd?' Faye mouthed at Brian, and Brian nodded towards Julie, who was standing quite close to the shrieking woman and staring up at her in awe. "Haven't you got a lovely voice," she said, "You sound just like the queen."

" – smoking drugs and ruining it for everyone else," Candice-Marie continued, paying Julie no attention. "I'm not putting up with this appalling behaviour for one more instant, you're setting a terrible example for our children! Jackie, come on, we're going to see the manager." And off they stomped.

"Poor Ant," said Mark, "He's got his work cut out with those two. I mean, he didn't exactly leap into action last time, did he."

"Excuse me," Tel shouted after the women, "Would you mind taking your children with you?"

One of the women bawled, "Tarquin! Zena! Eugenie! Harry! With us, please!"

The kids didn't move, didn't appear to hear. The four of them had moved over to the plastic table where the bread rolls were piled high, ripping open the packets, pulling the bread out in big chunks and pushing it into their mouths. The smallest one took a piece over to a barbecue and was about to put it on the hot grill before Olivia stopped her. The girl picked up a cheese biscuit from the wooden table as she passed and pushed it into her mouth. She immediately coughed and spat it out.

"Off you go, kids," Faye encouraged brightly. One of them briefly looked up at her, then down again at the bread. The bread griller moved over to the other barbecue and reached out for the tongs. Sophie put her arm out to stop her and she wandered back to the bread. The mothers disappeared through the wooden gates.

"Go to your mothers," Sophie said with a smile.

"Ooh, where's mummy gone?" Olivia cried gaily.

Nothing.

"Have you got any pop?" the oldest child asked, "I'm thirsty."

"Go and ask mummy."

"Is this pop?" another asked, picking up the peach-flavoured gin bottle. Sophie snatched it out of their hands.

Brian moved towards them and bent down to their scoffing faces. "Go to your mothers!" he growled. The smallest girl looked up at his enormity and began screaming. One of the mothers, the dark haired one, stomped back through the gate and screamed, "ARE YOU MAKING MY CHILDREN CRY?"

"NOT YET!" Brian boomed.

"TARQUIN! ZENA! EUGENIE! HARRY! COME OVER HERE AT ONCE!"

The children flew off like a flock of birds, screaming like seagulls that the big man had shouted at them.

The group looked from one to the other across the aftermath of strewn bread rolls and plates devoid of sausages and beefburgers.

"Way to set kids up to be regularly beaten at school with names like that," Brian said, shaking his head.

"I didn't think the music was that loud," said Jim.

"It wasn't."

Someone from the field shouted, "Put the music back on!"

So Brian did, and they regrouped on the driveway and started line-dancing again, laughing and occasionally breaking off to slurp at a drink. Julie even got Jim up, and they smooched along to the music while everyone else hopped and jumped with their hands on their hips. The music changed to a slow piece and they paired up, smooching along with Jim and Julie. Mark and Olivia danced awkwardly together, laughing a bit too much and leaving enough gap between them to drive a motorhome through, and then the next track had them all hopping and jumping again.

The two women and their brood of strangely-named children returned and stormed straight into their vans, herding the children inside and throwing evil looks in their direction, but they were having far too much of a good time to notice. As Alan Jackson sang out, a couple of women from the field came running over, halted by Candice-Marie, who charged out of her van and stood firmly at the entrance to the hardstanding area. "NO!" she cried, holding up a firm hand, "You can't come in here, this isn't a middle-aged rave, you know!" The women turned and wandered back to their tents, glancing over their shoulders and muttering, "Middle aged? Bloody cow."

Next track, a smoochy. Faye, quite puffed now, rested her head on Brian's broad chest to catch her breath. Sophie and Tel danced forehead to forehead, smiling at each other. Mark and Olivia danced a meter apart, holding fingertips and laughing.

"Unhand my wife at once!" snapped a voice.

They all turned.

There stood Richard on the driveway, his long face incandescent with rage.

CHAPTER 6

Mark dropped his hands to his sides straight away, feeling like he'd been caught doing something naughty. Olivia, however, who was definitely a bit 'squiffy', reacted differently.

"Oh Richard!" she cried, laughing, "You did make me jump! I wasn't expecting you back so early."

"Yes, I can see that."

"Come and join us." She staggered over to him and grabbed his arm. "We're having such a lovely time."

"Yes, join us," Faye said, "You're very welcome. There's even some food left. Isn't Olivia a brilliant cook?"

Richard glared at her. She wished she hadn't mentioned Olivia's cooking, he hadn't seemed very pleased about them 'eating his food' yesterday. "We bought all the food, Olivia just did a fantastic barbecue sauce for the chicken."

"Would you like a drink?" Sophie asked, "We've got pretty much everything, even a fine whisky. No ice though."

"Come and sit down, mate," Jim urged.

Richard stood dead still, eyeballing them one by one with his slitty little eyes. When he set his sight on Olivia again, who was now standing next to the table picking at the remains of the frittata, he said, quietly menacing, "Go back to the motorhome, Olivia."

"Oh, we haven't finished yet, have we," she giggled at everyone. "We're having such a *lovely* time. Line dancing!" she suddenly cried, "We must learn line dancing, Richard, it's absolutely – "

"Olivia, go back to the motorhome."

"But I'm not ready." She plonked herself down at the wooden table and finished off the dregs of her half glass of wine. "I really like this, what is it?" she asked Tel.

"Chianti. I think there might be another – "

"I think she's had more than enough," Richard snapped.

"No, I think I might have a tiny bit more. You should try it, Richard, it's – "

"Enough, Olivia!"

"Oh, you're such an old spoilsport, we were just having a bit of fun."

"After I told you not to fraternise with them again? After I distinctly told you *not* to leave the motorhome? You deliberately disobeyed me, Olivia."

"I got bored all by myself. You go out all day and expect me just to sit there and clean and read." Behind them came the crack of a tree branch and the rustle of some dry leaves, but everyone was too caught up in the moment to pay much attention. "I was *bored* to *sobs*."

Brian noticed that Richard's hands were curled into tight fists at his sides and he seemed to be struggling to control his inner rage. He'd seen this sort of thing in the warehouse before, enraged men, and knew situations like this could escalate out of control in the blink of an eye. "Richard," he effused with a huge smile behind his beard, "Please, sit down for five minutes and I'll get you – "

"No."

"Honestly," tried Sophie, rushing for a clean plastic glass and fingertipping her way through the bottles, "We'd love you to stay for just a little while, maybe you'll realise we're not such – "

"You are!" Richard hissed, "You are exactly how I imagine you to be!"

"That's not fair," said Faye, "We're all utterly adorable, give us five minutes and we'll – "

"Olivia," he said, his teeth and fists clenched tight, "I'm only going to say this one more time – "

"And then what are you going to do, stop my sweetie money?" Olivia didn't seem to be reading him very well at all. She'd only had half a glass of wine and was laughing in the face of some considerable wrath.

"Get back to the motorhome, Olivia. Go now, right this minute."

"Just hold on a sec," Mark said, stepping forward. Brian caught his eye and briefly shook his head. Mark took a deep breath and nodded, but he looked far from happy. His lips pursed together in an effort not to speak.

Olivia stood up and threw what could be mistaken for an angry look at Richard, although it was impossible to imagine Olivia anything other than giggly and highly excited. She huffed loudly as she extricated herself from the picnic table and, with a wiggle of her fingers and a genuine smile at everyone, she sauntered slowly and unsteadily back to the motorhome.

"She was really enjoying herself," Julie said.

"If I find you enticing my wife away like that again I'll – "

"You'll what?" Mark asked, "Take us all to task, one by one? Have you seen the size of him?" He nodded towards Brian, who threw out his chest in a menacing way. "I'd like to see you try it, *pal*."

"I'll … I'll have you all removed from the site."

Mark laughed. "Good luck with that. Have you met the owner? Idle bugger. Also, a very good mate of mine."

With a final furious glare, Richard spun on his heels and marched back to the motorhome. They all stood there, waiting, watching, listening, anxious about the woman with the cute overbite and bright smile. Silence. And then heavy footsteps and raised voices. Sophie caught her breath and held onto Tel's arm. Faye looked at Brian. And then one voice echoed across the campsite, high-pitched and indignant: "No, I will not!"

Faye looked at Brian and said, "Maybe we should … ?"

He raised a finger; wait. They all stood still, looking back at the grey motorhome in the corner of the caravan area. There was the clatter of what sounded like saucepans. Mark said, "He'd better not – "

Olivia's voice again, shrieking, "How dare you embarrass me like that in front of my friends, how *dare* you, Richard!"

"Give him what for, Olivia," Sophie grinned, and they all seemed to exhale at once.

"Where's your dinner? You show up early to try and catch me out, ruin the only bit of fun I've had in ages, and you want to know where your *dinner* is?" They could hear a door being thrown open and footsteps stomping across the hardstanding. Olivia appeared from behind the motorhome wearing oven gloves and holding a tin. She stood in the middle of the driveway and launched the tin as hard as she could into the air. The frittata travelled a good distance before it rattled across the gravel and then splattered into a steaming heap. "It's there!" she shrieked, "Go and get it if you want it!" And then, noticing them all standing there, she broke into a huge smile and wiggled her fingers at them again. "I'm a bit squiffy, you know."

"We noticed," Tel laughed.

"Go Olivia!" Faye said.

Richard appeared and pointed a finger at them all. "You will not encourage my wife to – "

"Oh shut up," Olivia scolded, pushing past him and stomping back to the motorhome. He followed. There were some heavy footsteps from inside before Olivia shrieked, "No, I'm not sleeping on the sofa tonight! I don't care if you don't like the smell of alcohol on my breath, *you* sleep on the sofa if it bothers you that much!"

"Whoa," Tel laughed, "Seems our quiet little Olivia has finally found her voice."

"It certainly does."

* * *

More than a little drunk and exhausted from all the dancing, they wandered back to their vans around 10 o'clock, with Candice-Marie shouting, "About time too!" They looked over at the sound of her voice. She was sitting on a folding chair on the driveway outside her VW with her friend, Jackie, both stony faced, their arms crossed firmly across their chests. "We've had to stop the tent people from getting in or we'd have been overrun with gatecrashers. You're all *very* inconsiderate, there are people trying to sleep, you know."

Brian looked at his watch. "It's 10 o'clock, woman, get a grip of yourself!"

"Don't call me *woman*! It's offensive."

"It's less offensive than what I want to – "

"Brian!"

"Okay, *thingy*," he said instead, "Get a grip of yourself, *thingy*."

"How dare you!"

"I dare, I'm drunk and I dare and I don't care," he laughed.

"Come on, Brian, time for bed."

"Said Zebedee, hopefully. Hopefully?" He looked at his wife's raised eyebrow and said, "No? I'll crack you with my charming powers of persuasion." The eyebrow lifted higher. "Fine, I'm tired anyway."

* * *

Nobody slept well that night. Brian started snoring as soon as his head hit the pillow, the thunderous noise reverberating across the entire campsite. Faye tried to turn him over onto his side but it was like pushing an immovable object. In the end she jabbed in some earplugs, but she could still hear him. It felt like the whole caravan was vibrating.

Sophie and Tel felt ill from all the alcohol they'd happily poured down their necks and the food they'd gluttonously stuffed themselves with. Tel sat curled up on the toilet floor with his head strategically positioned over the plastic loo, while Sophie lay on the bed hugging a washing up bowl. "I'm going to be sick," she groaned, just as Tel barfed, which made her heave again. They stayed like that all night, only occasionally moving to gulp water straight from the tap.

Mark lay in bed with his book. It was a good book

and, because he wasn't a big drinker, he was eager to find out what happened next. He was so engrossed he didn't hear the first crack of a branch outside or the rustle of dry leaves, he only noticed when his caravan rocked a little and a small voice cried, "Oomph." He sat up and looked out of the window. It wasn't fully dark yet and he could see the trees and the bushes and the shadow of someone or something running away.

Probably a deer.

He resumed his book.

* * *

With a huge snort Brian opened his eyes. He stared at the ceiling, his mouth as dry as the Arizona desert. He considered getting a bottle of water out of the fridge, but then remembered how much he'd had to drink the night before and didn't, in the end, dare move. He heard a tapping sound. He'd heard the tapping in his dreams, the tapping had dragged him from his sleep and was now keeping him from resuming sleep. A tiny voice cried, "Brian? Brian? You awake, Brian?"

"I am now," he boomed. "Who is that?"

"It's Jim. Have you got anything to drink in there, we're dying of thirst?"

Brian growled. The bed creaked. "Have you woken me up to ask for a drink?"

"Julie's thirsty too. Have you got anything?"

He groaned. Faye lay asleep next to him, totally oblivious in her bright orange earplugs. "Get a plastic glass and take it to the water tap!"

"What plastic glass?"

"The bulk-buy tower of plastic glasses outside Sophie and Tel's caravan. Good god, lad, could you not figure that out for yourself?"

"Okay. Thanks, Bri. Sorry, Bri."

* * *

Sophie was just vowing to never drink again as long as she lived for about the millionth time when she heard a noise outside, right next to where she was lying, separated from whatever it was by only a thin piece of tin. "Tel," she croaked, slowly sitting up, "Tel, there's someone out there."

"If it's a psychotic serial killer, unlock the door and let them in."

"I'm serious, Tel, there's someone out there!"

She unclipped a corner of the weird window blinds and peeked through. There was definitely someone outside, she could see them leaning over one of the tables. She heard the tinkle of bottles knocking together. "Tel, he's stealing our alcohol."

"Let him."

Sophie watched the dark shadow scurrying off with their head down, holding something shiny in their hand. She flopped back onto the bed. Her stomach flopped with her, and she leaned over the washing-up bowl, the booze thief now the furthest thing from her mind, survival was all that mattered now.

* * *

Olivia opened her eyes, stared up at the ceiling and groaned at the pain already throbbing in her temples. There was a circle of light on the ceiling and she focused on it, wondering if it was maybe a dream or a migraine. The light moved across the ceiling and down one wall on Richard's side. She followed it with her pulsating eyes. A car's headlights? A hallucination? Alien abduction?

The circle moved across the bedspread and Olivia watched it, slowly sucking in air, a panic building up inside her. "Richard," she gasped. He didn't answer, didn't move. Olivia raised her eyes up to the window, searching for the source of the light, and suddenly the light vanished and a dark, shrouded face appeared.

"RICHARD!"

She flung her arm out and whacked it against Richard's body. He sat bolt upright in bed and cried, "What? What is it?"

"There's someone out there!"

"Where?"

"Out *there*!"

She pointed at the window, but the face was now gone. Richard threw back the duvet and shimmied to the bottom of the bed, leapt up and bounded for the motorhome door, throwing it open and jumping down onto the gravel in his bare feet. He cried out in pain, making Olivia cry out in alarm from inside.

He spotted someone bent over the water tap between the motorhome and the scruffy caravan on the other side of the driveway. The someone turned their head to look back at him. Richard leapt over and was on them in a second, grabbing them fiercely round the neck and pushing them onto the ground.

"Hey! Hey!" they cried, "What the bloody hell are you doing?"

"Why are you lurking around our motorhome?" Richard demanded to know.

"I wasn't by your motorhome!"

"You were peering through the window at my *wife*!"

"No, I wasn't. It wasn't me. I saw someone there but they ran off into the trees. Let go of me!"

Richard let go of the man's neck but remained on his gravel-pained knees, breathing heavily over him. "What are you doing here?"

"I've just come for a drink!"

"Everything alright out here?" Mark asked, coming out of his caravan.

"Tell him to get off me, he's trying to kill me!"

Mark crunched his way over as Richard slowly stood up, the man lying on the gravel between them shouting, "I was thirsty! I just came to get a drink!"

"Jim?" said Mark.

"Yes!"

"You really are a bully, aren't you," Mark said to Richard.

"He was peering through our window!"

"I wasn't! Someone else was peering through your

window, it wasn't me!"

"Were you looking through my window earlier?" Mark asked.

Jim scrambled to his feet, two plastic glasses still in his hands. "Why is everyone accusing me of peering through their windows?"

"Because you're lurking around our caravans!" Richard hissed.

"I'm not lurking, I'm bloody thirsty. I came to get a drink, is that a crime now?"

"Someone was looking through your window, too?" Richard asked Mark.

"A little while ago. Couldn't see who it was though."

"It wasn't me!"

"Jim?" came a woman's voice, "Are you alright, Jim? What's happening?" Julie quickly picked her way down the driveway clutching a small blanket around her otherwise naked body. Jim was also naked. As was Richard. And Mark. "Why has no one got any clothes on?" she asked, "Is this like a nudist meeting or a swinger's party? Why did nobody tell me?"

"MY CHILDREN," screamed a woman from the top of the driveway, "ARE TRYING TO SLEEP!"

"STOP YELLING THEN!"

"YOU LOT ARE WAKING EVERYONE UP!"

"KEEP THE BLOODY NOISE DOWN!" came a voice from a tent in the field.

"SHUT UP!" came another.

"SEE!" hollered Candice-Marie, "YOU'VE WOKEN EVERYONE UP! YOU PEOPLE ARE JUST SO *INCONSIDERATE*!"

Jackie leapt out of her VW van and stomped onto the driveway next to her friend. "What's going on, Candice-Marie?"

"It's those bladdy people again."

"What do you mean, those bloody people?" snapped Mark.

"The same bladdy people who were making a nuisance

of themselves earlier," Candice-Marie barked back. "Oh my god! Why are you all naked? Are you members of some cult? Is this a cult rally?"

Richard was, by now, shuffling backwards to his motorhome with his hands covering his private parts. Jim and Julie were huddled over the water tap, mooning everyone as they filled the plastic glasses and gulped it down. Julie stood up, wiped her mouth and stared down at Mark. "Ooh, you're a big boy, aren't you."

"Stop eyeballing men's penises!" Jim snapped.

"I can't help it, can I, if they're happily flapping them about like that."

Mark covered his manhood and slowly retreated backwards to his caravan. Jim and Julie filled their plastic glasses and took them to their van, passing Candice-Marie and Jackie, who averted their gaze from their nakedness. Alone now on the gravel driveway, they both huffed and turned to their VWs, when Jackie suddenly let out a blood-curdling scream.

"What the fluffin' hell is it now!" cried someone in a tent.

"There's someone there!" she shrieked, pointing to the trees a short distance away, "I saw someone running through the woods."

Both women gripped onto each other. "Hello?" squeaked Candice-Marie, "Is there anyone there?"

Quick footsteps thrashed through the undergrowth and both women rocketed into high octaves and clutched at each other. A man in a nearby tent unzipped the door and pushed his head out like he was being born, "WILL YOU *PLEASE* BE QUIET!"

"THERE'S SOMEONE IN THE WOODS" Jackie cried.

The man's head disappeared and the canvas flaps zipped shut.

"They don't care that there's two vulnerable women on their own being stalked by a homicidal maniac," Candice-

Marie declared loudly.

"No, we don't," said the tent, "We just want some bloody sleep!"

"Men!" snorted Candice-Marie.

"Harridans!" snorted the tent.

Candice-Marie released her terrified grip on Jackie. Jackie latched back onto her like a limpet. "I can't be alone now, not when there's someone *out there*!"

"You'd better get the kids and come into my van then."

There followed the sounds of children being woken up, children not being very happy about being woken up and children sniveling their way from one VW to another. The sound of whining and thunderous snoring echoed across the campsite, followed by the sound of someone fornicating in a van on one side of the driveway and someone else retching on the other.

Faye, in her orange earplugs, slept through it all.

Day 3 - Sunday

Brian was dreaming. He was dreaming he was floating high up in the sky, amongst fluffy white clouds, his body weightless. He thought he could hear angels tuning up to sing in the distance. And then, a loud bang. In his dream he saw his heart burst out of his chest, still attached to blood vessels and other gooey stuff, thump loudly and largely in front of him, before flying back into his chest. The angels sang, his body floated. His heart flew out of his chest again, pounded once, and shot back in. And again. Thump. Thump.

Brian thought, *Am I having a heart attack*?

Thump. Thump.

Is this it then, the end?

Thump.

Did I tell Faye I loved her enough? Will she be okay without me?

Thump. Thump.

Brian opened his eyes. The clouds disappeared. The angels stopped singing. The world came into focus, and with it a loud thumping sound. The last beats of his heart? He reached over to Faye and shook her. She mumbled awake and turned to him, taking out the orange earplugs. And then he heard a woman's voice outside shouting, "That's it, children, wake them up like they woke you up last night."

Brian lifted himself up with some considerable effort onto his elbows, raised the blind and peered out of the window. There appeared to be a tribe of small people kicking a ball against his caravan.

"GERRAWAY!" he bawled.

Faye gave a little laugh. "It's only the same punishment you gave Jim and Julie when they were bonking all night."

"Bonking?" Brian eased himself down onto the mattress, grinning now. "Is that good for hangovers?"

"I'm not sure the bed's up for it."

"I wasn't asking the bed."

He leaned over to kiss her. She started to put her arms around him but then suddenly pushed him away. "Your teeth are full of barbecue, and my breath probably stinks."

"It does, but I don't care."

"Well I do."

Hangover forgotten, Brian quickly hauled himself off the bed and lumbered to the 'bathroom' to hastily scrub his teeth. Faye followed, dragging the duvet off the bed, and he passed her the electric toothbrush and toothpaste to use at the kitchen sink. They both stood furiously brushing their teeth with frothy smiles and groped each other with their free hands. Brian finished first and cried, "Yee-haa!" as he leapt back towards the bed.

"Brian, no! The slats!"

Too late, Brian was already committed to flying heftily through the air. In his head he thought, 'Probably not a good idea,' and tried to turn in mid-flight. He landed in the middle of the pull-out bed with all the elegance and weight of a hippopotamus. The slats between the sofas immediately caved on impact and Brian's giant body hit the floor beneath, the two 'sprung for extra comfort' seat cushions flipping up and pinning him firmly in place. His head rested at an acute angle against the drawers. He was wedged.

"Brian?"

"Yes, Faye?"

"Are you hurt?"

"Not that I'm aware, but I do appear to be ... " He gave a little wiggle, but nothing budged, not his bulk, not the cushions, nothing. One arm was pinned underneath him. He tried to pull himself up with his free arm but couldn't get a grip on anything. " ... stuck."

"Stuck?"

"Yes."

"Try to wriggle free."

"Tried."

"Lift yourself up with your free arm."

"Tried."

"Can't you – ?"

"Faye, I'm trapped."

"You can't move at all?"

"No, I'm just lying here like a sandwich filling for the fun of it."

"Okay, there's no need to be sarky. What should I do?"

"Pull me up."

"Pull you up? I'm not Wonder Woman, I don't have super-human strength!"

"See if you can pull one of the cushions out then."

Faye pulled at the bedsheet beneath him. She tried to move the vertical sofa cushions, but nothing gave at all. She attempted to remove the horizontal seat cushions in order to release the vertical cushions, but they were wedged in place too. Grabbing his free hand she pulled and tugged for a bit, but Brian was just too heavy and too stuck.

"Oh Brian," she gasped.

Brian's head wobbled up and down as he tried to unwedge himself, banging his head against the drawers, but the cushions held him in a vice-like grip and he couldn't lift himself up with one arm in such an awkward position.

"What are we going to do?"

Brian lay there, pincered between two sofas in the middle of his caravan, naked, and sighed heavily. He didn't want to say it but he said it anyway. "You're going to have to ... get some help."

"The fire brigade?"

"I was thinking more local."

"Who?"

"Mark," he sighed.

"Shall I get Tel and Jim too?"

"No, let's start with one before extending the humiliation."

Faye flung on her dressing gown and hurried out of the caravan. Brian lay there, trapped on his side on the floor, finding it quite hard to breath in the tight confines and trying not to panic about it. He braced himself for what was to come.

* * *

Faye knocked quickly on Mark's caravan door and got no immediate response, so carried on knocking, faster and harder, shouting, "Mark! Mark! Mark!" She finally heard movement from inside and Mark grunting, "Who is it?"

"It's Faye, we need your help."

"Just a sec."

Faye waited for what seemed like forever, hopping from one foot to the other and looking back at their caravan, where her husband lay stranded. Mark came to the door only moments later, zipping up his jeans. "You okay?"

"It's Brian, he's fallen."

"Oh my god, is he alright?"

Faye quickly beckoned him to follow her as she hurried back to the caravan, but Mark raced past her and leapt inside first. "Brian?"

"Mark."

"What are you doing on the floor?"

"Oh, you know, just relaxing."

"He's stuck," said Faye.

"How did you manage that?"

"Lustful haste, short flight through the air, lots of crashing and breaking, and voila."

Mark laughed in both relief and amusement. He braced himself at Brian's feet and reached out for his free hand. He tugged. He pulled. Brian wobbled his head, trying to free himself. Faye reached out for his wrist and started pulling too. With more seriousness now, Mark told her to move and stepped up, one foot on the end of each sofa, careful not to stand on the seating slats. He heaved at Brian's arm as Faye pulled on his foot, throwing herself back as hard as she could.

"One, two, three, *pull*," said Mark, as Brian threw his head up and down, feeling as if his arm and a foot were being pulled off. "One, two, three, *pull*."

"You're not moving, Brian."

"I'm not doing it on purpose, Faye."

"You're a bit of a hefty bugger," said Mark.

Mark tugged on the sheet for a while but still nothing budged. He managed to yank the horizontal cushions off and Faye tossed them outside. Together they gripped and pulled at the sheet, at the cushion wedged in front of Brian, then the back one, but they were really packed in tight and didn't give.

"I should mention ... that I'm finding it ... a bit hard to breathe."

"Oh god!" cried Faye.

"We're going to need more help."

* * *

Faye knocked quickly on the back doors of Jim's van. "Jim, Jim, we need your help! Jim! Jim! Julie! JIM!"

A groggy voice. "Whaddaya want?"

"We need your help." Silence. No movement. "Jim, it's an emergency, you have to come now!"

A cough. A tilting of the van. Muffled voices. And then one van door opened and Jim's bleary-eyes peered out.

"Brian's had an accident, he's fallen."

Like Mark, Jim was instantly awake, leaping out of the van naked and reaching back for his trousers, putting them on as he ran. An equally naked Julie lifted her head off the blow-up mattress and blinked at the light.

Faye hurried back to their caravan. Mark now had a knee on either side of Brian's head, reaching down behind his quite substantial neck and throwing his weight back to haul him out. "You're going t'pull my bloody head off!"

Jim took one look at Brian, lying sideways and naked on the floor between the sofas, and burst out laughing. "What is this, an orgy gone wrong?"

"Yeah, get the laughter over with," Brian gasped, "Then bloody help."

His free arm was pulled on by three sets of heaving hands, his legs were pulled, his legs and arm were pulled at the same time, and he did not move an inch – his weight held him down and the cushions pinned him in place. Brian gasped for breath.

"We need reinforcements," Mark eventually declared, and left the van.

* * *

He knocked quickly on Tel and Sophie's shiny door and waited. Knocked again. Knocked harder.

"People busy dying in here," came Tel's voice.

"Brian's stuck," Mark said.

"Stuck?"

"In his caravan."

"In his caravan?"

"Can you just come!"

"What's going on?" came Sophie's voice.

"Brian's ... just come, Tel, quick."

He heard them both groan before he ran back.

* * *

Tel stepped into the caravan, followed by Sophie. Despite the hangovers and the sleepless night, they still looked gorgeous, if a little green. They stared at everyone in the now crowded space, then saw Brian lying on his side on the floor between the sofas, naked.

"How did you get in that position?" Tel laughed.

"It was ... surprisingly easy. It's the getting up part that's ... difficult."

The five of them, struggling for space and leverage, pulled and tugged. Julie appeared and all six of them yanked at his feet, his arm, his head, the cushions, the sheet. Nothing would move. Brian gasped out loud in pain and frustration. He wasn't sure if it was panic or the pressure of the cushions, but he was really struggling to pull air into his crushed lungs now.

Tel looked at the end of the sofas. Everyone else peered inside them. A gazebo in a bag, expanding chairs, halogen oven, a box of lager, some blankets, a couple of cushions, medicine box, fire extinguisher.

"You pack a good caravan," said Sophie, impressed.

"I like to be prepared."

"For everything except ... a wedged husband."

"Well, if I'd known you were going to lustily launch yourself onto the bed I'd have brought a winch with me."

"Lustily?" Sophie grinned.

Faye grinned back and nodded.

"We're going to have to break him out," Tel said.

"Break the bed?"

"Yeah, release the pressure on the cushions. It's that, or call out the fire brigade."

"Break the bed!" Brian gasped, "Smash it! Get me ... out!"

"Don't suppose anyone's got a lump hammer, do they?" Tel asked.

"I have," said Jim, "In the back of my van. I'll get it."

There was much talk amongst the menfolk over the best trajectory for the hammer and the amount of force required to break the bottom of one sofa. The women stood outside to give them space, comforting Faye. Olivia anxiously came running over. "Is everything okay? Nobody's hurt or ill, are they?"

Inside the caravan, Jim prepared to swing the hammer.

"Don't bloody miss," Brian growled. "I don't want to be crippled for life because you have a shit aim."

Jim lifted the hammer behind him like a golf club and gave the bottom of the sofa a hefty crack. The wood remained in situ, didn't even splinter.

"Blimey, they don't make caravans like these anymore, do they," Mark said.

Jim raised the hammer again, swung it harder, and missed, hitting Brian full on the bottom of his foot. Brian whimpered breathlessly. Outside, the women waited anxiously.

"Third time lucky," said Mark, as Jim took nervous aim.

The wood broke this time with a satisfying crack. The three men tugged at the wooden frame and Brian was finally released its his tight restraints. They pulled a sofa cushion out and finally Brian was free. The men helped him up, just as the women clambered back into the caravan.

"You're all big boys around here," Julie grinned. "Give you a run for your money, Jim."

"I'm above average, Julie."

"Are you?" She licked her lips. "His is *massive*."

"I appreciate y'time and effort in rescuing me from murky depths of caravan floor," Brian said, snatching at the dressing gown Faye handed to him as she positioned herself in front of his nakedness with her arms outstretched like a policeman at a cordon line. "Now can you all bugger off while I try and salvage what remains of my dignity, and we'll never mention this again."

Julie was the last to leave, staring back at Brian with a cheeky smile.

"Out!" Faye cried.

They looked at the broken remains of their bed.

"I suppose a romp amongst the wreckage is out of the

question?" Brian asked.

Faye tutted. "Where the hell are we going to sleep now?"

CHAPTER 7

Later, after Brian had recovered a little and he and Mark stared at the broken sofa with screwdrivers in their hands for a while, Faye went over to Olivia's motorhome. Olivia was sitting outside at the wrought iron table, reading a book.

"How's Brian?" she asked, putting the book in her lap, pages open. In the bordering trees, a branch snapped and there was a dry rustle of leaves.

"He's okay."

"Was he injured?"

"Not physically, only his ego, although his ego was boosted somewhat when Julie told him he has a massive one."

"Massive what?"

"Massive manhood."

Olivia laughed, covering her mouth and flushing a little.

"How are you?" Faye asked, "You know, after last night?"

"Oh, I woke up with an awful hangover, but it's gone now."

"I meant with Richard."

"Oh, he was actually quite nice last night, seemed a bit alarmed, to be honest. I think I shocked him after I threw his dinner out." They both looked down the driveway, where the frittata tin remained but the contents had been consumed by some animal or a very hungry camper. "Lost my temper a bit I think, although I don't remember much."

"You were quite feisty, and you only had half a glass of wine."

"I know, but I don't normally drink and it went straight to my head. Lovely, though, I must ask Tel what it was, I might try it again."

"You little rebel."

"I know! Terrible, aren't I." Another tinkle of laughter.

"Maybe you should drink more often, keep the bugger on his toes."

"Oh no, I couldn't do that, I might become an alcoholic." The smile slipped from her face. "He was really moody before he went out this morning though, back to his old self. Left me a huge list of jobs to do so I wouldn't get 'bored' and 'wander off'."

"Don't do them."

"Oh, I *have* to do them."

"Do you?" An awkward silence, and then Faye, hearing Brian's voice in her head, added, "Listen to me, what am I like? Take no notice, I'm still in shock from my husband's wedged-in-ness. We're going out for lunch later, if you want to come?"

"Best not."

"You sure?"

"Yes, I've got loads of things to do, *loads*."

"Let me know if you change your mind. We'll be leaving as soon as Brian's figured out how to put the bed back together, which could take a while."

"I will, and thank you, Faye, thank you for being a friend, I don't have many. Well, none at all, actually. It's nice to have one."

"Sophie too, don't forget. Women power and all that."

"Yes, Sophie. Two friends. How lovely."

"Always here for you, Olivia. Don't forget that."

"I won't."

* * *

As Faye walked away, Olivia glanced over at Mark, sitting under the gazebo with a book. "Oh," she cried, and he looked up, "I think we're reading the same one." She held hers up for him to see and he laughed, "Oh yeah."

Somewhere behind them, in the trees, came the sound of quick, rustling footsteps, but neither of them noticed.

"How are you enjoying it?" Mark asked.

"It's very good. What page are you on?"

"132. You?"

"Not that far, 95."

Mark nodded and smiled.

Olivia lowered her head to the book on her lap and smiled too.

"There's a pub about a mile away does yer basic pub grub." Brian was sitting opposite the now bodged sofa, looking at his phone.

"I quite fancy a carvery."

"Carvery, carvery." Brian swiped his screen. "Nearest one is 10 miles."

"Oh, that's too far for a meal."

"The Hen and Pheasants in the village has quite a nice menu."

"We'll go there then."

"Okay, grab your coat, lass, I'm bloody starving."

"You're always starving. What about Mark, shall I ask if he wants to come, to thank him for rescuing you from the bed?"

"I asked, he declined, said something about reading a book and having a bit of thinky time."

Brian left the caravan for the first time since 'the incident' that morning and felt the whole world was watching the man who had fallen naked and got wedged. He lifted his hairy chin and strode to the car, hoping he looked like a man who didn't care. He did, in fact, care a great deal, as a man of imposing stature and as a Yorkshireman he didn't like to appear weak or exposed, but then he remembered what Julie had said and allowed himself a little smirk behind his beard. He clambered into the car and watched Faye zip up the awning and walk straight past the car. He sighed.

Faye tapped on the silver door opposite. "We're going out for a pub lunch, do you want to come?"

"No thanks, Faye," came Sophie's voice, "I think we're just going to concentrate on staying alive today."

"Okay. Use our reclining chairs in the awning if you want, and I'll leave the caravan door unlocked so you can help yourself to anything you need."

The silver door opened and Sophie poked her head out. "You're a star, Faye, do you know that?"

"Bloody star," Tel shouted.

Faye waved it away, embarrassed, and walked back towards the car. Brian's stomach rumbled. He watched his wife walk past again, unzip the awning, unlock the caravan door, zip up the awning again and, eventually, clamber into the passenger seat.

"Let's be off, woman, man needs feeding."

He'd just started up the car when the side door suddenly opened and Jim and Julie scrambled in.

"Where we going for lunch then, Bri?"

"Get out."

"But we're starving!"

"Get out."

"But we've got nothing else to do and we're *so hungry*."

"Get ... out."

Jim and Julie miserably scrambled out again. Brian dared to turn and look at Faye, who was wearing her downturned mouth and sad-eyed expression, and he knew there was no point arguing.

"Get in."

"Cheers, Bri."

"Though why you couldn't go for your own meal in your own vehicle is beyond me."

"We can't move the van or that bossy woman will pinch our space, she's watching us all the time."

"All the time," agreed Julie.

On the way to the pub Jim regaled them with the previous night's activities around the water tap. Faye gasped in horror, Brian howled with laughter.

"So, who was the stranger hanging round the caravans?" Faye asked.

"Nobody knows. Spooky though, innit."

The pub was nice, cosy, full. They managed to find a table and sat down. Brian stared at Jim. Jim smiled back.

"I'll get the first round then, shall I?" Brian said, standing up. They all moved round to let him out.

"I'll have a gin and tonic," Julie said.

"You'll have half a lager and like it."

"Pint for me, please, Bri."

He stared at Faye. This was all her fault. She looked up at him with a beaming smile and said, "I'll just have a glass of water, think I had enough to drink last night, give my liver a rest."

"Lucky liver," Brian mumbled.

When he returned to the table with a tray of drinks Julie's eyes fell to his jeans and she smiled. Brian quickly sat down.

The waitress came to take their orders. They spent an inordinate amount of time trying to decide what to have that the waitress left and came back again, and still they dithered.

"Just pick something!" Brian boomed, and the noise in the pub dimmed a little as people wondered where the voice of God had come from. Julie kept glaring at him across the table, looking 'down' and winking. Brian covered his face with the plastic menu until, finally, they gave the bored waitress their order.

It came. They ate. Brian, staring at his empty glass and then at Jim several times, to no avail, raised a finger at the waitress and indicated another round, which never came.

"Do you work at all?" he asked Jim, forcing himself not to add, 'Or do you just bum around in your van scrounging off people?'

"Builder's labourer, mostly."

Julie stroked his muscled arms proudly. "He's so strong."

"And do you work, Julie?"

"In a supermarket, but I want to start my own business

eventually."

"Doing what?"

"I don't know yet, maybe something to do with animals or children, or I might just sign on for jobseeker's allowance."

"Where do you live?" Faye asked.

"I live just down the road from Jim, don't I, Jim, with me mam, but we don't get on, always arguing, you know, and she keeps bringing men home, so I sofa surf a lot with my mates, at least until me and Jim find a place of our own."

Jim's head swiveled towards her, his fork halfway to his mouth. "What's that now?"

"Until we get our own place." She snuggled up to him.

"Hang on." His fork was back on his plate. "We've never talked about this."

"But you said you were leaving your wife – "

"No, *you* talked about me leaving my wife, I never talked about leaving my wife."

Faye and Brian glanced at each other. Brian noted that there were no more vacant tables for them to move away from the domestic dispute that was slowly brewing on theirs. He just wanted to eat his meal peacefully, arguing – observing or participating – gave him indigestion.

"You said you wanted to spend more time together, Jim."

"I said it would be good to spend a *weekend* together."

"But we're in love." She looked devastated. "I thought you wanted to take me away for a special weekend, just the two of us, to plan our future?"

"I did, I am. I live for the here and now, Jules, I'm a free spirit."

"Except for the wife," Brian said.

"I don't plan ahead, Jules, I go with the flow."

Brian and Faye lowered their heads and concentrated on their meal. "Good chicken," Brian muttered. "It is," mumbled Faye. The atmosphere at the table had turned 'sparky'.

"But ... but we're in love, Jim."

"Don't be soft, Jules, we've only known each other a few weeks."

"Six weeks, Jim, that's enough time to – "

"No, it's not and it isn't." He glanced briefly at Brian and Faye. "All this leaving Bethany and setting up home together is just in your head, I never said any of it."

"So why did you want to bring me away for a special weekend then?"

Jim huffed and slammed the knife and fork down on his plate. "If you really want to know, me and Bethany had a massive argument, so I left her to calm down for a couple of days. You were nagging me to take you away somewhere, and I thought I'd kill two birds with one stone."

Brian sucked in air. Faye suddenly found something interesting to look at on the other side of the room.

"So this weekend with me is just because you had nowhere else to go?"

"I thought we could have some fun, have a laugh, and we have. Drop it now, Jules, okay? Let's just enjoy ourselves while it lasts."

"While it lasts?" Julie looked at Jim with eyes brimming with tears and her lower lip quivering. She turned to Brian, who looked down at his meal, then at Faye, who said, "Sorry, love." She leapt up from the table and ran through the crowded pub, howling loudly. Jim sighed.

"Best get after her, lad, put her straight on a few things, eh?"

Jim huffed and left the table.

"Young love," Faye said, shaking her head.

"Young lust, more like."

"Poor girl."

"Poor wife." Brian stabbed a forkful of chips, then said, "Special weekend?"

"A blow-up mattress in the back of a van? Wouldn't impress me much."

"Ah, but you're more used to the finer things in life, like

me." He gave her a huge grin behind his beard and she gently punched his arm.

They ate whilst watching Jim and Julie through the window, pacing up and down in the car park outside, waving their arms and clearly having an argument. They watched as the two came together and hugged, Julie looking up at Jim's face and Jim looking up at the sky. They came back into the pub arm in arm, Julie wiping her eyes. Jim headed for the bar and Brian breathed a sigh of relief, until he heard him saying, "Just add it to our bill."

"He's definitely leaving his wife," Julie said, now wearing a beaming smile.

Faye and Brian just nodded.

They talked about other things after that, boring things, safe things, like their meal, the décor, the weather. Julie snuggled up to Jim. Jim just looked perplexed. Brian didn't want to prolong the torment any longer than necessary so didn't ask for the dessert menu, even though he could have killed for an apple pie and custard, he just motioned for the bill. It came and sat in the middle of the table.

"So, half each?" Brian ventured.

Jim pulled a face. "I'm just a bit short at the moment, Bri."

"Then why did you come out for a meal then, Jim?"

"Because we were hungry."

Brian paid, and drove them all back to the campsite gently fizzing with resentment.

* * *

Meanwhile, back at the camp.

Mark and Olivia were sitting outside their respective vans reading their books on opposite sides of the driveway. Every now and then they'd look over at each other and nod. Mark was impressed with the speed of her page turns. Eventually he shouted over, "Which chapter you on?"

"Five. It's very exciting."

"Six is even better."

"Oh, don't tell me."

"I won't."

The sun shone, the birds sang, and somewhere in the trees specks of light reflected off two shiny objects pointed towards them. They didn't notice.

Mark's phone rang. He picked it up off the table beside him and looked at the screen. Janis. He didn't want to talk to Janis. He pressed the red button and put it down, went back to his book. It immediately pinged with a message. Sighing, he read it. 'Emergency!!!! Please come ASAP!!!!'

Mark sighed again, wondering if it was a ruse to get him to come home so she could smother him with lies and false promises. Moving to the front of the caravan so Olivia couldn't hear, he called her.

"Mark, you have to come!" she screamed, against a backdrop of loud hissing, "Something's broke! There's water everywhere!"

Mark immediately raced to the other side of the caravan, where he'd parked his van. "I'm on my way," he said, pulling the keys out of his pocket.

He was still clutching his book, his finger holding his place. He threw it onto the passenger seat, his place lost.

"Everything okay?" Olivia shouted over.

"Emergency at home," he said.

Drowned out by the sound of the van starting and spinning on the gravel, a voice in the woods muttered, "Damn it."

Olivia, seeing the van logo, gave a surprised, "Oh!"

* * *

Outside the Airstream, Sophie and Tel were lying on their patch of grass *behind* the silver bullet, next to the VW van. Since their door opened on the wrong side, being American, they could hardly lie on the gravel pitch at the 'front'. They heard but didn't see Mark's van driving out of the caravan area. It was a perfect summer's day and, despite opening all the windows, the inside of the Airstream had become a bit whiffy in the heat. Sophie had borrowed a blanket from Faye's awning, feeling guilty about taking someone else's property, even with their permission, and they were both now lying on it wearing shorts and t-shirts. Every now and again Candice-Marie's face peered at them through her window.

"So, what do you think of it so far?" Tel asked, staring up at the sky.

"I like it. I didn't think I would."

"I got that impression."

"But the people are so nice."

"They are, remarkably so."

"Do you think it's just our group that are like that or do you think all campers are so generous?"

Tel gave a short laugh. "Let's find out, shall we? CANDICE-MARIE!"

Her head immediately popped up in the window. "What do you want?"

"Could you nip to the reception shop and get us a couple of choc ices from the freezer?"

There was a long silence, and Tel instantly regretted involving the horse-faced woman with the cut-glass accent when her face disappeared from the window. It had seemed like a funny way to prove a point in his head, but now he wasn't so sure. Candice-Marie duly appeared on the edge of their grass. She opened her mouth to speak, paused, sniffed, and said, "What's that smell?" She bent and sniffed at her VW, and stood up again, frowning. She looked at Tel. "You want me to *what*?"

"We were just talking about the kindness of campers. It was a joke. Not so funny now, of course."

Sophie sniggered.

"Can we have a choc ice, mummy?" The children wandered over, and Sophie whispered, "Uh-oh, you've done it now."

"I don't think they do organic choc ices in that poky little shop."

"Oh please, mummy, *please*." They quickly progressed into full whine mode. Tel wished he'd kept his mouth shut and not drawn Candice-Marie and her children into their sphere of existence. He wanted them to go away so they could carry on enjoying the sunshine in peace.

"You see what you've done now?" Candice-Marie snapped at him.

"I apologise."

"Now they want choc ices!"

"Can we, mummy, can we?"

"I'll pay for them," he offered. He reached into his shorts pocket and pulled out a note. This should cover it."

Candice-Marie leaned forward and snatched it from his outstretched hand. "I suppose it will have to do, now you've put the idea into their heads." The children went hysterical and rushed off to gather Jackie's children, screaming, "Choc ices! We're having choc ices!"

With a final withering look at them both, and another quick sniff at the air, Candice-Marie stomped off.

"You're welcome," he breathed, watching them all charging towards the reception shop.

"Proved your point pretty well there," Sophie snorted.

"Does that answer your question about the kindness of campers?"

"Pretty definitively, I'd said. Ours are special."

"I think they are."

They lay on the blanket in the sun, staring up at the wispy clouds in the sky, holding hands and feeling deliciously lazy.

"What *is* that smell?"

* * *

"Right, Sunday afternoon nap it is." Brian climbed out of the car and headed for the caravan, desperate for some peace and quiet. Jim and Julie skittered off to their van, ignoring Jackie, who was poised to acquire the hardstanding pitch opposite her friend the minute the white van moved. Jim quickly unlocked the back doors and they dived in, slamming them shut behind them. Brian heard them giggling, heard Julie squealing and Jim growling playfully, and thought, 'On a full stomach?' He felt a twinge of envy, then shuffled into a more comfortable position on the sofa, the one which hadn't been smashed to pieces and hastily repaired and was therefore safe to hold his weight.

Outside, Faye waved over at Tel and Sophie, who were standing mere inches from the back of their Airstream. They distractedly waved back.

"Everything okay?" she called out.

Inside the caravan Brian groaned, "Don't do it, Faye, don't do it." Just to make sure he got the peace and quiet he and his full stomach so desperately craved, and to not hear the sound of Jim and Julie bonking in the van next to him, Brian took out his hearing aids and put them on the table between the two sofas. He could still hear Tel yelling, "We seem to have a bit of a problem."

"I am not moving, I am not moving."

"What is it?" He heard Faye crunching her way across the driveway. Silence. And then, "BRIAN!"

"Not moving."

"BRIAN!"

Her feet crunched closer, calling out his name. The caravan door opened and Faye said, "They've got a problem."

"Don't care."

"They're not sure what to do."

"Ask Mark."

"Mark's not there."

"Still don't care."

"But it apparently stinks."

"Can't smell nowt in here."

"Brian!"

"What?"

"Get up and help them!"

"I don't want to, I want an afternoon nap."

"But they said it really pongs and the horse-faced woman keeps telling them to do something about it!"

"Use earplugs for nose plugs. I don't care, Faye!"

"But Brian."

Brian let out a furious growl and sat up. "They're lawyers, do they not have the brainpower to figure it out themselves?"

"It's more a practical problem than a brainpower problem."

"What makes you think I can fix whatever it is?"

"Because you can fix anything, Bri."

"Your flattery won't work on me, woman."

"Please, Brian. Pretty please?"

He knew then that he'd lost. He would get no peace, no afternoon nap, until Faye had stopped worrying about other people. He stood up, let out another, deeper growl, and stomped over to the silver bullet.

It certainly did pong over there.

"It's making my children feel sick," Candice-Marie said, as soon as Brian turned up, "You have to do something."

"We're working on it," said Tel.

"What seems to be the problem?"

"We don't know. It pongs to high heaven inside the Airstream, and it's not much better out here."

"They're retching!" cried Candice-Marie from inside her van, "*Do* something, it absolutely *reeks*!"

"Give me a chance, woman, I just got here!"

"I'm offended by you calling me 'woman'!" she screeched.

"Never visit Yorkshire then, love, that's my advice."

"Don't call me love, I'm not your love."

"No, I am," Faye snapped, "If you shut your gob for two minutes they'll be able to get on with it."

"Get on with it then!"

"I am!" Brian looked at Tel and said, "Are you telling me you don't know what that smell is?"

"No. What is it?"

"You've clearly led a very sheltered life."

"How so?" Tel asked, as memories of public school and Oxford lit up in his mind.

"It's shit."

"What is?"

"The shit."

"What?"

Brian sighed and pointed at a box embedded into the side of the Airstream.

"Yes," said Tel, excitedly, "It does seem to be coming from there."

"And there's a very good reason for that."

"What reason is that, Brian?"

"That, lad, is your toilet cassette, and," he added glancing at the now brown gravel beneath, "You appear to be at full capacity."

"What's a toilet cassette?" Sophie asked.

"Well, you know you use the toilet in your caravan."

"Yes."

"Where do you think it goes?"

"Into the drainage system."

Brian paused for a moment to take this in. "No, it's collected in the toilet cassette, which needs emptying at least once a day."

"Emptying? Every day?"

"We do ours first thing in the morning, before the rush."

"There's a rush?"

"You don't want to be standing in a queue with a plastic box full of your own excrement for too long in rising temperatures."

"No, I guess not."

"You'll need plastic gloves."

"I'll get them," Faye said, and raced back to the caravan, grabbed keys from inside, opened up the front compartment and pulled out a box and a small, folded trolley.

"You're going to have to do something about that smell," Candice-Marie shouted through her window, "We can barely breathe over here."

"And yet you're still able to talk," Bri said in mock surprise.

"Here," said Faye, handing over a box of plastic gloves. "They're working on it, love," she told Candice-Marie, "No need to make a fuss."

"I'm not fussing, I'm choking! And would everyone stop calling me love!"

Brian nodded at the gloves, now in Tel's hands, and then at the side of the Airstream. "Open the compartment and remove the cassette," he bellowed.

"How?"

"If one inspects the compartment one will notice it has a lock on it."

"I see it."

"Unlock the lock."

"With?"

"A key."

"What key?"

"Your caravan key."

"Oh." Tel reached into his shorts pocket and pulled out the keys, unlocked the compartment, opened it and heaved.

"Now," said Brian, "Push the retaining flap down and – "

"Sorry," Tel gasped, pinching his nose, "'Retaining flap'?"

Brian pointed at the thing that held the cassette in place. Tel nodded, holding it down while he twisted to look up at Tel for further instructions.

"Pull it out."

Tel started pulling, then reeled back, choking.

"Yes, well, you should empty it more often."

"I didn't know I had to empty it at all," he heaved, "Nobody mentioned having to empty and cart off our own effluence on a daily basis."

"Because it's common sense that what goes in must come out."

"I'm a lawyer, not a plumber."

Sophie was now pressed up against the VW van, holding her nose and gagging, wondering why she was gagging when her sore stomach was already empty.

"Are they going to be much longer?" Candice-Marie asked her through the closed window, "It's spoiling our holiday."

"Go somewhere else while they fix it then," Faye snapped.

"Go where?"

"I don't know, you've got the whole of the Cotswolds to choose from."

"Why should I?"

"To get away from the smell."

"I don't have to if I don't want to."

"Then stay and put up with it, just stop moaning."

"I can moan if I want to!"

Faye tutted and turned her back on her.

Olivia appeared at the end of her motorhome holding a towel across her face. "What's going on, Faye? What's that awful smell?"

"Toilet cassette emergency, could blow at any minute."

"Oh no!"

Tel slid the cassette out an inch and Brian cried, "Oh my god, what the hell have you two been eating?"

"Not so much eating as regurgitating," Tel gasped, turning his head away as he braced himself to pull it out some more, "Which is pretty much what I want to do right now."

"Imagine how much worse it is for someone who didn't create it!"

"Okay, it's loose."

"I don't need all the gory details."

"No, the cassette, it's loose."

Sophie dry-retched.

"Pull it all the way out."

"You're kidding me!"

"Look at my face, does this face look like it's kidding?"

"I guess the beard does look a bit agitated."

"Agitated? It's curling up in horror. Pull it out, man. How else are you going to empty the bloody thing?"

Tel pulled on the cassette and it shifted in its compartment. The stench was indescribable. Even Brian had to take a few steps back. Both Sophie and Tel were gagging. Tel suddenly let go of the cassette, half sticking out of the Airstream, and ran across to the other side of the driveway. "I can't do it, Bri!"

"Get back here!"

"I can't, I just can't."

Now the kids inside Candice-Marie's VW were retching, as were a couple of the people on the tent field, one of them shouting, "What the hell is that farkin' smell?" Faye was the only one standing still and silent, not covering her nose, not pulling a face or heaving, just watching peacefully.

Brian stood there, trying not to breathe too much or too deeply. The crisis had reached its climax. There was nothing else left to do.

"Okay," he bawled at everyone, "There is an emergency Plan B, but it's going t'cost you."

"Christ, anything!" Tel spluttered, "Just make it stop!"

"Faye, name your price."

Everyone looked at Faye, who smiled and shrugged and said, "Well, I'd quite like a bottle of real champagne, if that's okay with you, Tel?"

"Not quite sure what's going on," Tel said, "But if you can end this pungent nightmare, by whatever means, I will personally present you with a *crate* of champagne."

Faye's eyes widened. She looked at Brian and mouthed, 'A crate!' Then she mouthed, 'How many is that?'

Brian held up six fingers and Faye's eyes widened even more. "Woman," he said, with a broad sweep of his arm, "Do your thing."

Faye walked up to the Airstream and pulled on a pair of gloves. She extricated the toilet cassette and hoisted it onto the small, unfolded trolley as if wasn't a stinking mass of putridity. She screwed on the lid, secured it onto the trolley with a bungee rope, and stood up straight. "Done," she said.

"You'll need to empty it too," Brian said.

"But that's not my remit," she said. "You empty the toilet cassette and the wastewater every morning, and I fill the aqua roll."

"I think, for six bottles of champagne, you might make an exception."

"But I don't know how to empty it," she said, "I've never done it before."

"You empty it down the hole and rinse it out with the short pipe provided. In fact, take Tel with you, I'm sure you can figure it out between you."

Faye and Tel walked off with the cassette in tow towards the chemical disposal point next to the shower block. Tel walked quite a distance away from Faye. Several campers yelled at them as they passed.

"How ... how did she do that?" Sophie gasped, amazed.

"Congenital anosmia," Brian said.

"Congenital ... ?"

"Born with no sense of smell."

"No smell at all?"

"None whatsoever. Ideal for situations like this, not so good when you come home from work to find the house filled with gas from a unlit oven and Faye watching TV in the living room, totally oblivious. Now, you'll need to sluice out that void before they come back."

"Can't Faye do it?"

"You could ask, but I suggest you do it yourself, not everything in life can be delegated." Sophie nodded, understanding. Brian turned on his enormous feet and strode off across the driveway. "There's an expanding hosepipe in the boot of my car," he called back, "Attach it to the water tap down there and hose it out, it should be long enough. Then fill a bucket with water and a bloody good slug of disinfectant and wash it out. Hopefully we'll all be able to breathe again. Use double the amount of blue."

"Blue?" Sophie called after him. "What's blue?"

Brian plodded through the awning. "I am having an afternoon nap and I do *not* wish to be disturbed. JIM!"

"What?"

"KEEP T'BLOODY NOISE DOWN!"

"Blue, Bri? What's blue?"

* * *

Mark pulled up outside the semi-detached house. The front door immediately opened and Janis came running down the garden path to the kerbside, waving her hands in the air, totally hysterical. "Oh Mark! It's awful!" she cried, throwing herself against his chest and sobbing, "I was so scared."

"How bad is it?" He prised her away.

She looked up at him with tear-filled eyes. "The kitchen's flooded."

He huffed and walked off up the path. She followed. "I think the boiler burst or something, all this water just started coming through the kitchen ceiling."

"The bathroom's above the kitchen."

"Maybe a pipe burst in the bathroom, I don't know, I haven't looked."

Mark stepped into what was once his home, might be again, just without Janice in it. He was keeping a tight hold of his emotions, his whole body was clenched with the effort. Just looking at her – petite, pretty, pathological – made his anger bubble deep inside. He had to control himself.

He took the stairs two at a time and opened the bathroom door. No squirting pipes, no dripping from the ceiling from the boiler above, just a bath full of water, the taps still on full blast, the water cascading down the bath panel and across the floor. He turned them off and sighed. Another ruse to entice him home, only this time it was going to cost him.

"I'm sorry," Janis said from the doorway, "I must have forgotten about the bath."

Mark pushed past her into the hallway and bounded down the stairs to the kitchen. It wasn't too bad, just damp wallpaper really and a couple of bubbles in the ceiling. "Keep the small windows open and put the radiator on full in here, should dry it out."

"I will. Do you want a drink?"

"No."

"Where are you staying?"

"At a mate's."

"Which mate?"

"Stop it, Janis."

"I just want to know you're okay." Tears slipped down her face. Crocodile tears, Mark thought. He didn't trust anything she did or said any more. "How have you been?" she sniffed.

"I'm getting there, but these stunts don't help, Janis."

"I can't help it, I miss you."

Mark pursed his lips and exhaled through his nose. "I can't do this."

"Stay. Just for a bit. We can – "

"We can't. I can't."

"But it's been nearly a month, Mark. How long are you going to punish me for?"

"I'm not punishing you," he said, surprised. "You broke my heart."

"I didn't. Nothing happened. Mark, you don't understand – "

"I understand enough." He headed towards the front door. She threw herself in front of him, grabbing hold of his sweatshirt. He gripped her shoulders and gently but firmly moved her aside, striding quickly down the hallway.

"Don't go!" she called after him, "Please, Mark, we have to talk."

He left the house, slamming the front door behind him.

He didn't go straight back to the campsite. He called in on the garden centre to check on things. His Sunday staff seemed pleased to see him, and he was happy that they were keeping everything ticking over nicely. They were a good bunch. Some of them tried to commiserate but he didn't want to hear it, it was still too raw.

Afterwards he drove around for a while, trying to get his thoughts together. Seeing Janis has been like a punch to the stomach again. He couldn't look at her or think about her without feeling pain.

He found himself on a dual carriageway and slotted a Meat Loaf CD into the stereo, turned the volume to high, and pressed hard on the accelerator.

CHAPTER 8

While Brian slept like an asthmatic dinosaur inside the caravan, Faye made herself comfortable in a chair on the grass patch between their caravan and the back of the motorhome, reading. Olivia poked her head out of the window. "Ooh," she said, "Are you reading?"

"Yes. Come join me if you want."

"I can't."

"You can."

Olivia's head disappeared from the window and she quickly appeared at the front of the motorhome, book in one hand, ornate metal chair in the other. She put it down on the edge of the gravel and sat down.

"Come sit with me," Faye laughed, "I don't bite, I promise."

"I'm not allowed."

"Don't be silly, of course you're allowed."

"Richard said I'm not to leave the pitch today on account of my appalling behaviour yesterday. He's very cross with me."

Faye was speechless for a moment. Sophie, who'd just come out of the Airstream after washing her hands for about the millionth time, overheard and said, "You're not allowed to leave the pitch, did I hear that right?"

Olivia looked embarrassed now. "Richard doesn't want me to get into any more trouble." Sophie was striding across the driveway and Olivia squirmed awkwardly in her seat. "He doesn't mean anything by it, he's just looking after me."

"Controlling you, more like," Sophie said. "Are you a psychopathic serial killer who needs to be monitored and restrained at all times?"

"Not that I know of."

"It's always the quiet ones," said Faye.

"He can't detain you like that, Olivia."

"Oh, it's not detaining, he's just taking care of me. Daddy was the same, I wasn't allowed out to friends' houses or allowed to bring them home, he said it made me too giddy. Richard says I'm easily led and overly generous."

Sophie looked at Faye, who, hearing Brian's warning voice in her head and knowing she was prone to getting drawn into other people's dramas, discretely shook her head. Sophie nodded, and said brightly, "So what are we all doing?"

"Reading." They held up their books.

"Gosh, I don't remember the last time I read a book just for pleasure."

"I've got some in the caravan if you want to borrow one? Borrow, mind, I'm very possessive about my books, I want it back."

"Faye, you're amazing."

"You get the chair out the awning and I'll find you one. What do you like?"

"I don't know," she said, following her, "I can't remember. What are you reading?"

"Some cozy mystery set in Cornwall." The volume of Brian's snoring increased slightly as Faye opened the caravan door. "How about something funny?" she whispered, "I've just finished a great book called Tipping Point, it's very good, very funny."

"Okay."

Sophie dragged the chair out to the patch of grass and positioned it next to Olivia. Faye came back out with a book and dragged her chair over too, so they were all sitting together, them on the grass and Olivia on the gravel pitch within her 'boundary'. She handed Sophie the book. "What are you reading, Olivia? Is it an old book, it has no cover?"

"Oh, I take the dust jackets off, Richard can't stand to see battered jackets on the bookshelf so I take them off."

"Quite fussy about things, isn't he, this husband of

yours."

"He's got OCD and a germ phobia, it's very difficult for him."

"And for you, I imagine."

"Yes. It's a thriller," she said, raising the book and hastily changing the subject, "Mark's reading the same one, isn't that funny."

At that moment a man stepped out of the trees between Mark's caravan and Olivia's motorhome. He was tall, wearing a black hoodie, black jeans, black trainers, and sunglasses. A pair of binoculars hung around his neck. They couldn't see his face, just a hint of a stubbled chin poking out. They watched in silence as the man came around the water tap and stepped onto the gravel driveway.

"Hello?" Sophie said.

No reply. The man took a few steps forward and came to stand next to them. He slowly turned his head. They still couldn't see his face but they could feel his eyes on them. Faye recognised him from the pub the night before and felt the sudden urge to call for Brian. Olivia looked terrified; he seemed to be focusing on her.

Sophie stood up. "Can I help you?" she asked in a clear, calm voice.

The man slowly shook his head, stared at them for a few moments more, and moved on. Tel came out of the Airstream just as the man was striding past. 'Who's that?' he mouthed at Sophie, throwing a thumb back. She shrugged. The man slowed his pace to stare at Candice-Marie and Jackie, sitting outside their VW sipping wine, and carried on. They all watched the man leave the caravan area and walk through the tents on the field, not pausing to glance at any of them. Small children moved out of his way, their eyes following the tall, dark stranger. He crossed the field towards the bell tent at the far corner.

"He was in the pub last night," Faye breathed, "Nobody knows who he is or where he comes from. Never speaks, apparently."

"Creepy," said Olivia.

"What was that all about?" Tel asked, coming over to join them.

"Don't know, he just appeared, said nothing, and went again."

"It's that bloke that lives in the corner tent," Faye said. "Mark said he keeps himself to himself?"

"Not so much today," Sophie said. "He came out of the trees and just stood there, staring at us."

"Maybe he's our nighttime prowler?"

"Maybe," Faye said. "What's he doing wearing a hoodie on a day like this? He must be sweating buckets."

"And what was he doing in the trees?" Sophie said in a scary voice, "Is he the tree monster, coming out at night to steal our souls."

Olivia gave a cry of alarm, but Faye laughed. The tension was broken.

"So, what you all up to then?" Tel asked.

"Guess," said Sophie, waving her book.

"Reading."

"You'll make a fine lawyer some day with observational skills like that."

"You're funny, do you know that?"

"I do."

"Join us," said Faye.

"No, I fancy a walk around. Want to come, Soph?"

"I might stay and read with the women folk."

"And we're not at all offended that you didn't ask us, are we, Olivia?"

Olivia laughed.

"You be okay with the tree monster lurking around?" Tel asked.

"We'll be fine, we have our sharp tongues to fight off marauders."

"Don't rate their chances. Okay, see you in a bit."

"See ya, babes."

"Ooh, get you," Faye said, as Tel loped off, "Learning the common lingo now, are we, babes?"

"When in Rome," she replied.

"Should we be offended by that?" Faye asked Olivia, quickly adding, "Oh, no point asking you, is there, you speak better than she does."

They laughed. They opened their books and read, stopping from time to time for a quick chat about the birds landing on the grass in front of them or the people in tents on the field, or to comment on the volume of Brian's rumbling snores, before diving back into their books again.

It was nice, a pleasant hour was spent. Until the VW children started screaming blue murder and didn't stop. Candice-Marie began pacing up and down the top of the driveway, one hand holding a mobile phone to her head, the other holding a glass of wine. They could clearly hear her shrieking.

"But *mummy*, I've had them all week and *all weekend*! Yes, I know they're my children and I'm responsible for them, but I deserve a break, don't I? Benjamin's in Cornwall until tomorrow. No, he didn't want to come with us, he's far too busy."

Candice-Marie was huffing and puffing and rolling her eyes at Jackie, while the children mildly battered each other and screamed blue murder. "*Please*, mummy," cried Candice-Marie, "Me and Jackie just want to go out for a couple of hours without the children, that's not too much to ask, is it? I can wait two hours for you to drive here, that's not a problem." She raised her glass at Jackie and they both took a swig. Then she screeched, "What do you mean, you won't come? They're *your* grandchildren! No, not all of them, but we're desperate, mummy, can't you come? What? I can't believe you'd abandon me like this in my hour of need! Mummy? *Mummy!*"

Candice-Marie stared at her mobile screen and turned to Jackie with wide, disbelieving eyes. "She won't do it," she cried,

"She says she's *busy*! I can't believe it, Jackie, I just can't believe it."

Jackie slumped in her chair, then turn to scream, "WILL YOU STOP FIGHTING! I can't take much more, Candice-Marie, really I can't."

"Me neither." Candice-Marie turned in the driveway and spotted the women sitting together. "Hi," she cooed.

"No," said Faye.

"No, what? I haven't asked anything yet."

Silence. The women bent their heads, pretending to read. Candice-Marie came closer, smiling broadly. "I don't suppose any of you would mind babysitting while – ?"

"No."

"I'm not good with children," said Sophie.

"Oh, I couldn't possibly, Richard wouldn't – "

"It would just be for a couple of hours at the *very* most."

"No."

"Sorry."

"But me and Jackie are so tired, we just need a little – "

"NO!" boomed Brian, opening the caravan door and stepping down into the awning, "We're not having any screaming, fighting kids here, I'm on holiday."

Candice-Marie huffed loudly, clearly trying to think of a more persuasive argument to get what she wanted. "An hour," she said, "Just one hour."

"No," said Faye and Brian together.

Candice-Marie pouted and stormed back to her VW, shouting, "You're all incredibly selfish people!"

"Can you believe that?" Sophie laughed, "Trying to force her children onto complete strangers!"

"It's the entitled generation," Faye said, "I see it all the time."

"Blimey."

"If you're trying to immerse yourself in the common lingo, 'bloody 'ell' would be a more appropriate term."

"Bloody 'ell."

"You still sound posh!"

"Bloody hell," Olivia tried.

"Oh my god, it's the queen!"

"Farking hell, then."

"Olivia!"

In the midst of their giggling Faye heard a click and a hiss. Her head swiveled over to Brian, sitting under the awning. "Isn't it a bit early, Brian?" she asked, as he sucked thirstily on a can of lager.

"It's 5 o'clock somewhere!"

"Oh!" cried Olivia, looking at her watch and jumping up, "It's 5 o'clock here, Richard will be home for his dinner soon and I haven't found all my pocket money yet."

Before any of them could ask about pocket money, Olivia picked up her chair and dragged it round the back of the motorhome.

Sophie spotted Tel coming back from his walk and hurried over him.

Brian yelled, "Alone at last, woman! Fancy a quickie?"

Faye laughed so hard she almost wet herself. She got up to go and kiss him, but then Jim and Julie appeared. Julie immediately rushed up to Faye and threw her arms around her, howling, "He's going back to his wife!"

"Farking 'ell," Brian sighed, "It's like a Coronation Street on wheels round here."

"I have to!" Jim was saying, "Bethany will be expecting me, and I've got work tomorrow."

"I'm expecting you to stay with me!"

"I can't, Jules, I've got to go."

"What about me? What am I supposed to do now?"

"You can ... you can stay here with Bri and Faye, can't she, Bri?"

"Not a chance."

"Just for a couple of hours, while I sort things out with Bethany?"

"Not for any length of time. This really isn't our

problem."

"Faye?"

"Sorry, Jim."

Julie howled louder. "Why do you want to sort things out with her? You said you wanted to be with me!"

"We've been through this over and over again, Jules, I never said that."

"Stay with me!"

"I can't!"

"You're aware that this is our awning, our caravan, our holiday?" Brian asked.

"Sorry, Bri, but this is an emergency."

"Your emergency, lad, not ours."

"What am I going *do*?" Julie wailed, "My friend's gone on holiday and hasn't left me a key to her flat, and my mom said she won't have me back unless I change my attitude. I'm all alone and homeless. Don't leave me like this, Jim!"

"I've got no – " Jim's phone rang and he seemed relieved to answer it as he walked out of the awning with it clamped to his ear. "Beth," they heard him say, quite cheerfully, "I was just about to… What?" Jim moved further away, onto the driveway, down to the entrance of the caravan area. Julie disentangled herself from Faye and ran outside, watching him. "Jim?" she called.

"I'll be crossing this campsite off our favourites list," Brian told Faye.

Faye went and stood with Julie and they both watched Jim turned at the entrance and distractedly come towards them again. "What do you mean, it's over? Don't be daft, of course it wasn't me with another woman at the Hen and Pheasant, your mate's just winding you up."

"Tell her, Jim," Julie shouted, "Tell her, or I will."

Jim turned again, heading back to the entrance. Faye was really struggling to hear him now. Julie just stood there on the driveway, watching and waiting. "Jim!"

"No, that's just some other camper, we're pretty tightly

packed in here. No, Beth, I love you, I wouldn't do that. Honestly, Beth, your mate's got it wrong, I haven't even… Beth, wait, I can explain every… Of course I'm coming home, it's where I live! What do you mean, it's not my house, it's yours? Beth! Beth?"

Jim took the phone away from his ear and just looked at it, his mouth half open.

"You didn't tell her!" cried Julie.

Jim looked up, stunned. "Bloody 'ell," he gasped.

"Farking hell would be a better in a situation like this," boomed Brian.

"Brian!"

"What? Olivia can say it but I can't?"

"Jim?" cried Julie. "Where are you going, Jim?"

The two women watched Jim jump behind the wheel of his van and start it up.

"Jim?"

On the other side of the driveway, just outside the entrance to the caravan area on the grass, Jackie leapt up from her chair and watched too.

"JIM! WHERE ARE YOU GOING?"

He threw the van into reverse, roared backwards, stopped, and skidded out of the caravan area, sending up a plume of dust. He roared through the entrance gate and was gone, his engine disappearing into the distance.

Julie turned to Faye, who suddenly wished she wasn't there. "He's gone, Faye. He's gone and left me!"

"I know. I'm sorry."

"What am I going to do?"

"I don't know, love."

Jackie's VW suddenly roared into life, revved up its engine and lurched off the grass, across the driveway in front of them and onto the now empty hardstanding pitch that Jim had so recently vacated. She slammed on the brakes, making the VW and it's concertina roof rock, and leapt out, thrusting her fist in the air in triumph. Candice-Marie came running over to help celebrate with a freshly poured glass of wine, followed by four still fighting, screaming children: *"Give me my pencil!" "It's not your pencil, it's mine!" "Mummy, mummy, he won't give me my pencil!"*

"You got it in the end then, Jacks!"

"All good things come to those who wait." Jackie turned to Julie and Faye, and gave another victory punch in the air.

"Has he gone for good?" Candice-Marie asked a sobbing Julie.

"I don't know."

"Are you any good with children?"

"I don't know."

"I'd take that as a no," said Faye, putting her arm round Julie's shoulders and leading her back to the awning.

"We'd only be an hour," Candice-Marie called after them.

"She's not staying here," Brian boomed as they came into the awning.

"I'm just going to calm her down with a cup of tea, Brian."

"That's all, just tea no overnight stays, no counselling sessions until the early hours of the morning, no adoptions or offers of a home for life completely free of charge."

Faye tutted. She sat Julie down in a chair and went to put the kettle on. Julie looked at Brian. Brian looked back, not sure what to say or do, just knowing he didn't want to get involved in whatever this was. They both heard a vehicle crunching on the gravel driveway, coming towards them, and Julie was up and out again. "Jim!" she cried. Only it wasn't Jim, it was another van, a bigger one, with a colourful logo on the side.

Brian watched the van sidle past his awning and leapt up with his can of lager, glad of the escape. He followed it to Mark's caravan, behind which he parked the van, out of sight.

"Mark."

"Brian."

"Colourful van you've got there."

"Yes."

"Is it yours?"

"Is this like twenty questions and I get a prize at the end or something?" Mark slammed the van door shut.

"Just seeking refuge from the latest drama, but if it's a bad time ... " He turned to walk off again.

"No, no, it's okay." Mark pulled a bunch of keys from his pocket, opened up the front locker of the caravan and pulled out a fold-up chair. He handed it to Brian and they both sat underneath the gazebo. "Sorry," Mark said, "It's been a shitty afternoon."

"Same here."

"I'll bet you my shitty afternoon was worse than your shitty afternoon."

"Want to talk about it? I may be deaf but I've got my hearing aids in and I'm a very good listener."

"No. Thanks. It is my van, the logo on the side might have given it away."

"Mark's Marvelous Garden Centre? Aye, a bit."

"Garden centre's just down the road. Had it for about 10 years now, does alright."

"You might want to give the landlord some advice about his landscaping." Brian indicated the dead shrubs around the caravan area.

"I did. I planted those." Mark suddenly laughed. "I said privet would be better but he wouldn't listen. I even put in an irrigation system, but Ant's too lazy to even turn on a tap."

Richard, tall, thin faced, miserable-looking, suddenly appeared, stepping over the line of dead bushes they were looking at and walking quickly to the motorhome.

"Good day?" Brian boomed.

Richard glanced their way, gave a tiny nod, and disappeared inside. They heard Olivia's high voice cheerfully asking about his day, and Richard grunting and hissing about the 'people outside' and 'trusting she'd behaved herself'.

"Bit of a git, isn't he," Mark said.

"Aye."

"I see her sitting outside the motorhome every morning for about 10 minutes, then he comes out and tells her the price of something."

"Price of what?"

"Dunno, he just says twenty pounds and 66 pence, or something like that."

"Odd."

"He's odd, but then, other people's marriages always seem odd, don't they, except yours, of course, Bri."

"Mine?"

"Yeah, you and Faye seem to have it all worked out. An inspiration to us all, really."

"You'd be surprised."

"Would I?"

Brian looked across at Faye, fussing over Julie in their awning. "She left me once, not long after we got married. I was still getting used to being a husband and not doing a very good job of it. I'd work all week, go out drinking with lads in the evenings and weekends, then every other weekends I'd go up t'Yorkshire t'see family. Faye would come with me sometimes, but she worked weekend shifts at the care home so she got left at home a lot on her own. Came home one weekend and she'd gone, back to her mother's house, left a note to say she'd had enough of me never being around and she'd be better off on her own."

"What did you do?"

"Couldn't lose her. Stopped all the drinking. Well," he said, glancing at the can of lager in his huge hand. "Begged her for another chance, I mean, really laid it on thick with flowers and apologies and promises, but I won her round in the end. Heart of gold, that woman."

"Happy wife, happy life."

"Never a truer word, but it takes effort on both sides."

"Yeah, but sometimes the effort isn't enough." Mark

sighed, then nodded towards Faye. "What's happening there, then?"

"Jim left."

"Without Julie? Another git who thinks he's God's gift. He's not, he's a scrounger, always has been. Bethany's lovely too, deserves much better than him. Don't know how long he's been stringing this one along."

"Six weeks, apparently."

Mark laughed. "And they say women can gossip!"

"I'm not gossiping, just relaying facts. I heard all about it over a very dreary lunch."

"Yeah, well both women are better off without him. Not that I'm qualified to hand out relationship advice, of course."

"They can be hard."

"Impossible, I'd say. I'm thinking of giving up and becoming a monk."

"Is that why you're hiding your van, so the wife can't find you?"

"Janis hates camping, this would be the last place she'd look." He looked down at his hands. "Things fell apart at home, had to get away for a bit, you know? Can't bear to look at her at the moment, not sure if I ever can again."

"Things have a habit of working out in the end."

"Nah, not this time, this time something broke and I don't think it can be fixed."

"We all have our breaking point."

"Are you reading from your Little Book of Men's Placating Platitudes?" Mark laughed.

"Of course. I'll lend it to you if you like, but, speaking as a man of great age and experience, it's true, things do usually work out in the end, if you want it bad enough."

"Not sure if I do, not now." Mark smiled at Brian, who was smiling across at his wife. "You two are really happy, aren't you."

"We strive to be."

"I envy you."

"It doesn't come easy."

"Lots of teeth grinding determination," Mark laughed.

"On her part, not mine." He stared at the women in the awning, one crying, one comforting. "Woman's too kind for her own good, but the Yorkshireman won't be best pleased if the girl ends up sleeping in our awning tonight."

Candice-Marie and Jackie were still high-fiving their hardstanding takeover while their kids bickered around their legs. "They're on the warpath for a babysitter," Brian said.

"Imagine coming across them in your local pub!"

"Terrifying. Those cut-glass accents could slice a man in half at thirty paces."

"Tel and Sophie alright?" Mark asked. "I only went out for the afternoon and the place falls to pieces!"

"Yeah, they're good. Nice couple."

"They are. She's stunning."

"She is, but never tell my wife I said that."

"Scouts honour."

Brian suddenly became uncomfortable in his chair, shaking his empty can and sticking out his tongue. "Very dry down here, isn't it."

"Beer?"

"Good man."

* * *

"Do you know what I think we should do tomorrow?"

They were lying on the bed with their legs resting up on the aluminum walls.

"What?"

"Go out and buy one of those big television sets with a built-in DVD player."

"Why?"

"So we can lie in bed and watch films. How decadent would that be, on a week day, watching films while everyone else is at work?"

"You've certainly changed your tune from when we first arrived."

"I just feel so ... relaxed. Do you feel it?" Tel nodded. "You don't realise how much stress and pressure you're under until it stops. I feel like I've been released from a long sentence of hard labour, and there's so much I want to do."

"Such as?"

"All the things I've never had time for before, like lounging around doing nothing, sunbathing on a sunny day, *not* thinking about court cases or legal precedents."

"I hear you."

Sophie turned on her side to face him, smiling. "So let's go out tomorrow and buy a TV, a load of DVDs, and ice-cream, and cakes! Bugger the diet, I'm on holiday. And hiking boots, I've always wanted to own a pair of good hiking boots, and we could go off somewhere, find a mountain and climb it."

He laughed. "I don't think there's many mountains in the Cotswolds."

"A hill then. Just something different. Something fun. How long have we got the Airstream for?"

"Technically until Friday."

"Let's have fun till Friday then." She leaned down and kissed him.

He pulled her on top of him. "I'm all for that," he said.

* * *

It was a pretty short conversation, considering its enormity.

"I did *not* go to the Hen and Pheasants with another woman!"

Bethany, who was standing at the front door preventing him from entering the house, thrust a phone screen into his face. It was a photograph of him sitting with Julie, Brian and Faye at the Hen and Pheasants.

"That's not me."

"How about this one?" She flicked the screen to another photo. "Or this one? That not you, either? Your long-lost twin, is it? Your doppelganger? How about this one, where you're kissing some bint in the pub car park?"

"I can explain – "

"Save your breath. Your stuff's in the garage. You are no longer my husband and you no longer live here."

"But this is my home!"

"No, it's *my* home, that I pay for, that I invited you into when we met, and now I'm kicking you out. I've had enough, Jim, it's over. End of."

"Beth, let's sit down and talk about – "

The front door slammed shut.

* * *

Julie was, of course, thrilled to have him back and threw herself around his neck as soon as he stepped out of the van, which he'd now parked on the grass field next to some tents. "Jim, you came back for me!" she squealed.

He sighed, leaning against his van as Julie clung to him like a monkey.

"I knew you'd come back," she said, covering his face in kisses, "I knew you couldn't leave me."

She was almost choking him, clamping her legs around his waist and gripping him tight. He staggered into Brian and Faye's awning. Faye was there, reading. Brian came rushing over from Mark's caravan shouting, "No!"

"I told you he'd come back, didn't I, Faye."

"Yes, love, you did."

"Wife not have you back then?" Brian settled himself into his chair.

"Brian!" Faye snapped, "You don't have to be so abrupt *all* the time!"

"Well, lad?"

"It was … I … she … "

"Couldn't squirm your way back in and had nowhere else to go. We're old, lad, we're not stupid."

"No," said Julie, "He came back for me, didn't you, Jim. We were meant to be together."

Jim sighed again, struggling to keep balance with Julie hanging off him.

Brian peered up at him with suspicious eyes. "Why are you here, in our awning, looking expectant?"

Jim pried Julie off his person. She gripped onto his arm, reaching up to smother the side of his face with kisses. He felt very depressed. "The back of my van's full."

"Of?"

"Stuff."

"What stuff?"

"My stuff."

"Has she thrown you out?" Julie squealed, jumping up and down with excitement, "Have I got you all to myself now?"

"And?" Brian boomed.

"We've got nowhere to sleep."

Across the campsite echoed the roaring boom of Brian yelling, "ABSOLUTELY NOT!"

CHAPTER 9

Nobody slept much that night, for the third night in a row. This time it wasn't Brian's snoring that kept them all awake, or the dark stranger lurking about their caravans, or a naked Jim searching for water, it was something else.

Candice-Marie had charged over as soon as she heard Jim and Julie had no place to sleep, loudly announced by Brian, who yelled something about being on holiday and not being a mobile hotel for stray waifs. She said they could stay in her tiny VW awning in exchange for a spot of babysitting, "Just for an hour," she said, "Two hours, tops."

So Jim and Julie extricated the mattress and the blankets from beneath his pile of belongings in the van, struggled to blow it up whilst four children kept throwing themselves across it, and attempted to make a bed in the awning as four hyperactive children bounced up and down like it was a trampoline. Candice-Marie and Jackie excitedly and hurriedly got ready, ordered a taxi at 7.30 and, with barely a look back at their abandoned, riotous children, high-heeled it down to the entrance gates 'for an hour, two hours, tops'.

The noise of four children set free was horrendous. Faye and Brian couldn't concentrate on reading books in their awning, Richard and Olivia couldn't hear the film they were trying to watch on TV, and Sophie and Tel couldn't lounge around on their bed making decadent plans because they could hardly hear themselves speak. The kids reached a fever pitch of screeching, and then started kicking footballs against the caravans.

"Clear off!" Brian bawled at them, and they laughed with overwrought amusement and scampered off, but they didn't stop.

They ran around yelling at the top of their voices and pounding with their hands on the caravans, red-faced and sweaty and totally out of control. Shouting at them to stop just seemed to make them worse, they knew they were too quick to catch.

Jim and Julie ran after them trying to round them up and herd them back into the VW but they kept escaping. Then, after almost an hour of mayhem, they started picking up stones from the gravel driveway and lobbing them.

Brian slammed down his book and stood up.

"Don't kill them, Bri."

"I'm gonna ring their bloody necks!"

"They're just kids."

"Who should be asleep in their beds! What the hell are Jim and Julie doing?"

He found out what they were doing when he stepped out of the awning. Jim had a child under one arm and was chasing after another, and Julie was carrying one having a massive tantrum to the VW; the child's legs were like pistons and the noise coming out of its mouth would have made the devil himself wince. The caught children wriggled free and rejoined the riot. Jim and Julie looked exhausted.

"RIGHT!" Brian boomed, "THAT'S ENOUGH!"

His voice echoed across the field and into the distance. The kids stopped dead in their tracks at the sight and sound of such a big man.

"YOU!" he hollered, pointing down at what looked to be the oldest, a boy, whose eyes widened as he peered up at the giant, "GET TO BED! AND YOU! AND YOU TWO! OFF YOU GO BEFORE I BITE OFF YOUR HEADS AND *COOK THEM FOR MY DINNER*!"

"Brian!"

"HUSH WOMAN, I'M PICKING THE *TASTIEST*."

Four small mouths fell open. A little girl began to cry. Another girl began to scream in terror, followed by another, and another. Jim and Julie rushed to grab each of them tightly by the wrists while they were transfixed with terror and dragged them, still hysterical, into Candice-Marie's van.

"AND I DON'T WANT TO HEAR ANOTHER SOUND OUT OF YOU UNTIL MORNING!"

"Bit harsh," Faye said, when he lumbered back into the awning, quite pleased with himself.

"Got t'take a firm stance if you want t'keep control."

"Is that what you do with your men at the warehouse, tell them you'll bite their heads off and eat them if they don't do as they're told?"

"Of course."

A short while after the children had finally settled down and gone to sleep, the adults went to bed and slept too.

But their peaceful slumber didn't last long.

At 2.45am there was a rumble in the distance, which got closer and closer until it thundered across the campsite, waking everybody up.

"What is it?" Faye asked, as Brian raised the blind and peered through the window.

Brian couldn't see. Two single bright lights came through the entrance gate and down the driveway towards them, and the thunder came with them, vibrating the caravans. Brian hefted himself out of bed, threw on his dressing gown and went outside, where he met up with Tel and Mark, who'd come out to see what was happening and were standing together on the driveway.

"What the…?"

"Alien abduction?"

"Those are normally quiet, aren't they?"

"Normally?"

The lights and the noise stopped next to the entrance to the caravan area. Two motorbikes, big, roaring beasts. On the bikes, quite difficult to see in the dark, were two riders in black leather and dark helmets. Behind them, easier to see because of the amount of flesh on display, sat Candice-Marie on one bike and Jackie on the other, their legs flailing in the air and their shrieks of laughter high enough and loud enough to shatter the nerve endings of a saint.

The first rider kicked down his stand and leant his bike against it. Candice-Marie went with the lean and fell off. She writhed on the ground, shrieking with laughter. Jackie tried to clamber off the back of her motorbike to help her friend, but fell head first into a dead bush. The first rider got off and tried to lift Candice-Marie to her feet, but the heels of her shoes kept twisting and her legs kept buckling and she would not stop laughing. The second rider just looked down at Jackie, writhing in the bush.

"Phnnn nnnnph phnnnn?" said rider through his helmet, as the motorbike engines idled and the women shrieked and screamed.

"Sorry, we can't hear you because of the *noise*."

The rider turned off his engine. The other followed suit. The sounds of screaming children filled the void from the VW van and from several out on the field of tents.

Sophie appeared. "What's going on?"

Tel pointed at the women on the ground. The children, all four of them, burst out of the VW van, screaming hysterically as they ran towards their mothers, lying prone on the ground, both of them laughing uncontrollably. When the children spotted the giant man looking down at them with his hands on his hips they screamed even more, huddling together in a hysterical mass around their prone mothers. Jim and Julie came racing out of the awning.

"Do these women belong here?" the rider said.

"'Occifer," cried Candice-Marie from the ground, "I've never sheen this*h* man before in my laife."

"MUMMY! MUMMY!" screamed the children.

"State of them!" said Mark.

"Been in the biker's bar all night," said the rider, shouting to be heard above all the screaming. "Pissed as arseholes, they were. Are still, likely to be for quite a while."

"Ars*h*eholes!" screamed Jackie from the bush.

"MUMMY! MUMMY!"

"Couldn't understand a word they said, but they were loud, weren't they, Kev?"

The rider on the other bike nodded his helmet.

"Thought we should bring 'em home, though it were 'ard keeping them on the back of the bikes. No cars, y'see, at a biker's bar, and no taxi's gonna take them in this state."

"MUUUUUMMY!"

"We had to stop a couple of times when they fell off, but they din't seem injured or nuffin'. They're your problem now. Good luck to you."

The rider got back on his bike and kicked up the stand. They started up their thunderous engines, drowning out the sound of terrified children, turned on the gravel driveway and roared out of the entrance gate, leaving the two high-heeled and highly intoxicated women writing on the ground surrounded by their traumatized children.

"Shall we just leave them there?" Mark asked.

"It's more an ethical question," Tel said, "Can one abandon a fellow human in their hour of need?"

"I could," Brian said.

"No, you couldn't," Faye bawled out of the caravan window. "Pick them up and put them in a campervan."

Brian huffed. The two women rolled onto all fours and tried to crawl, collapsing in hysterical laughter. Their children fell upon them, equally hysterical. Voices in the field were yelling for them to 'be quiet'.

Tel huffed. Candice-Marie lifted her head up with some considerable effort, her hair strewn across her face, and hissed, "Get back, you beasts. Don't come near us, all men are rapists!" Then she threw up.

"I'm not going near that," Mark said, holding a hand over his mouth.

"Faye."

"What?"

"They're saying all men are rapists. Should we help

them and risk police swat teams descending down on us, or help them and risk being covered in vomit?"

Mark dry-heaved.

"Help them, of course!"

"And the rape charges?"

Faye hurried over, just as Candice-Marie threw up again, and Jackie, seeing it or smelling it, threw up too. Mark gagged again and turned away. Faye tutted. Somebody from the tents yelled, "Shut the hell up, we're trying to sleep!"

"And we're not?" Faye yelled back.

"Bloody caravanners!"

"Bloody tenters!"

"Faye," said Brian, gently touching her arm, "Concentrate on't task in hand, love. What should we do with drunken, vomiting, men-hating women?"

"We don't hate men," Jackie squealed, "We love them. They just don't love us." She started sobbing into the dried-up bush that was covered with the liquid contents of her stomach. Her children sobbed along with her. Candice-Marie tried to drag herself over to her friend, despite the weight of children on her back, but gave up when Jackie threw up again.

"Put them in the van," said Faye.

"And the vomit, love of my life?"

Faye looked up at Brian, who was smiling innocently down at her. "I've got some spare blankets we can wrap them in," she said.

"*More* spare blankets?"

"You can never have enough blankets, Brian."

"Clearly not, my love. A blanket for every occasion, it seems."

Tel stepped towards Candice-Marie. He bent over and attempted to grab hold of her waist without touching anything wet. He stood up again, shaking his head and shrugging his shoulders. The children continued to howl. Faye dashed back to the caravan and returned with two blankets.

"Are those new?" Brian asked. "Exactly how many blankets do we have, my love?"

Faye looked at the women, then at the blankets in her hand. As she was deciding whether to keep her Dunelm special offer blankets 'as new' or not, Jackie threw up again.

"MUMMY! MUMMY!"

Mark was stepping backwards down the driveway. "Sorry," he said, still holding a hand over his mouth, "This isn't my thing at all."

"No?" said Brian, "What's a good caravan holiday without a few litres of fresh puke?"

Mark bent over and threw up.

Just as Brian was deciding to sell the caravan due to chronic lack of sleep and impending madness, he caught Richard and Olivia peering out of their window at the bottom of the driveway. He raised a hand. "IT'S OKAY, NOTHING TO SEE HERE, JUST SOME GENERAL PANDEMONIUM! DON'T WORRY, WE'LL TAKE CARE OF IT!" He turned back to the women on the ground, covered in frantic children, muttering, "You stay in your nice, cosy van and let the plebs quieten things down for you!"

"Brian," said Faye, "You've gone all Basil Fawlty."

"Just the last of my marbles exploding, Sybil."

"What are we going to do?"

He took a deep, calming breath. "Why do I have to deal with this?"

"Because you're the biggest, and you're a manager, you know how to deal with things like this."

"Things like this? Yes, we get a lot of this in the warehouse; drunken women, screaming children, lots and lots of – "

"Just make it stop, Brian, before we all lose our minds!"

"RIGHT, CHILDREN!" he hollered. The children were jolted into silence and stared up with wide eyes at the giant man. "I won't shout if you promise to listen. Are you going to listen like good children?" The children nodded their heads, their mouths open, rapt. "Now this lady here," he put his arm on Faye's shoulder, "this is super nanny, she's everybody's nanny, she's your nanny. Say hello to super nanny, children."

The children mumbled hello. Faye breathed on her fingernails and buffered them on her dressing gown, quite pleased to be called a super nanny.

"Now, children, I want you to do whatever super nanny tells you to do, okay?"

Faye stopped buffering and whispered, "What should I tell them to do?"

"Super nanny wants you to get off your mummies now," Brian said. The children shuffled off their mummies' backs and sat on the ground beside them. "Your mummies are a bit poorly and – "

"I see where you're going with this," Faye said, "I got this, Bri. Children, your mummies are a bit poorly, they've got poorly tummies. Have you ever had poorly tummies?" Four little heads nodded. "Horrible, isn't it, especially when you feel sick and you throw up." Behind them, Mark dry-retched again.

"Jeez," hissed Tel, "Get a grip of yourself."

"I can't help it, I have a very sensitive gag reflex."

"Now, children, we're going to look after your mummies and make them feel better again, would you like your mummies to be better again?" Four faces nodded. "I want you to get into your own beds and get nice and comfortable. We'll make your mummies better and we'll bring them to you so you can all sleep together, would you like that?" More nods. "Off you go." Four snotty, tear-stained children got up and ran to their vans, each pair followed by Jim or Julie.

"S'locked," Jim cried from Jackie's van.

"Frisk her," Brian said to Faye, "Get the keys out of her bag. Go on." Faye was glaring at him. "I can't do it, I've never seen the inside of *your* handbag. Plus, you can't smell and I – *bleugh* – can."

"Okay, okay!" With fingertips, Faye pulled Jackie's bag from the puddle of vomit and gingerly opened it. As she was rifling through for the keys she picked out a bottle of very expensive perfume. She sprayed some on herself and, turning to Brian, asked, "Is this nice? Do you like it? Might not be able to afford it but – "

"Faye!"

"Yes, Brian?"

"The keys."

"I'm looking, I'm looking!"

She threw the keys back to Jim, who opened up the door and helped the sniveling children inside.

"What do we do now?" Faye asked, looking down at the groaning heaps of flesh and regurgitated alcohol.

"We could hose them down?" Tel said.

"Mark, get the hosepipe out of the boot of my car and hook it up. I'll tell you when to turn the tap on."

"We can't hose them down, Bri!"

"We can hardly lie their festering bodies next to little children, can we."

Faye and Sophie gently turned the women over. Sophie winced at the rising smell, but Faye was oblivious to it. Once on her back, Candice-Marie raised a limp hand up into the dark sky and screamed, "Oh my god, Jackie, I've gone blind!" Jackie didn't answer or make a noise as they rolled her over, she'd gone to sleep. Just to make sure, Sophie put two fingers on the pulse of her neck and nodded with some relief at Faye.

Mark came running up with the end of the hosepipe in his hands, handing it to Brian, who handed it to Faye, who said, "Okay, turn it on." Mark ran back down, puffing, and turned the tap.

The water dripped limply from the end of the hosepipe. Faye put a finger over the end and sprayed it, as gently as she could, over the women's faces, hair and bodies. The rancid water poured into the dead bushes in a smelly stream, and Mark dry-retched his way back to his caravan.

"We'll have to take their clothes off," Faye said, "They can't sleep in wet clothes, they'll catch their deaths."

"In summer?"

Sophie and Faye were just pulling at Candice-Marie's incredibly tight leather skirt when two police cars raced through the entrance gates with their sirens wailing and their blue lights flashing across the field. The sirens gave a *whoop whoop* as the cars skidded to a halt on the driveway in front of them.

"You have got to be kidding me!" Brian breathed.

Four police officers got out, two men, two women. "We've had a report of a disturbance involving two women being attacked," one of them said.

Brian indicated the women on the ground with a huge hand. "Drunk," he said, "As skunks. We're not attacking them, we're trying to help them."

"We'll be the judge of that."

Tel quickly stepped forward. "I'll handle this," he said.

The two female police officers helped Faye and Sophie strip the groaning, semi-conscious women down to their bras and pants, using the blankets to shield them from the crowd of disturbed campers milling about on the field and then wrapping them up. A policewoman followed Brian as he carried Candice-Marie into her van and placed her carefully between the two children on the double bed. They immediately cuddled up to her and they all looked quite cosy together, until Candice-Marie turned on her side and started retching. The police officer quickly found a bowl under the sink and Brian placed it next to her head. They left swiftly.

Jim and the other female police officer carried Jackie into her van.

Tel stood with the male police officers, explaining the whole situation to them. They eventually drove off, leaving them all standing in the middle of a now silent campsite, absolutely knackered. Faye and Sophie hurried to the showers, while Brian hosed the smelly puddles into the bushes. Tel picked the women's wet clothes up with a stick and put them in a binbag.

They got back to bed at about five in the morning.

Day 4 - Monday

A whispered voice and an incessant tapping cut into her dreams.

"Faye! Faye!"

"What?"

"Are you awake?"

"Guess!"

"So, you're awake?"

"I am now!"

"It's the kids."

"What about them?"

"They're awake."

"What time is it?"

"It's 7 o'clock."

"Oh god."

"Oh god," said Brian, stirring from his sleep and raising the blind on the window. On the other side stood Jim, behind him, Julie, and behind her, two kids rubbing their eyes and whimpering. Behind them, in Jackie's VW van, two small faces were pressed against the window, silently crying.

"What should we do?" asked Jim.

Faye wriggled to the end of the bed and grabbed her dressing gown, left the caravan. Brian lay on his back, staring at the ceiling, trying to remember what a normal holiday was like. It was, he sensed, not going to be a good day. He briefly wondered if he could cut his losses and simply make a bolt for home when he heard Faye saying, "Just bring them in. Get the other two as well. I'll give them some breakfast."

"Oh god," groaned Brian.

Suddenly the awning was full of small people, like a load of disgruntled ETs, and Faye was rifling through the caravan cupboards for bowls and spoons and boxes of cereals. "You getting up any time soon?" she snapped.

"Only if I really have to."

"You really have to."

"Why?"

"Because we have a situation on our hands."

"Is it our situation, though?"

"It is now."

"Why is it?"

There was a pause, and then, "Because we're nice people who help other people."

"I don't want to be a nice person anymore, Faye, I want to stay in bed and pretend I'm on holiday."

"So do I, but if I'm not, you're not."

Brian grumbled as he struggled off the bed and furiously wrapped his dressing gown around his enormous body. Then he entered the awning.

Faye had put one of her infinite blankets on the floor and the children sat on it, crossed legged. As Faye was handing out bowls and spoons, filling them with Cornflakes and trying to tip milk in without spilling it all over the place, Jim said, "Any chance of a cup of tea, Faye, I'm parched?"

"Of course, Jim, I'll just use my telekinetic powers to put the kettle on, shall I?"

Jim looked at Julie, who shrugged. Brian, noting that Jim was sitting in his seat, coughed loudly until he looked up, then he nodded towards the caravan. "Help yourself," he said, not a little sarcastically, "We don't provide a waiter service here."

Jim and Julie jumped up and jumped in. Seconds later came the sound of clinking mugs and spoons. "Do you want one, Faye? Brian?"

"Oh, how lovely of you to ask," said Brian. "Yes, I'll have my own mug of my own tea, with my own milk and my own sugar. Thank you so much, so very kind of – "

"Brian!"

"Faye."

"You're not helping."

"Nor do I wish to. I am, as of this moment, a conscientious objector. Do not involve me in any further – "

"BRIAN!"

He recognised the urgent, desperate tone of his wife and clamped his mouth shut – it was much too early for a domestic.

"Can you *please* give me a hand?"

"Can I at least have a cup of tea first?"

Jim leaned down from the caravan and handed him a mug. Faye reached out and grabbed hers. "Didn't know how many sugars you wanted," Jim said, "So I've put two in each."

Faye pulled a face, she didn't take sugar, but Brian said, "Drink it, we're going to need all the sugar-rush help we can get this morning."

"Alright if we make ourselves a bacon sandwich?" Jim called out.

"I rest my case," Brian said, adding, "Forget the sugar, we should just pour whisky into our mugs to take the edge off the pain."

"I want mummy," said a child.

"I want *my* mummy," said another.

"I suppose we should check on them," said Faye. "Julie, be a love and just see if they're okay, would you?"

Julie sauntered off, while Jim stayed in the caravan, happily frying bacon. "Hurry up, Jules, it'll be done in a bit."

Brian forced himself to smile at a child and it immediately burst into tears. He sipped his super sweet tea and made a note to only book child-free campsites in future.

Jim stepped out of the caravan carrying two plates. He put one on the table Brian was sitting at and threw himself into a chair with the other.

"Is that for me?" Brian asked.

"No, that's Julie's."

"Oh, you didn't do us one?"

"There's no bacon left."

Brian made a rumbling noise in the back of his throat.

"Faye!" It was Julie, shouting from Jackie's van. "FAYE!"

"Oh god, what is it now?" Faye rushed off.

Brian, piqued and hungry, snatched up the bacon sandwich next to him and started eating it. "You can share yours," he snapped at Jim.

"Brian!" came a distant voice.

Brian made a noise in the back of his throat again, louder this time.

"BRIAN!" More desperate this time. Brian leapt up, as did Jim, and both men hurried to the VW van next door.

"What is it?" Brian asked Faye, who was standing next to Julie, who was sitting on the bed shaking Jackie quite violently.

"We can't wake her, Bri!"

"I'm not surprised, the amount of alcohol that came pouring out of her last night. She'll be hungover but she'll be fine." He paused, then said, "Is she breathing?"

"Yes, but it's very shallow."

"Alcohol induced coma, seen it many times. She just needs to sleep it off."

He left to return to his sandwich, except when he reentered the awning his sandwich was gone and two children sitting on the blanket were suspiciously munching something other than Cornflakes. Brian was about to question them about it when he realised there were two missing. He peered into the caravan and found them sitting on the floor in front of a cupboard, surrounded by biscuit crumbs and merrily chomping their way through a pack of chocolate bars. "WHAT ARE YOU DOING?" he roared, and the children screamed. "FAYE! FAYE!"

Nothing. Brian pointed at the caravan door and cried, "Out!" The children burst into a fresh bout of tears and ran out, throwing themselves down next to the other children on the blanket, who also burst into tears.

"FAYE!"

"What is it now?" she asked, hurrying into the awning.

"They're making a lot of noise!"

"Then make them stop!"

Julie slipped into the awning. "She's awake," she yelled above the hysteria, "But she wishes she wasn't. Never seen anyone so hungover. I've given her some paracetamol and bottles of water. Blimey, it's noisy in here. Where's my sandwich?"

"Brian and the kids ate it," Jim said, pushing the last of his into his mouth.

"Make me another then."

"There's no bacon left."

"Egg sandwich?"

Jim got up and went into the caravan. Brian raised his hands, acknowledging the fact that he'd totally lost control and wasn't quite sure how it had happened. Faye was fussing around the children, trying to make them stop crying, but they seemed fully committed to it now.

He stood up. "I'm going outside," he boomed, "I may be some time."

* * *

Mark was sitting under his gazebo with a book, trying to read despite the pandemonium he could hear further up the pitches. He saw Brian exit the awning and come walking towards him with his hands in his dressing gown pockets. He sat himself down next to Mark.

"How's it going?" Mark asked with a grin.

"Bad, it's bad, and my gut's telling me it's only going to get worse as the day progresses. I was thinking of just going home and leaving them all to it."

"Stay here a bit until it calms down. Cup of tea?"

"Love one. No sugar, I've had my weekly quota from some syrup sludge Jim cooked up earlier, along with the last of our bacon."

Mark laughed from inside his van, "He doesn't do bad for someone who turned up with nothing, does he. Do you want a bacon sarnie?"

"I would." There came the satisfying, sizzling smell of

frying bacon, and Brian exhaled all the tension from inside him. "When you say 'stay for a bit', what would you consider to be overstaying my welcome?"

"If you crawled into bed with me later," Mark laughed.

"At this point in time I'd be happy with the floor."

The noise from his awning suddenly abated and Faye came out, followed by four small people. She glanced around briefly and Brian hissed, "Hide me!" Mark leaned out of the caravan and threw a tea towel over his head. Brian picked it off and held the small rectangle of material between finger and thumb. "And you thought this would do what?"

"First thing to hand, I'm all out of invisible cloaks."

"Brian!" Faye called over to him, and he groaned. "Brian, I'm just taking the children for a shower."

He nervously raised his hand, hoping that nothing would be expected of him. Thankfully, Faye turned and led the children to the shower block like the Pied Piper of Hamlin, with Jim in the rear and Julie keeping them on the path like a sheep dog. Brian sighed in relief, just as Mark put two mugs of tea and two plates of bacon sandwiches down on the table next to him. "You, my lad, are a bloody star."

They ate and drank in silence for a while, blissful, beautiful silence, and then, when they'd finished, they both yawned.

"Quite a night," Mark said. "Are the yummy mummies still alive?"

"Barely, though I suspect they might wish they weren't."

"Can't remember when I last saw someone that drunk."

"In our youff, before we knew better. They should know better."

"Wonder why their husbands aren't with them."

"Too busy earning money for them to spend, I guess."

"They're very..." Mark searched his mind for the right word. "Entitled."

"Faye says it's a generation thing, they expect everything t'be done for them, given to them, and are genuinely horrified when they don't get it, simply can't understand why their every need isn't met. They'll be the fall of mankind, you mark my words."

"Ey up," Mark whispered, nodding right. "Watch this, happens every morning."

They both turned to the motorhome as the door opened and Olivia stepped out. She smiled her sweet smile when she saw them, and sat neatly on an ornate metal chair. "Morning," she called over.

"Morning."

There was a thumping noise from inside the motorhome, and then Richard stepped out. He had his back to them and didn't see them, so they carried on watching. Olivia stood up, still smiling but looking awkward. "How much?" she asked Richard.

"£17.53."

"Lovely." She glanced over at them. They quickly turned away and pretended not to be listening.

"I'd like a lamb casserole for dinner," Richard said, "with some baby carrots, and not so much mint sauce this time."

"Okay."

"And ... " He looked off into the distance for a moment, then said, "Apple crumble and custard for pudding. I'll be back around five, so have it done for then. You can catch a bus into the village to buy supplies."

"Shall I use the card?"

"Yes, but only for food, nothing else. And no gallivanting about," he said firmly, "Straight there, straight back."

"Yes, Richard."

He bent to kiss her lightly on the cheek and strode off through the dead bushes gripping the straps of his backpack. Olivia glanced over at them. "No rest for the wicked, is there," she giggled.

"You're not wicked," Mark said, surprising himself, then surprising himself more when he found himself saying,

"You're very, very lovely."

"I'll second that," Brian boomed, raising his mug of tea.

Olivia giggled again, then climbed into the motorhome, where they heard her moving about and, eventually, a vacuum cleaner being turned on.

"What was that about, the money thing?" Brian asked.

"No idea, it's a different amount every morning." His gut instinct was telling him it was something a bit sinister, and he trusted his gut instinct after what had happened with Janis and... He pushed the thought from his mind, thinking about Janis was like wrapping a dark, heavy blanket around himself.

"The kids are coming back," he said as a distraction.

"Oh god."

They watched Faye, holding the hand of the smallest child, and Jim and Julie lead wet-haired children back to the caravan area. She dispersed them at the entrance and they ran to their vans. "Oldest help the youngest to get dressed," Faye called after them, "And don't bother your mothers, they're still feeling poorly."

Brian noticed that Jim and Julie swooped straight into his awning and, through the plastic windows, he watched Jim settle straight into his chair. He made a growling noise at the back of his throat.

Faye looked over at Mark and Brian, sitting under the gazebo sipping tea, and shouted, "I'm going to need a hand with these children, Bri."

"You have Jim and Julie, how many more hands do you need?"

"Your hands," she said.

"My hands are busy," and he again raised his mug of tea, which was empty but Faye wasn't to know that.

"Brian!"

"What?"

"We need to decide what to do with the children if their mothers are out of action."

"Are there no workhouses?" he boomed dramatically.

"BRIAN!"

"I don't know, they're not my children!"

"They're not mine either!"

"Then set them free, Faye, just resist the urge to care."

"Like you, you mean?"

"Very much so!"

Faye tutted and ducked into the awning, where he heard her asking Jim and Julie if they wanted another cup of tea and Jim asking if there were any biscuits. He wondered again if anyone would notice if he slipped away in the car and went home, wearing only his dressing gown to avoid being sucked into the chaos again by getting dressed.

"Was that a spat I just witnessed from the golden couple?" Mark laughed.

"Spat for now, may turn into all-out war later if she doesn't curb her constant desire to help people."

"It's good that she cares."

"Says the man sitting comfortably under his gazebo without a care in the world."

"Is that how I look, like a man without a care?"

"You have the look of a man who's deeply troubled about something, and again I offer my services as a good listener who may or may not dispense some wise words of advice."

"I doubt you'd have any experience of … "

"Of?"

"Nothing."

"Keeping it in won't do you any good, lad."

"It's still cooking."

"Well, I'm here all week."

Silence, and then, "Thanks, Bri."

"Any time."

More silence as they both stared off across the caravan area and the camping field beyond. Then, very slowly, Mark said, "It's not the thing itself that hurt the most, it's the thing that came after it, you know?" Brian did not know but kept quiet. "The truth, I suppose, said out loud is a very powerful thing. Devastating, in fact. I always did my best, gave her pretty much everything she wanted, but I always got the sense that it wasn't..."

"Enough?" Brian suggested.

"Yeah, and then she told me it wasn't enough and that just destroyed me." He stared down at his empty mug of tea. "It was like putting on a pair of glasses and seeing everything clearly for the first time, seeing her clearly for the first time, you know? Other people told me, of course, but you don't listen, do you, you think they're just jealous or making trouble, but ... I can't look at her in the same way anymore, and I feel a fool that I didn't see it before. Nothing's the same, everything's changed."

"Sometimes change is a good thing."

"Hurts though, a lot." He took a deep, calming breath. "It's just going round and round in my head, s'driving me nuts. I read to distract myself, but when I stop it all comes rushing back again."

"Have you tried talking to her about it?"

"Can't even look at her, Bri."

"Is it forgivable, this thing?"

"I don't think it is."

"Have you considered couples counselling? It works for some."

"Seems too big to talk about. Talking won't fix this."

"Letting it out into the world might diminish it's power and allow you to deal with it better." Mark said nothing, so Brian asked, "Is it a big thing for her, too?"

"Well yes, but only because – "

"BRIAN!"

"Just a minute, my love!"

"BRIAN!"

"I'm thinking of overstaying my welcome," he said to Mark, breaking the tension.

Mark looked relieved and laughed. "Feel free, but I draw the line at sharing my bed."

Brian stood up, took a deep breath and muttered, "Once more into the breach, dear friends, once more."

"Good luck."

"Luck won't help me, lad," he said, stoically walking away, "Stamina and teeth grinding determination is what's required, and lots of it."

CHAPTER 10

"Morning." Sophie stepped out of the Airstream wearing jeggings and a sweatshirt with a sequined unicorn on the front, and still managed to look like a supermodel on a catwalk with her long legs and elegant gait. Tel stepped out behind her, looking every bit as gorgeous in jeans and a t-shirt.

"Morning," Faye called across, as she helped four sets of children put their shoes on in the awning. "You two are up early, it's not even 8.30 yet. I thought you'd want a lie-in after last night."

"And what a night it was!" Tel gasped.

"How are they?"

"Still alive, thankfully, but not conscious."

"I'm not surprised." Sophie stood outside the awning in the sunshine, breathing in the fresh air and feeling very, very relaxed. Which was more than could be said for Brian, who grumbled like an angry bear in his chair as he furiously completed a puzzle in a crossword book with Jim watching over his shoulder. "So, what are you two up to today?"

"Survival," Brian barked, "We're just concentrating on surviving the holiday. We're thinking of booking Beirut for our next trip."

Sophie laughed. Faye rolled her eyes. "We planned to visit Blenheim Palace today, but I'm not comfortable leaving the kids."

"God forbid they should look after their own children after boozing all night," Brian grunted.

"Come with us if you want," Faye suggested.

Sophie looked at Tel, who shrugged. He was surprised at his capacity to 'go with the flow' these last few days, a hitherto unexplored region of his psyche, when he'd always been so organized and fully in control before. He even liked his new jeans and t-shirt look. He'd never previously owned a pair of jeans.

"We have plans," Sophie said excitedly.

"And one of them is to find a hotel room with a comfy bed and take a blissful afternoon nap."

"Highly recommend a good afternoon nap," said Brian.

"Tel's taking me for breakfast at Sainsbury's."

"Way to show a girl a good time, Tel."

"We're doing things we've never done before."

"And breakfast at Sainsbury's was top of your list, was it? Not quite the same ring as breakfast at Tiffany's, but each to their own."

"No." Sophie laughed. "But it is on the list, as is buying a TV for the Airstream so we can lounge around watching films all day if we choose."

"Nice. There you go," Faye said to a small child, "All done." She watched the child run off to join the others, who had formed a small group with some tent children playing football on the field. "I just don't know if we should leave them."

"Leave them," barked Brian, "We're not taking them with us."

"Have you tried waking them up?" Sophie asked.

"Julie gave them a firm shake earlier. Well, it was more of an attack really, I thought Jackie's head was going to come off, but they're both out cold."

"Call the fathers," Sophie said. "Their children, their responsibility."

"Here, here," boomed Brian.

"I don't know their phone numbers."

Sophie smiled. "It'll be in their mobiles."

* * *

Faye, Sophie and Julie stood in Candice-Marie's VW van. It reeked of regurgitation and body odour, although Faye was oblivious to this. Sophie gave the dead-looking woman on the bed a firm shake, but Candice-Marie just groaned and rolled over, dragging the duvet over her head. "Definitely not capable of mommy duties today, I'd say. Where's her phone?"

"Here," said Julie, holding a handbag in one hand and rifling through it with the other.

Faye took the phone and the bag. "I was just looking," Julie said. She pressed the start button on the side and the screen lit up. She swiped up and the screen read, 'Use fingerprint or enter password'. "Oh."

"Give it here." Julie grabbed the phone back and threw herself across the bed, making Candice-Marie rock and groan again. Roughly pulling a hand out from beneath the duvet, she pressed the woman's fingers to the back of the phone until the home screen appeared. She passed it back to Faye.

"What's her husband's name?" she asked, scrolling through the contacts, of which there seemed to be many. "She certainly seems to have a lot of friends, but no ICE contact."

"ICE?" said Julie.

"In Case of Emergency, so the police know who to call if you're involved in an accident or something."

"Grim."

"Practical." Faye continued scrolling, reached the end of the list, and started scrolling up again, searching for a name that stood out or one that read 'husband'. Nothing.

"BRIAN!" she suddenly yelled, making the two women jump, "BRIAN!"

"WHAT?"

"WHAT'S THE NAME OF CANDICE-MARIE'S HUSBAND?"

"HOW THE HELL SHOULD I KNOW?"

"DIDN'T SHE CALL HIM WHEN SHE WAS ARGUING WITH JIM ABOUT…? Oh." She turned to Julie, who shrugged. "ASK JIM IF HE CAN REMEMBER THE – "

"HE DOESN'T KNOW."

"Oh."

From far, far away came a little, high-pitched voice.

"WHAT?"

And again, a tiny voice, followed by Mark, yelling, "OLIVIA SAYS IT'S BENJAMIN."

"THANKS."

Faye called the 'Ben Mob' contact. It went straight to voicemail. There was another one, 'Ben Office', so she called that, putting it on speakerphone.

"Good morning," came a woman's voice, "Brothers Architects, how may I help you?"

"Yes, hello, I'd like to talk to Benjamin, please."

"Which Benjamin? We have two Benjamins in the office?"

"I don't know his surname. He's married to Candice-Marie."

"Porter," said the woman, "Benjamin Porter."

"Can you put me through to his office, please."

"He's in a meeting at the moment and isn't taking calls."

"But this is an emergency."

"What kind of emergency?"

"A family emergency. It's about his children."

"Oh my god!" the woman suddenly cried, "Not the children! BEN! BEN! QUICK, IT'S THE CHILDREN, SOMETHING'S HAPPENED TO THE CHILDREN!"

"Hello?" came a man's slightly breathless voice, "My children? What's happened to my children?"

"It's nothing to worry – "

"What's happened? What's wrong?"

"My name is Faye Bennett, I'm on a campsite in the Cotswolds. Your wife and her friend went out last night and got drunk. They're both incapacitated and we're worried about the children being – "

"Have you pulled me out of a very important meeting to tell me my wife got drunk last night?"

"More than drunk, she's – "

"Put Candy on the phone."

"Well, that's the point, Candy can't – "

"Put her on the phone, *now*."

"She's out cold."

"Then wake her up!"

Sophie snatched the phone off Faye and, in her finest lawyer voice, said, "Mr Porter, your wife and her friend are unconscious and there are four little children running amok on the campsite. They're currently in the care of complete strangers, so I suggest you come immediately to – "

"I can't come now! I'm in the middle of a very important – "

"What's more important than your children?"

"This deal, for a start."

'Wow,' mouthed Faye.

"How far away are you, Mr Porter?"

"I'm back in Oxford."

"How long would it take you to get here?"

"Normally about 40 minutes, but I can't come now, it's completely out of the question. Look," he snapped, exasperated, "I didn't want her to go bloody camping in her stupid hippy van in the first place. If she wants to get pissed that's on her and has nothing to do with me."

"And what do you suggest we do with your children?"

"Just keep an eye on them."

Sophie pursed her lips. "Jackie's husband, do you know how to contact him?"

"He's here with me now." He huffed. "Just give us a minute," and the line went dead.

"Unbelievable," Faye said, "No sense of urgency."

They waited. Julie gave Candice-Marie a couple of desultory shakes. Faye stared out of the window at the children playing outside. Sophie vowed to look up the legal ramifications for child abandonment at the earliest opportunity and sue them both.

"Hello?"

"Yes, I'm still here, with your children."

"We'll be there between 5 and 6 o'clock this evening,

depending on traffic. Give them strong coffee, that usually works, and – "

"Mr Porter," Sophie said, very slowly and very clearly, "If you're not here within the hour I'm calling the police and, in my capacity as a Senior Partner at a major London law firm, I shall insist that they charge you with child abandonment *and* child endangerment. You have one hour before I call the relevant authorities." And she ended the call.

"Marvelous!" Faye cried. "Do you think they'll come?"

"They'd better," she said, exiting the smelly van, "It wasn't an idle threat."

"You can charge them with child abandonment?"

"No idea, I work in corporate, but I can certainly call the police. You ready, Tel?"

"I certainly am!" he cried, jumping in behind the wheel of his sports car.

* * *

The fathers arrived at 9.45, both in one SUV. They parked on the driveway between the two VWs and each clambered straight into their wife's van. There was some one-sided shouting of 'dragged me out of work' and 'hairbrained plans to live a hippy lifestyle', followed by a bit of van rocking, before they clambered out again, holding their noses. The children, spotting them from the field, came running over and wrapped themselves around their legs. "Mummy's sick," one of them said.

"Yes, I gathered." He looked around the caravan area and saw Brian and Faye, Jim and Julie, standing outside the awning, watching. "Are you the ones who called?"

"Yes."

"It wasn't necessary to threaten us with the police."

"Our lawyer thought it was."

"Is she really a lawyer?"

"Yes, a very good one."

"Where is she?"

"Out."

The man huffed. "Get your stuff together, kids, we're going home."

The children started whining about staying to play football with their new friends, but the men ignored them. One roughly tore down the awning on Candice-Marie's van. Jim dashed over to retrieve his airbed and sleeping bag. The awning was pushed inside the van and one of the men, Benjamin, climbed behind the wheel. The other herded the children into the back of the car, still whining about being taken away, and then carried a limp Jackie to the passenger seat.

"What about the van, Mike?"

Mike looked at the VW next to Brian and Faye's caravan and, with real emotion, said, "Burn it for all I care. I knew it was a bad idea to let them charge around the country in the stupid things."

"You just leaving it then?"

"Yeah, she can collect it tomorrow and drive it straight to the scrapyard."

"I could drive it for you?" Jim suddenly said, and everybody looked at him.

"Don't you have work to go to?" Brian asked.

"No."

"Why not?"

"I rang in sick."

"Are you sick?"

"Yeah, I told 'em I'd split with my missus and was too upset to work." He said this as Julie snuggled up to him, repeatedly kissing his face.

"Yes, you look devastated."

"I am, mate, I am."

Brian rolled his eyes.

"You can drive the van back to Oxford?" Mike asked.

"Yeah, for twenty quid."

"Okay, you're on."

"Damn," Jim hissed under his breath, "I knew I should

have asked for more." He prised himself away from Julie and raced towards Jackie's van. The man threw him the keys and they set off, out of the campsite, in a convoy, the car full of children leading the way.

"Thank goodness for that," Brian said, "I thought we were going to be stuck with them all day."

"Well at least we know they're safe now."

He wrapped an arm around her shoulders and kissed the top of her head.

"What's that for?" she asked.

"For being a lovely woman." Faye smiled and rested her head briefly on his chest. "Right, grab your stuff, we're off to Blenheim."

Julie stood in the awning, gently swinging her arms from side to side. In a little girl's voice she said, "Can I stay in your caravan until Jim gets back?"

Faye asked Mark and Olivia if they wanted to come along but they both said no – Olivia because she wasn't really allowed to leave the pitch except to go shopping, and Mark because he wanted to stay and finish his book.

"What page you on?" he called over to Olivia after everyone had left and the caravan area was suddenly quiet.

Olivia was sat outside the motorhome at her bistro table. "Page 376."

"Bit ahead of me then."

"Yes. It gets very exciting."

"No, don't tell me."

"I won't."

They read quietly. Behind them, in the trees, a dark shadow slithered closer to the edge of the camping area and came to a stop behind the water tap. Olivia and Mark were too engrossed to notice, even when the shadow stepped on a branch and it cracked. A head peaked out behind a tree trunk and watched them. An hour passed, and the shadow moved from one tree trunk to the next.

After a while Olivia closed her book and said, "Well, I'd

best go shopping."

"You're leaving the pitch?" Mark said with a laugh.

"Yes, Richard wants a lamb casserole today."

"So going shopping isn't against the rules?"

"They're not rules," she laughed, "They're just ... *guidelines* to make sure I don't do anything silly."

"Are you prone to silliness?"

"I guess I must be," she giggled, standing up.

"How silly can you get?"

"I don't know, it's been so long I can't remember."

"Shall we find out?"

Olivia looked across at him.

"I could do with going shopping myself," he said. "We can go together if you like, if it's not against the guidelines."

Olivia seemed flustered for a moment. "Richard told me to catch the bus. I don't think he'd be pleased if I went in your van."

"No, no, I was thinking of taking the bus myself, take the stress out of driving. We'll just catch the same bus into Woodstock, coincidentally."

She still seemed unsure.

"It's okay if you'd rather go alone."

"No, I'd ... I'd quite like the company actually."

"Good."

* * *

They stood at the bus stop outside the campsite, glancing at each other and smiling awkwardly as they waited for the bus. Olivia had brought a shopping trolley.

"You have enough change for the fare?" he asked.

"Yes, Richard left me some pocket money."

"Pocket money?"

"Yes." She laughed. "I get pocket money, but I have to find it first."

"Find it?"

"It's a little game Richard likes to play. He hides money all over the house, or in the motorhome, and I find it while I'm cleaning. If I find it all he knows I've cleaned thoroughly."

Mark was lost for words for a moment, then asked, "Is it fun, this game?"

"Fun?"

"Yes, aren't games supposed to be fun?"

She'd stopped smiling. Mark felt bad about that, so he said, "About this silliness you're prone to," and the smile returned.

"What about it?"

"I dare you to ... get on the bus using only one leg."

"One leg?"

"Yes, *hop* on."

"Hop?"

Mark nodded, a big grin spreading over his face. He saw her eyes widen with excitement when she said, "I will if you will."

"Yer on."

Mark tripped trying to hop onto the bus and splayed across the floor in front of the driver and the lower deck passengers. Olivia rushed to his aid, but he jumped to his feet like a gymnast, pulling a muscle in his groin as he did so. He raised his arms at the gawping passengers and cried, "Nul points." Some of them laughed.

When he finally limped over to the seat next to Olivia she was in the midst of a fit of giggles. "I'm so sorry," she kept saying, "But you were like a starfish on the floor."

Mark liked hearing her laugh and kept the fit of giggles going by saying, "I dare you to pull a face at the next passenger that gets on the bus."

"No, I couldn't!"

"You could."

Olivia concentrated as the bus pulled up at the next stop and two elderly ladies clambered on. When one glanced around, looking for a seat, Olivia stuck out her tongue, making the woman do a double-take, which set off her giggles again. She stopped when the woman gave her a look that could have halted a charging elephant in its tracks. They gave their seat up to the two women and raced upstairs, laughing like naughty children, and threw themselves down on the front seat.

At the next bus stop Olivia said, "Knock on the window and pull a face at the first person that looks up."

Mark leaned forward and pounded on the window. A woman with a child in a buggy looked up, and Mark put this thumbs in the corner of his mouth, his fingers at the corners of his eyes, and pulled them together. He looked like a gargoyle. The woman's mouth fell open and she hurried onto the bus. They were both trying to stifle their giggles when a voice cried up the stairs, "Oi! What you doin' pulling faces at me like that?"

"Sorry," Mark called back, and burst into laughter again, which set Olivia off.

By the time they arrived at the village they were in full hysterics and walked to the Co-Op falling against each other. They stood outside for a while waiting for the hysteria to subside, but every time they looked at each other they couldn't stop themselves. People walking into the shop gave them funny looks, which made them laugh even more. They felt like children.

"Oh, I haven't laughed so much in ages," Olivia said, wiping tears from her eyes.

"You have a nice laugh, you should laugh more often."

They finally managed to calm themselves enough to enter the shop, one tiny trolley each, Olivia's shopping trolley in hers. Mark proceeded to lob items into his from a distance, underarm, overarm, tossing them over his head, playing the fool because he liked the sound of her tinkling laughter. He didn't care that people were looking at him, he felt happy. He realised he hadn't felt happy in a very long time.

Olivia quickly picked up a bag of baby carrots and some potatoes, then stood with Mark at the book display. "I've got that one," she said.

"Me too!"

"And that one."

"That was good. Have you read this?"

"Yes, not as good as his last one though."

"No, I much prefer the one I'm reading now."

"Yes, he's very good."

"He's my favourite. We should both get the same book and read it in silly voices."

"Like Mickey Mouse?"

"Or Arnold Schwarzenegger; *I need your clothes, your books and your motorcycle*."

Olivia laughed. "Which one?"

Mark picked up a blue book and read the cover like the voiceover for a film, "Seven Days. Three families. One killer."

"Ooh. Or this one." She picked up a book and lisped, "Thuthanne hath a job she lovth, for a both she loathes."

"A both?"

"Boss."

Mark nodded, and they each put a copy in their trolleys and continued shopping.

Olivia dithered at the meat counter, picking up shrink-wrapped packs of lamb and muttering, "Too much fat for Richard. Too big. Probably too small."

"This one," Mark said, and threw a random lump of meat in her trolley. "Come on, let's get some sweeties!"

Olivia followed, carried along by his energy and his enthusiasm. She felt very naughty. In the confectionary aisle she baulked at a large bar of Cadbury's chocolate he handed her, saying, "I can't, Richard doesn't let me have chocolate except on special occasions, he says he doesn't want a fat – "

"Richard's not here, is he," Mark said, "Eat it before you get home. Eat it on the bus and smother it all over your face."

Olivia burst out laughing. "You're bonkers."

"Fun though, isn't it."

In the bread section Olivia noticed a display of fresh croissants, and cried, "Oh, I love croissants!" Mark threw four into a brown paper bag and put it in his trolley, "My treat."

Olivia chose a bottle of red wine, a Chianti, and Mark took it from her to read the label in a terrible French accent. She picked up another and read it aloud in perfect Spanish.

"Hey, you're fluent!"

"I am."

"A woman of many talents."

She blushed and followed him to the flower display.

"What's your favourite flower?" he asked.

"Sunflowers and – oh, look at those germini, aren't they lovely!"

"Daisies," Mark said, picking out a pink bunch, then picking out a bouquet of sunflowers.

"Are those for me?" she asked.

"They certainly are."

"Richard doesn't like cut flowers, he says they look – "

"But Richard isn't here," Mark said with a wink. "I'll put them on the table outside my caravan, and you can look over whenever you want and know that they're yours."

"Oh, that's so lovely," Olivia said, putting a hand on her chest.

"Too serious, must do something silly immediately."

"Put your head in the flowers," she said, and he did, and she laughed, and he felt happy.

* * *

Faye and Brian pulled up outside their caravan late afternoon, and slowly got out, groaning.

"Didn't realise the place was so big," Brian said, leaning on the bonnet and staggering stiffly towards the awning, under which Julie sat, doing one of his crosswords.

"Beautiful though."

"Beautiful and very, very big. My feet are killing me."

"Mine too. Cup of tea?" She sensed him looking at his watch and added, "It's too early, Bri."

"It's 5 o'clock somewhere, and besides, I deserve it after walking 173 miles round a stately home."

"Don't exaggerate, it was only a hundred or so. Hi, Julie.

Jim not back yet?"

"No. I tried calling him but he didn't answer, and then I found his phone in the van, along with his wallet. Did you have a nice time?"

"Lovely. Exhausted now though."

"I'll make you a cup of tea."

"Lovely."

Brian's eyes were drawn to a splash of colour at the end of the caravan area, and saw Mark sitting outside his caravan with a huge bunch of flowers lying on the table next to him.

"ADMIRER, MARK?"

"THEY'RE NOT FOR ME."

"FOR THE WIFE?"

"NO. YOU WOULDN'T HAPPEN TO HAVE A VASE, WOULD YOU?"

Brian turned to Faye, who'd collapsed in a chair with her arms and legs splayed wide. In the caravan Julie busied herself with kettle and cups. "Do you have a vase?" he asked her, intrigued.

"A vase?"

"Yes, a tall thing you put flowers into."

"Why, have you bought me flowers? I didn't see you buy flowers."

"It's not for me, it's for Mark."

"Mark has flowers?" Faye glanced over. "So he has. Nice. Admirer?"

"He says not. Do you have a vase?"

"In a caravan?"

"Well, you appear to carry Dunelm's entire stock of blankets, towels and sheets, maybe you have a selection of vases stashed away somewhere."

"No."

"NO, MARK."

"NOT TO WORRY."

"Oh," she suddenly cried, "I have a big plastic bottle of cordial from Asda, cherries and berries or something, don't like it. He could use that, but he'll have to come and get it himself, I can't move."

"I'll get it," Julie said. "Where is it."

"In the cupboard under the sink."

"Next to the flux capacitor and the hen's teeth," Brian laughed. "Oh, and don't touch the inflatable medical theatre she has stashed in there."

"Are you making fun of my preparedness, Bri?"

"Of course not, my love, I wouldn't dare, and I don't have the energy."

Faye looked at him with slitty eyes. He smiled back, then staggered to his chair and fell into it, reached out, pulled his Halfords coolbox closer and took out a cold can of lager. He leaned back, sighing with satisfaction as he pulled back the tab, avoiding Faye's still slitty eyes.

"What shall I do with the cordial?" Julie asked.

"Just tip it away and rinse it out."

There was the sound of glugging, and then Julie stood in the caravan door with a giant plastic bottle. Faye reached up and took it from her, put it on the table. Julie reappeared with two mugs of tea and handed one to Faye, who mimicked Brian's sigh of satisfaction as she brought it up to her lips. She sipped, he gulped.

"MARK!" Brian suddenly hollered, making Julie spill her tea as she went to sit back on the blanket, "WE HAVE A TALL RECEPTACLE FOR YOUR FLOWERS."

"You've stained my blanket with your bawling, Bri."

"Not to worry, I'm sure you have a spare somewhere."

An hour later, while Faye and Brian were still sprawled in their chairs, hardly able to move, and Mark sat outside his caravan, next to a plastic bottle of flowers, reading and casting quick glances over at Olivia, who was sat at her bistro table, reading, Tel's red sports car roared into the caravan area and skidded to a stop outside the Airstream. They both looked very happy. Sophie elegantly climbed out and beamed at them. "The fathers turned up then?" she said, noticing a distinct lack of screaming children.

"Yes, about an hour later," Faye said. "Did you have a good time?"

"The best. We went *wild*!"

"How wild?" asked Julie.

"*Wild* wild."

"Tattoos?"

"Well, not that wild."

"Piercings?"

Sophie puckered her mouth and Julie went back to her almost blank crossword puzzle. Brian said, "I hope you haven't done all of them while we've been gone."

"No," said Julie, "This is my first one. S'hard."

Sophie coiled herself down onto the blanket. She was wearing a whole new outfit, very casual in an expensive way. "We had breakfast at Sainsbury's, which was very nice."

Julie started quietly, and seeming unconsciously, singing about living like common people. Sophie pushed her and she fell sideways, tipping her mug of tea over the blanket. Faye groaned, Brian laughed.

"Then we went shopping in Oxford and bought some appropriate clothing and trainers," she said, lifting up a Nike shoe, "Purchased a load of films, and Tel bought me a gorgeous bracelet, look." She held out her arm and Faye cooed at the delicate chain around her wrist. "I can't stop looking at it."

"It's beautiful."

"You deserve it," Tel said, coming to lean against the corner of their caravan with an equally huge smile. He had a large and seemingly heavy box in his hands. "We got something for you too, Faye."

"For me?"

"As promised, for your toilet talents." He lifted up the box and put it on the table. "One crate of champagne, the good stuff, mind, this is from a very exclusive wine shop in Oxford, not Sainsbury's."

"Oh!" Faye cried, jumping up and opening up the box.

"Look, Bri, proper champagne! Oh, that's so nice of you, thank you."

"No, Faye, thank you for coming to our rescue, we literally couldn't have done it without you."

"Having no sense of smell has its advantages," she said. "Drink?"

"You'll need to chill it first."

"Here," Brian said, holding up a cold can, then another for Sophie, which she opened and sipped at delicately.

"Me too," said Julie.

Sophie looked at her bracelet again and continued, "Then we had the *best* sleep in a hotel room with the comfiest bed on the planet."

"Just sleep?" Julie grinned.

"None of your business."

"Just askin'."

"And then we stopped off at Sainsbury's on the way back and bought a TV set."

They all looked over at Tel's sports car, seemingly devoid of a TV set.

"Miniature TV, is it?" Brian asked.

"No, actually it's quite a big one. We had to wait around in the car park for ages until a van turned up."

"The driver agreed to bring it back for us," Tel said.

"For a small fee, of course. In fact, here he is now."

Sophie jumped up, as did Julie. Faye and Brian mostly used their arms and a lot of grunting to get out of their chairs and stagger out onto the driveway. A decorator's van pulled into the caravan area and a man jumped out. "Nearly lost you back there," he said, going round to the back and opening up the doors.

"Sorry, couldn't resist putting my foot down for the last bit."

"You wanna help me get it out? I don't do heavy hauling, bad back."

Tel disappeared behind the open doors, then peaked his

head out at Brian. "Could you lend a hand?"

"I can barely carry myself, lad, let alone a TV set."

Mark ran up. "Occurring?" he asked jovially.

"You're cheery!"

"I am. I quite like it. I might carry on doing it for a bit."

"You should, looks good on you."

"Ta. So, what's occurring?"

"Tel needs a hand with his TV set."

"Okay." Mark went to the back of the van. He immediately started laughing.

"What's so funny?" Tel asked.

"You haven't thought this through too well, have you, mate."

"Just grab the other end and help me get it out."

There was some moving, some scuffling, and then Tel reappeared from behind the van door, walking backwards. Brian exploded with laughter. Faye's mouth fell open. Julie cried, "Bloody 'ell!" as Sophie glanced at them all, confused.

"Best one they had," Tel said over his shoulder, a bit peeved at all the laughter when he'd expected gasps of amazement. "It has an a9 Gen 3 Processor for excellent picture quality, and Dolby multi-dimensional surround sound."

Mark finally appeared, carrying the other end of the box and quaking with amusement.

"How big is it?" Brian asked.

"88 inches."

"So, almost as big as the Airstream then." He wiped tears from his eyes.

"Why are you all laughing?" Tel snapped, as he and Mark leaned the enormous box against the silver bullet. "This is a state-of-the art TV!"

"It may be, but … " Brian could barely get the words out. "… how are you going to get it in your teeny-tiny caravan?"

CHAPTER 11

Tel and Sophie had bought a good selection of DVDs.

"You've never seen any of these?" Julie asked, glancing through the titles.

"No."

"How come?"

"Too busy studying."

"Too busy working."

"Which one shall we watch first?"

They were all in Brian and Faye's awning. Tel had finally realised what all the laughter was about when he looked at the giant box containing the TV and then at tiny door to the Airstream. After much debate about the law of physics and the removability of Airstream windows, they put it in the awning, to Brian's great delight. Mark and Tel set it up, while Faye and Sophie got the drinks and, to Sophie's great delight, made popcorn with parmesan cheese.

"These taste like feet," Julie whined.

"Don't eat them then."

"But I like popcorn."

"Just lick off the feet dust off then."

Julie stuck out her tongue, then threw a glare at Faye and said, "Oh, ha ha."

They had watched The Martian, which everyone liked except for Julie, who said, when it was over, "Well that was rubbish, it didn't have any Martians in it at all!" It took ages for them to stop laughing, while she stared at them quizzically. They were now enthralled with Avatar. Outside the open awning sat a group of small children, all rivetted to the colourful screen. From the corner of his eye Brian noticed some adults with blankets or cushions sitting down on the gravel outside too, and then some more.

The baddy in the film was just about to fire at the big tree where the blue people lived, when Jim suddenly burst into the awning.

"JIM!" Julie cried, jumping up and latching onto his gasping body, "WHERE'VE YOU BEEN? I'VE BEEN SO WORRIED!"

"You're in the way!" someone sitting outside yelled.

"We can't see!"

"Water," he gasped. Faye let him collapse into her chair, where he sat with his eyes closed, breathing heavily. Julie rushed to get him a glass of water.

"Where you been, lad?"

"Yes, Jim," cried Julie, handing him water, "Where have you been? You've been ages! I was so worried."

"It's been ... a nightmare." He gulped at the water. "I drove ... the van to Oxford." He gulped more water. "Parked it in their driveway – big house – and then ... then they just carried the women into the house, gave me 20 quid and slammed the door in my face, didn't offer me a lift anywhere or anything. I was going to catch a bus back, but I left my wallet in the van."

"Yes, I saw it," Julie said.

"Then I thought, bugger it, and went to call a taxi, but my phone is in the van too. So ... " Another gulp of water.

Someone outside shouted, "Put the film back on!"

"So I had to walk back."

"You've walked all the way from Oxford?"

"Yeah."

"Oh my god, Jim!"

"It's only 10 miles," Brian said, "About three hours walk. Did you get hijacked on the way?" He laughed, then stopped suddenly and said, "Oh."

"Oh, what?" said Julie.

"Nothing."

"No, come on, what?"

"Nothing."

"Jim?"

"What?"

"It only takes three hours to walk from Oxford, you've been gone since 10 this morning, that's ... that's ... "

"Seven hours," someone from outside shouted, "Now put the film back on!"

"Where've you been, Jim?"

"Let me rest, Jules."

"Where've you *been*?" He didn't reply, and she spun round to Brian. "You know, don't you! You know where he's been!"

"I know nothing," Brian said, "I've been walking my legs off at Blenheim Palace all day, how the hell would I know where he's been?"

"But you said 'oh'."

"So?"

"'Oh' means something. You know something. Tell me what it is."

"Are you putting the film back on or what, only the kids are getting a bit restless out here?"

Brian squirmed uncomfortably in his chair. He didn't know for sure but he could guess where Jim had been because it was, to him, perfectly obvious. When he looked at Mark, who'd dragged his own chair over to watch the films, he knew that he knew too. He glanced at Faye and she very slightly shook her head.

When nobody answered, Julie jumped up and flounced out of the awning, through the small crowd sitting on the ground outside. One of them said, "I wanna watch the film," while someone else said, "No, this is better than Coronation Street. Where you been, pal?" he asked Jim.

30 seconds later, Julie made her way back through the crowd and into the awning again, where she stood, arms folded, saying, "I've got nowhere to go."

"I'd go home, love," Faye said gently. "I don't mean now,

but perhaps tomorrow, go home and make it up with your mum."

"I've got no one except you, Jim. I'm all alone and you left me and you won't tell me where you've been."

Jim let his head fall back on the chair, staring up at the white canvas ceiling.

"Tell me where you've been. I know you're keeping something from me, you're all keeping something from me."

Someone outside said, "See, I said this would be a good bit, didn't I."

"She's very good."

"Just tell me where you've been!" Julie cried.

"I went to Bethany's," Jim sighed.

Silence, except for a couple of outsiders sucking in air.

"What? You went ... what?"

"I just wanted to check she was okay."

"You went to Bethany's? Why?"

Jim took a deep breath. He lifted his head and looked up at Julie. Everyone held their breath and waited for him to speak. "I asked her if ... she'd have me back."

"You idiot," someone from outside said. "You shouldn't have told her, now you've broken her heart. Look at her face, the poor cow."

Inside the awning, on a blanket laid out over rubber camping tiles, Tel leaned closer to Sophie and whispered, "Is it me or is all this just a little bit ... surreal?"

"It is a bit odd," she breathed back, "But maybe this is what happens in the real world, of which we clearly know nothing. Maybe Coronation Street is more accurate than we assumed."

"You watch Coronation Street?"

"Not on a regular basis but, you know, every now and then."

"You asked her to take you back?" Julie gasped. "Why, Jim? Why?"

"It's my home!" he cried, exasperated. "Well, strictly

speaking it's her home, she never added my name to the mortgage, bought it before we got together, but it's where I live. Without Bethany I have nothing. Of course I want her to take me back, otherwise I'm homeless, Jules, I'll have nothing except what's sitting out there in my van."

"You have me, Jim."

"You're homeless too, Jules. Together we have nothing."

"Except each other."

"It's not enough."

"But we love each other."

"No, we don't, we're just two sad people clinging on to each other for comfort."

Tears spilled down Julie's twisted face. She threw herself down on the blanket and Sophie suddenly found a head in her lap, sobbing loudly. She gently patted Julie's head, not really knowing what else to do, as Julie started wailing.

Outside, a child started to cry, and then another. Someone asked if they could have the film back on now. Julie howled, and Mark started arguing with Jim about upsetting her *and* his wife and that he was just a bloody parasite who wouldn't know what love was if it hit him in the face.

"Oh, and you're such an expert, are you?" Jim countered, "How's Janis these days, still chasing after anyone with a hefty bank account, is she?"

Mark stood up, angry. Jim stood up, furious. Brian stood up and boomed, "ENOUGH!" With some stiff-legged effort he moved to the edge of the awning and rolled the door down, saying, "Show's over, folks, go home now."

Everyone outside groaned and grumbled, "But we wanted to see what happened next." They slowly dispersed back to their tents.

Brian turned to face those inside. "I know some of you are having a rotten time right now." He looked at Jim, slumped morosely in the chair, and then at Julie, who was wailing inconsolably in Sophie's lap. "Mostly of your own making, it has t'be said, but this is my holiday. I want to chill and relax, and so far it's been a complete circus, with screaming children and drunken mothers, the police, bed quests and cries f'water in middle of night. I would," he said, closing his eyes and taking a deep breath, "like to enjoy rest of my holiday in peace and quiet, is that too much to ask?"

"No, Brian."

"Sorry, Bri."

"Oh, it's not your fault, some of you just have chaotic lives, but please, could you contain your chaos a bit? I want a decent night's sleep, I want to spend time with my wife and read and have afternoon naps and take country walks. Not now, of course, Blenheim killed off all my leg muscles, but you know what I mean."

"Yes, Bri."

"Sorry, Bri."

"He's overtired," Faye said softly. "Come and sit down, love."

"We'll go," Sophie said, keen to get rid of the noisy head in her lap.

"Yeah, we'll leave you in peace," Mark said.

"No, no, stay and finish the film. I think," he said, hauling himself up into the caravan, "I think I'll just go to bed."

They finished watching the film without speaking, the volume just loud enough to hear, and then left, very, very quietly, Sophie gently extricating herself from under Julie, who had fallen asleep. Jim was asleep in the chair too. Faye pulled the sleeping bag over Julie and draped a blanket over Jim, and went to bed

Day 5 - Tuesday

"What's that noise?"

"I don't know."

"It sounds like a hissing snake fighting a growling dog."

"I think it's Jim and Julie, quietly arguing."

"Quietly? They've woken me up!"

"Well, I suppose they've got a lot to sort out."

"Do they have to do it in our awning?"

"They've got nowhere else to go."

"There's a bloody great forest outside, why can't they do it there?"

"Shush or they'll hear you."

"Shush? Shush! Why should I shush when they're hissing like bloody steam engines in my bloody awning!"

"Just go back to sleep."

"Why, what time is it?"

"It's early."

Brian lifted his head and stared at the clock on the wall. "You're kidding me!"

"Don't make a fuss, Brian."

"It's ffff-fluffin' 5 o'clock in't fluffin' morning! For god's sake, what does a man have to do around here to get a decent night's sleep?" He half turned, grabbed a pillow and started punching it, muttering incoherently. The van gently rocked. Outside, Jim said, "You awake, Bri?"

Brian brought the pillow up to his face and howled into it.

"Careful, you'll give yourself a hernia," Faye said, turning over. "Just go back to sleep."

"I can't go back to sleep because I'm fluffin' bursting with adrenalin and a deep-seated desire to *kill people*."

"Bri," Jim whined, "Can you just tell her – ?"

Brian roared like a lion. He wriggled off the bed on his butt cheeks, flung open the door to the toilet cupboard and snatched his dressing gown off the peg on the back. Faye lifted her head. "Don't kill them, Bri."

Brian huffed, violently pulled on his dressing gown, then violently tied up the belt and stormed outside.

Jim immediately stepped forward, saying, "Tell her she's got it all – "

Brian stopped and thrust an open hand into Jim's face, instantly silencing him.

Julie stepped towards him, saying, "How can he go back – ?"

Brian thrust his other hand inches from her face. When she, too, was silent, he snatched his hands back, furiously picked up a couple of blankets from the chairs, unzipped the awning and stomped out to his car. He unlocked the door, threw the blankets inside, hauled himself into the driver's seat, started up the car, and speedily reversed down the driveway until he was outside the caravan area, where he spun the car right, clunked it into first gear, and took off down the field, bouncing like a Space Hopper over the ruts.

* * *

"How's Bri this morning?" Tel shouted across, when Faye was opening up the awning.

"Don't know," she said.

"You don't know?"

"No."

"Why don't you know?"

"Because he's not here."

Tel stepped across the driveway, suddenly realising that their black car was gone. Sophie followed him. "Where is he?" she asked, concerned.

Faye threw an arm out towards the field of tents, and said, "He's out there somewhere."

They both looked. They didn't see the car, or Brian, just the tents and a few people scurrying to the toilet block. Inside the awning, Julie was curled up in a chair chewing on her nails, and Jim had his arms crossed tightly over across his chest. "It wasn't my fault," he said.

"Are you saying it's mine?" Julie snapped. "I wasn't the one trying to crawl into the sleeping bag!"

"I was *cold*!"

"Where's he gone, Faye?"

Faye sighed. "He took off early this morning, bounced across the field doing about 40 miles an hour, and then disappeared behind the tents. I assume he's down the bottom, sleeping in his car, or else he ploughed through the hedge and went home."

"Should we go and look for him?" Sophie asked.

"Not unless you want your head bitten off, he wasn't in the greatest of moods when he left, probably best to just leave him."

"It's *not* my fault," Jim said again.

"What did you do?" Tel asked.

"Nothing!"

"They were arguing, woke us up. Brian was pretty angry about it, I think he's suffering from chronic sleep deprivation."

Jim tightened his arms. Julie threw dirty looks across the table at him.

"He does this at home when things overwhelm him," Faye said. "He goes off to his shed and pounds around for a bit, hammers some stuff together, then calms down and comes out with a bird box or a bird table he's made by way of apology, and then we – "

"Have great make-up sex?" Julie said.

"No." Faye paused. "Not always. Anyway, he'll be fine once he catches up on his sleep."

Tel and Sophie looked down the field again. At the bottom, in the left-hand corner, they saw the mystery man come out of his tent, turn, and physically jump at something unseen on the other side of the field. He turned his hooded face up towards them, staring at them as they stared at him. Tel half raised a hand, then thought better of it. "Well, he's definitely down there somewhere, judging by mystery man's reaction. Oh wait, there's Brian's car now, he's coming back."

"Right," Faye cried, "You two, out!"

"Out where? We've got nowhere to – "

"Don't know, don't care. He'll be like a bear with a sore head and definitely won't want to see you two, so out!"

Jim and Julie stayed as far away from each other as they could as they shuffled miserably out of the awning. Jim looked at Tel and said, "Can we – ?"

"No."

"But we – "

"Absolutely not."

They loitered on the edge of the driveway, glancing at each other and looking lost.

Faye rushed into the caravan to put the kettle on. Sophie and Tel watched the car bounce across the field, crunch across the driveway, and come to a stop in front of them. Brian's face was set as hard as stone behind his beard as he got out. He nodded at them, glared at Jim and Julie, who dropped their heads like naughty children, and stomped into the awning.

"Wife!" he cried.

"Husband," she yelled.

"I'm back."

"Kettle's on."

"Make it a strong one, lass."

"Two bags, going in."

He threw himself into a chair and stared up at them. Sophie suddenly turned her head, covering one side of her face with her hand. "You okay, Brian?" she asked.

"Yes, *fine*."

"Can we … get you anything?"

"Pair of underpants?" Tel sniggered. "Shorts, perhaps?"

"I just need tea and some peace and quiet." Sophie was still covering her eyes. "What's the matter with you? It's not even sunny."

"It's going to rain today," Faye shouted, tinkling spoons in mugs.

"Do you have a headache? Faye, do we have any paracetamol?"

"No, no, I'm fine. It's just … " Sophie still wouldn't look at him, she looked at Tel, who grinned and said, "Your, er, manhood's hanging low there, Brian."

Brian snapped his legs together and winced.

They turned and moved towards the red sports car. "We're out exploring all day," Sophie shouted, "Won't hear a peep out of us."

Brian turned his gaze to Jim and Julie, still standing by the side of the driveway as if waiting to be called back into the awning. Brian said nothing, he just glared. They shuffled off towards their small van, the sports car honking its horn at them and making them jump as it roared past. They got in and drove off.

Faye came out of the caravan carrying two mugs of strong tea. "Here, get this down yer neck. We'll have a nice relaxing day reading our books, no point going anywhere, the weather forecast is terrible."

"Sounds good to me."

* * *

Rain had been lashing down all day, pounding relentlessly on the roof of the awning and even louder inside the caravan. Brian had to lift the canvas roof up every 15 minutes to drain the heavy bulge of water that accumulated. Rain cascaded down the plastic windows and lashed against the caravan, making it rock and the awning flap. All windows were steamed up and, when he wiped it away to peer outside, his only view was of jet-black sky and muddy puddles. Once he saw Olivia moving around inside the motorhome. She spotted him as she glanced out of her window and waved, he waved back. Sophie and Tel were still out, and Jim and Julie hadn't returned and now he was starting to feel a bit guilty. Even Mark had dashed out a little earlier, a jacket over his head as he ran to his van and drove off, seemingly in a hurry.

He was bored with his book and bored with crosswords. He thought about watching a film on the enormous TV set but, afraid of the awning leaking on it, he'd unplugged it and covered it with multiple black bin liners. Faye had thrown a blanket over it, purely for decorative purposes, he thought. He didn't fancy watching anything on their tiny TV in the van, he wasn't in the mood and he probably wouldn't be able to hear above the noise of pounding, incessant rain. He was just bored, and the sound of the downpour was getting on his nerves.

Faye had cooked him a breakfast and made him a sandwich for lunch, and appeared at regular intervals with nuts and bowls of olives and biscuits with mugs of tea, but he was starting to feel a bit stir crazy.

"I feel a bit stir crazy," he said.

"Read your book."

"It's boring."

"Start another one."

"Don't want to."

"You're like a little kid who can't go out to play."

He sighed. "How's your book?"

"Interesting, if I can read it."

"I'll shut up."

He paced up and down the awning, occasionally stopping to check the tension on the poles. He flopped into his chair and sighed, got back up again, sighed again, and went into the caravan, started opening up cupboards. "Do we have any – ?"

"Crisps are in the top cupboard."

He found them, picked one, put it back again. He wasn't actually hungry, just bored. He glanced at the clock. 4 o'clock. It had been raining for five hours solid and showed no sign of stopping anytime soon. He went back into the awning and started pacing again.

Faye slammed her book shut. "I can't concentrate with you stomping around like a petulant giant."

"I'm *bored*."

"Do you want a game of chess?"

He pulled a face and shrugged.

"Draughts?"

He pulled another face and shrugged.

"Cards? Swingball? Ludo? Snap? Poker? Char- ?"

"Strip poker?" he said with a hairy grin. "We could have sex, there's nobody around, and even if there was they wouldn't be able to hear us over the sound of the *endless bloody rain*."

"You're not using my body as a relief for your boredom, Bri."

"Why not? We used to."

"We did it out of passion, not boredom, there's a difference."

She tutted and got up, went into the caravan. Brian wondered if she was going to pull the bed out so they could romp all over it, carefully due to the hasty repair, but he saw through the window that she was lying on the sofa reading her book.

Brian sighed again and wiped the steam from a plastic window, wondering if it would ever stop raining.

* * *

Mark was inside his caravan, listening to the rain, when Janis's name suddenly lit up on his mobile phone. He took a deep breath to steady himself. He wasn't going to answer it, was considering maybe blocking her, but she'd only call back, best to grab the bull by the horns now and get it over with.

"Mark!" She sounded breathless. What emergency had she concocted now, he wondered, set fire to the house? "He's here. Tom's here. He wants to talk to you. Where are you?"

"I don't want to talk, not to him and especially not to you."

"We have to sort this out, Mark. We all need to sit down and talk it through."

"I can't think of anything worse. I'd rather stick rusty nails in my eyes than hold a conversation with you two. Why can't you just leave me alone?"

"Because I love you."

He gave a short laugh.

"I love you, Mark. Please, just come home, talk to Tom, he'll tell you that nothing happened, *nothing*, Mark."

"I know nothing happened."

"Then why – ?"

"It's what happened afterwards that ... that ... "

"I don't remember what happened afterwards, Mark."

"No, you were too drunk, but I do, I remember it very clearly. In fact," he said, pushing his palm against his forehead, "it's all I can think about, what you said in the car after we left the party."

"I don't remember what I said! Tell me what I said!"

"It changed *everything*," he suddenly hissed.

"What? *Mark!*" Neither of them spoke for a moment, and then she said, "You should at least have the decency to tell me what I've done and give me a chance to defend myself, even murderers get a chance to defend themselves. I was drunk, I can't be held responsible for anything I said when I was *drunk*. You're being ridiculous about the whole thing, playing the victim when *I'm* the victim here. You just left me with no explanation, all huffy and indignant, making out that a bit of harmless flirting was the worst thing in the world, but it's not, Mark, what you did was worse, much worse."

"I saw you, Janis," he said quietly. "I saw who you really are, and I didn't like it, didn't like it one bit."

"What are you talking about?"

"Your mask slipped, Janis. I saw what was underneath."

She was quiet. He could hear her breathing. And then, quietly, fiercely, she hissed, "I'm giving you one last chance, Mark, come home now or don't come home at all. You're not in charge here, I am. You were always punching above your weight with me, you were lucky to have me at all, but you were too stupid to realise it. I'm calling the shots now, I've always called the shots, and I'm telling you, get here now or I swear to god I'll make your life a living hell."

"There she is," Mark said, "There's the real Janis, throwing yet another strop to get what she wants. Well I'm sick of it, sick of our life together and sick of you. I'm not doing this anymore."

"Get back here right this minute or I'm tearing this house to pieces, I mean it. I'll take you for every penny I can get and leave you alone and destitute, do you hear me? I'll make you pay, Mark, I'll make you *suffer*."

Mark relaxed the palm pressing against his forehead, against all the thoughts that had been whirling round in his head for weeks, and felt suddenly very calm. She'd moved in after six weeks, was talking about marriage after six months, insisted on an extension and a new kitchen, new everything, then they got married and more demands, always wanting, always taking. A whirlwind of demands, buffeted along by her incessant need for more, more, more.

"Send Tom home," he said, "I'll come. I'll talk. Let's end this once and for all."

* * *

Later that same afternoon Richard called Olivia.

"I'm staying here at the village tonight," he said, and she could hear the rain lashing down in the background. "Most of the roads are flooded and impassable."

"What, you're staying out all night?"

"That's what I just said, there's no need to repeat what I said, Olivia."

"I'll be on my own all night in the motorhome?"

"Yes." He already sounded annoyed.

"What time will you be back in the morning?"

"I'm going to see a couple of churches over by Cirencester tomorrow, no point coming back to the campsite and then travelling out again, so I'll be back around seven tomorrow night."

"Tomorrow night!"

"Watch your tone, Olivia."

"I'm annoyed, Richard. I've been on my own all day, now all night and all day tomorrow too. This is supposed to be *our* holiday."

"You know this is something I have to do, I have a deadline."

"What deadline? You don't have a publisher. What deadline, Richard?"

"My own deadline, I want to get the book finished before Christmas, it won't research and write itself, you know, and I want to start on the second in the New Year."

"A second? Oh Richard, can't you get a taxi back? I don't want to be on my own all night, what if that man comes creeping around the caravans again?"

"Olivia, I've just told you, the roads are impassable, there's floods everywhere. Now stop being a child and grow up."

"But Richard – "

"Olivia, I'm drenched to the skin and covered in mud, I don't need an interrogation from my wife. I'm booking into a pub for the night and I shall see you tomorrow." And he hung up.

* * *

Brian glanced at his watch for the hundredth time. "Right!" he cried, "It's 5 o'clock. I'm off to the pub. You coming?"

"Ooh," Faye cried from inside the caravan, "Warm wine, how can I resist?"

"I've got to get out of here before I lose my mind."

"You lost it ages ago."

"I'm sure you'll seem funnier once I have a pint inside me."

"Shouldn't we eat first? There's no food there, we shouldn't drink on an empty stomach."

"I've grazed my way through the whole day, I don't need food, I need a pint in the company of other human beings!"

"Okay, okay, I'm coming."

Brian raced out to the car for the wax jackets and a golf umbrella, and ran back in again. They bundled up and set off, both holding the brolly against the lashing rain but they were still drenched within seconds. They noticed that half the tents had disappeared, given up against the elements and gone home. Those that remained were buffeted by the wind and streaming with water. Muddy puddles were everywhere.

As they passed through the entrance gates Brian spotted a white van in the car park. There was someone sitting behind the steering wheel. As they got closer they could hear music blaring, Celine Dion singing All By Myself.

"JIM!" Brian hollered, pointing towards the pub, "PINT?"

The door opened instantly and Jim leapt out, raced into the pub and held the door open for them. It was empty inside, except for a family at the far end who were huddled around a fire that wasn't lit. The three gathered at the bar. Ant, the landlord, was nowhere to be seen.

"Where's Julie?" Faye asked.

"I took her home. Her mom hugged her at the door so I guess she'll be alright."

"Good. What about you, what are you going to do?"

Jim shrugged. "Dunno. Go to work and find somewhere to live I guess."

Faye nodded. Brian peered down the length of the empty bar and bawled, "CAN WE GET SOME SERVICE AROUND HERE?"

Ant came round from the back, sighing. "What can I get you?"

"A hearty welcome and some convivial atmosphere?"

"Eh?"

"Three pints of your finest lager, my good man."

They'd just picked their drinks up and were deciding which empty table to sit at, when Mark burst through the door, soaking wet and wearing a face like thunder.

CHAPTER 12

"Whisky!" he barked at Ant, "A double."

Ant, the landlord, slowly turned and searched the shelf of spirit bottles. "Come on!" Mark barked.

"You okay?" Brian asked.

Mark nodded quickly, staring at Ant, who had picked up a bottle and was meticulously reading the label. "Whatever it is, that'll do, just tip it into a glass."

Ant started searching under the bar, moving things around before standing up straight with a spirit measure in his hand.

"Other pubs have optics, you know, you should consider modernising a bit." He said this between tightly clenched teeth, and Brian nodded at Faye, who understood immediately and led Jim to a table.

"What's up, lad?"

"I'm fine." He watched Ant delicately pouring whisky into the spirit measure, stopping twice before saying, "Is it up to the mark inside or up to the top?" Mark reached out, snatched both the bottle and the glass out of Ant's hands and poured a generous glug, which he knocked back in one before pouring another. He reached into his wet jacket pocket, pulled out his wallet and slapped a £20 note onto the bar. Ant took it, saying, "Bad day, eh? Weather don't help. How's that wife of yours?"

"Wife? Blood-sucking harridan, more like."

"Want to talk about it?" Brian asked.

"No." He emptied the glass and poured another. Ant watched him, horrified. Mark glanced up at Brian and said, quieter, calmer, "No. Thank you. You're a good man, Brian."

"And I apparently get better looking the more you drink,

according to my ... "

"To your wife, yes, you can say the word, Bri, I'm not opposed to wives per se, just mine in particular." Ant's eyes had now left the bottle and he was staring openly at Mark. "What's up with the missus, then?"

Mark slammed the whisky bottle down on the counter, spun around and took a few steps away from the bar. He stopped, seemingly not knowing where to go or what to do. He looked confused and very, very angry.

"S'up, Mark?" said Jim. "You made it up with Janis yet? Oh no, or else you wouldn't be here, would you." He started laughing. Faye nudged him but he took no notice. "Finished, is it? Yeah, I can tell by your face it's finished. Ain't worth it, these wives, these women, they just hold you back, ain't that right, Mark."

"Shut up, Jim," Faye hissed.

"You and me," Jim continued, raising his beer glass at Mark, "We're free spirits, we are, can't be held down by no woman. We're birds of a feather, you and me, birds of – "

Mark lunged forward, slamming his whisky glass down on the table and putting a hand tight around Jim's neck. Jim's eyes bulged. "Din't mean nothing," he gasped.

"Stop it!" Faye cried.

"Whoa-whoa-whoa!" Brian leapt forward. He tried to grab Mark's arm, but Mark snatched it away. Lowering his face to Jim's, he growled, "We are *not* birds of a feather, me and you, *mate*, we are *nothing* alike."

"Okay, mate, okay, keep your hair on."

Mark let go and straightened up. Jim rubbed his neck. Faye stared up at Brian, who said, "Sit down, Mark, sit down and calm down. You okay, love?"

Faye was visibly shaking. "Yeah, just a bit taken aback."

"You've upset my wife!" he bawled.

"Sorry, Faye," said Mark, "Just got a bit ..."

"I know."

"Jim?" Brian snapped.

"Why have I got to apologise? I didn't do anything." Brian glared at him. "Sorry, Faye."

"It's okay."

Brian turned to the barman, who suddenly thought to say, "No fighting in here."

"No, no fighting. Another round, I think."

"Who's paying?"

Brian stepped back to the bar. Ant stepped away from him until his back was against the shelf of spirit bottles. "I am," Brian said, slapping down a plastic card. "Another round, and ..." He looked back at the table, where Faye was trying to comfort both Mark, who was shaking his lowered head, and Jim, who was making a fuss over his neck. "... keep them coming."

He'd just sat down again with a tray of drinks when the door to the pub opened. Rain and wind gusted in. The man from the tent at the bottom of the field stepped inside, soaked hoodie dripping down onto his sunglasses. He slowly looked around, keeping his hand on the door as if prepared for a quick exit. Ant shouted, "You can't come in here with muddy boots."

The man raised his chin, all you could see of him, and opened the door wider. A pile of dripping wet people in muddy boots shuffled in with small, equally wet children. A frantic woman said, "Our tent blew down, everything's soaked!" The children started whimpering. More people came in after them until there were about eight of them standing next to the bar, drenched and miserable.

Mark instantly leapt to his feet. "Turn the heating on, Ant, it's freezing in here. And get those electric radiators from the guest rooms, we need to dry these people off before they catch pneumonia."

Faye rushed to help the campers take off their wet coats, as Brian and Jim sat in their seats, watching and quietly sipping lager. "We'd just be in the way," said Brian, and Jim nodded.

Ant stood behind the bar, motionless, as Mark and Faye

guided the group towards the log fire at the far end of the room that wasn't lit, helping them take off their jackets and putting them on the back of chairs. Their clothes underneath were wet too and they all started shivering. "Get some logs for the fire, Ant. Ant! Come on!"

Ant finally started moving. "Gis a hand with the radiators," he said to the man in the sunglasses, still standing by the door. The man hesitated, pulling his hoodie down lower over his face, and then followed him. A short while later they returned hauling small electric radiators under their arms. Mark grabbed them and plugged them in every available socket, switched them on and arranged them around the shivering group. "Logs?" he asked.

"Only got one pair of hands, Mark, gis a chance." He disappeared again. The man in sunglasses hesitated for a moment, then followed.

"So," said Jim, watching the now noisy crowd, "What do you think of it so far, this holiday of yours?"

"I'll give it foive."

Ant and the man in sunglasses returned with logs and Mark busied himself stoking up the fire until it gave out a comforting, crackling heat. Somebody asked for a hot drink to warm them up. Somebody else asked for hot food. Mark looked at Ant, who shrugged. Mark was just about to ask if Ant was capable of boiling a kettle when the pub door burst open and Sophie, sodden and thunderous, stomped like an enraged supermodel to the bar. Everyone suddenly went very quiet and stared at her. Even soaked to the skin she looked gorgeous. She threw herself onto a stool and snapped, "Can I get some service around here?"

Ant hurried over. "What can I get you?"

"A whisky. A big one. What's that?" she asked, as Ant put a glass down on the counter.

"It's a shot glass."

Sophie leaned forward across the bar and Ant stopped unscrewing the cap on the whisky bottle. "Do I look like a woman who needs a thimbleful of alcohol?"

"Pint?"

"Somewhere in between."

Ant tentatively put a tumbler on the bar. His hand shook as he trickled whisky into the spirit measure. "More than that," Sophie growled. "Oh, give it here." She snatched the bottle off him and filled the glass an inch, stopped, then glugged in another inch, while Ant stood and watched, mesmerized by her beauty and wondering why everyone seemed to think it was okay to pour their own drinks all of a sudden. Sophie put down the bottle, pulled a damp purse from her dripping bag, took out a £20 note, slammed it down and took a gulp.

Brian raced over and gently pulled the glass from her mouth. "Take it easy, I think we've all seen enough vomiting women recently."

"Bloody men," she hissed.

Faye came rushing over. "Sophie, what's up?"

"Bloody men," she hissed again.

"Come and sit down. Take your wet coat off."

The two women wandered arm-in-arm over to the table where Jim sat. Brian followed. The sound of loud children and equally loud parents ramped up again. Mark was yelling, "Just put the bloody kettle on, for god's sake! What do you mean, you've only got three teabags? You've got a bloody shop full of tea right next door!"

"Brian gives it foive," Jim suddenly said, as Faye was comforting Sophie, who looked pretty furious about something.

"What?" Faye asked.

"Brian, he gives this holiday a foive."

"Generous, I'd say." To Sophie she said, "What's happened?"

"He did the worst thing he could possibly do."

"Oh dear. What did he do?"

"He ... " She took a swig of whisky and cringed. Brian

widened his eyes at Faye and mimicked throwing up with a splay of fingers from his mouth. Faye gently took the glass off Sophie, who suddenly snarled, "He *proposed*."

"Tel proposed?"

"The bloody idiot! He's spoiled everything now, and I was really enjoying myself, too, I actually thought he might be the one, and then he does that!"

"But ... that's a good thing, isn't it?" Faye looked at Brian, who shrugged.

"We've only been seeing each other a few months, not even a year yet."

"Sometimes you just know," Faye said soothingly, looking again at Brian, who winked at her.

"It's not that." She picked up her glass again, took another swig. "Tel's ferociously ambitious, wants to shoot up the corporate ladder as quickly as possible. Joins the company, starts dating the boss's daughter, and oh, next thing you know he's asking the boss's daughter to marry him. I mean, it's not very subtle, is it."

"You're the boss's daughter?" Jim said, his interest suddenly peaked.

Sophie glared at him and he leaned back in his seat.

"He adores you," Faye said, "Anyone can see that."

"Or does he just see me as a step up the ladder? It's the third proposal I've had in 18 months, Faye, that's just not right, is it."

"You not looked in a mirror lately?" Brian said. "I'm surprised it's only three. Hell, I'd propose to you if I wasn't already – "

"Married!" Faye snapped.

Sophie looked over at Brian and her eyes softened a little. A tiny smirk played at the corners of her full lips. "Are you flirting with me, Brian?"

"Would it help?"

"Maybe."

"You're an utterly gorgeous and incredibly intelligent

woman," he said, ignoring the laser beams coming from his wife's eyes. "You have beauty and brains, an irresistible combination. Any man would be more than proud to have you as his wife, so you can hardly blame them for trying to keep such a rarity to themselves. How was that?"

"Not bad." She was smiling now. "So, you don't think it strange that every man I date wants to marry me, the boss's daughter?"

"I think it's strange that you think it's strange."

"You think, ambition aside, Tel might actually be serious?"

"I've seen the way he looks at you, lass, watches you, follows your every move. He's like an adoring puppy. You can't fake that."

"Brian," said Faye, and he braced himself for spousal retribution, "You're an old romantic at heart."

"You've just noticed, after 21 years?"

"It's 23, Bri."

"Aaand there go my Brownie points."

They were all laughing now, until Olivia, sodden from head to foot and wearing an evil expression on her normally sweet face, burst into the pub. "Bloody men!" she screeched with real feeling, "Bloody, *bloody* men!"

"All of us?" Brian shouted over. "Men in general or man in particular?"

She squelched up to the bar, next to where the man in sunglasses gently dripped onto the muddy floor, and pounded her clenched fist against it. "Drink! I need a drink! Will somebody *please* get me a drink!"

Ant came running over from the fireplace, where he'd been busy explaining to everyone that he Didn't Do Meals and everyone was arguing that it said 'Food' outside on the board. "What can I get you?"

"Whisky, and lots of it."

Feeling very de ja vu, Brian stepped up. "I'll get you a drink, Olivia, go and sit down."

She stomped over to the table and threw herself down next to Sophie, who raised her glass and said, "Here's to bloody men."

Brian came back with another tray of drinks, placing a glass in front of Olivia. "What's that?" she asked.

"Coke."

"I don't want *Coke*, I want a proper drink. What's that?" she snapped, nodding towards Mark's now abandoned drink on the table.

"Whisky."

Olivia snatched it up and downed it in one, gasping and cringing, before nodding at another glass and coughing, "Who's is that?"

"Mine," said Sophie, and grabbed it before Olivia could.

Olivia tutted, then swayed a bit on her chair. "Oh, it's strong, isn't it."

"Neat whisky usually is," Sophie said, "Drink some Coke to water it down before you slip into an alcoholic coma."

"What's up with you?" Brian asked. "You don't seem your usual, cheerful self."

Olivia opened her mouth to speak, when Mark threw himself down on a seat and said, "Ant's bloody useless, he can't even make a cup of tea that doesn't taste like dog piss."

"Eloquently put," Sophie said.

"They're all starving hungry and he's got no food. He probably has, he's just too lazy to cook it."

"Cook?" said Oliva.

Mark noticed his empty glass and looked at Brian, who nodded towards Olivia, who was now unsteadily standing up and saying, "I can cook. I'm a very good cook. What do they want?"

"It's okay, Ant's probably not insured to have drunken women in his kitchen."

"I'm not drunk," she said, swaying slightly, "I'm just very, very angry."

"Why are you angry, Olivia?"

"Because," she said, flopping back into her chair, "my husband is a dick."

Sophie gasped out loud. Jim burst out laughing, and Faye was all wide eyes and open mouth.

"He is, he's a dick. He's just called me to say ... can I have a sip of your drink?"

"No," said Sophie.

"He's just called me to say ... Do you know that man at the bar's wearing sunglasses?"

"We do."

"How incredible. You can't see his eyes but I think he's staring at us."

"Ignore him. What's Di- Richard done?"

"He said the world's flooded, he can't get back, and he's staying over in some village pub. So now I'm supposed to be on my own all night *and* all day tomorrow while he stomps around the bloody Cotswolds looking at old churches! I'm just going to call him Dick from now on, he'll hate that but it will serve him right." She gave a little, tinkling laugh, then her face fell serious again. "Leaving me all on my own when we're supposed to be on holiday, expecting me stay in and not talk to people, just like at home. Well, I'm fed up of it. Seeing you pair," she said to Brian and Faye, "And you two," she said to Sophie. Then, noticing there weren't two, only one, she said, "Where's Tel?"

"He proposed," Jim cackled, "Bad move, apparently."

"Shut up, Jim."

"Oh," Olivia said, putting a hand on Sophie's shoulder, "You haven't broken up, have you? He's so lovely, just like you, and he totally adores you, you can tell. Not like Richard, who just likes to boss me about." She started furiously mimicking her husband in a silly voice, "*Don't do this and don't do that. Cook my meals, clean the motorhome from top to bottom because I have a stupid germ phobia, and don't you dare mix with people, don't you dare have any fun.* God forbid I should have any fun! Well, I'm a grown woman and I've had enough of being told what to do. I've had it all my life, I want to do what I want to do for a change."

"Here, here," said Mark. "Celebratory drink?"

"I'll have what you're having," Olivia said.

"You won't," he laughed.

"Oh. Bit mean."

"I'll run you to a shandy."

"Okay. Can I have some of yours?"

"No!" said Sophie.

"Meanies, the lot of you."

At the bar Mark was arguing with Ant. "Look, think of the money you can make, you're missing a great opportunity here, they're all starving and all you have to do is cook them some food."

"Please, anything," one of the steaming group around the fire cried, "Toast."

"Got no bread."

"You've got a shop right next door that's stocked every day by the mobile baker!"

"It's raining!"

"Oh, I give up." Mark picked up the tray of drinks and turned, just as Olivia ran past him, shouting, "Where's the kitchen? I can cook, I'm a very good cook. What do they want?"

Suddenly everyone from the far end of the room was shouting.

"Egg and chips?"

"Beans on toast?"

"Egg and chips?"

"Any steak?"

"Egg and chips it is then," she giggled, and disappeared into the kitchen, closely followed by Ant, and then Mark, who said, "Better get her a strong coffee before you let her near any gas appliances."

"Oh, stainless steel," Olivia was saying, running her hand across the surfaces. "Where do you keep the eggs?"

"Is she okay?" Ant asked, nervously watching her falling against the fridge door, "She seems a bit ... drunk."

"Hence the strong coffee, mate. You do have coffee, don't you?"

"Yeah, course."

"Then put the bloody kettle on."

"There's no eggs," Olivia cried.

"On it, Olivia." Mark moved to the rain-lashed back door, turning before he opened it and saying, "I'm going outside. I may be some time."

"Good luck, darling. Oh, and get some bags of frozen chips. And tins of baked beans."

Mark walked outside with a big smile on his face, hardly noticing the rain at all.

* * *

The pub was buzzing. "Never seen it so busy," Mark told the group at the table. "This place could be a gold mine with the right management."

The remaining campers out on the field had given up the fight against the elements, or perhaps been lured by the smell of chips, and had come in from the storm to recover. Tea and coffee were flowing, courtesy of Faye, whilst Olivia, still slightly tipsy but now high on coffee and cooking, served up plate after plate of chips, egg and beans, including meals for their table.

"Wife," Brian cried, tucking in, "You're a mind-reader!"

"I could hear your stomach rumbling from the kitchen."

Even the man in sunglasses, sitting at the bar, got a plate and cutlery thrust in front of him. His hoodie head seemed shocked for a moment, and then he dug in, eating like a man who couldn't actually see what he was eating but enjoying it anyway.

The now warm and dry crowd heaped praise upon Olivia as she brought out meal after meal, but she just giggled and brushed it away with a wave of her tea towel.

"You can barely take your eyes off her," Brian quietly

said to Mark.

Mark, himself a little tipsy, grinned and said, “Isn't she amazing.”

“Crush?”

“Maybe. Nah. Maybe.”

Sophie and Jim had clearly found some common ground and were laughing hysterically on the other side of the table, while the man in sunglasses just sat at the bar, eating blindly, turning his head towards them from time to time and scribbling in a damp notebook.

“So, what happened earlier?” Brian asked Mark, “You know, before Sophie and Olivia stormed in like raging dervishes?”

“Ended it with Janis.” He sighed and sipped his beer. “Suddenly the fog lifted and I knew it had to be done.”

“Not fixable?”

“Nah, not after what she said.” He shuffled more upright in his chair, staring at the people around him without really seeing them. “Caught her kissing her sister's husband, my brother-in-law, at a party. Nice chap, wouldn't harm a fly, totally paralytic he was. I was furious.”

“Nobody wants to see their wife kissing another man.”

“I knew it wasn't serious, they weren't having an affair or anything like that, it was just a drunken kiss. Janis had probably thrown herself at him, it wouldn't be the first time, but Tom's a decent bloke, I trust him not to do the dirty.” He suddenly laughed. “Rang me the next day, poor sod, almost crying, begging forgiveness and saying she just wouldn't leave him alone, was after him all night and finally cornered him upstairs. I actually felt sorry for him, Janis can be very persistent when she wants something.”

Brian remained silent. They both watched Faye and Olivia hurrying to and from the kitchen, feeding people and serving up hot drinks.

“I could have forgiven her for that, but in the car on the way home ...” He pulled a face at the memory. “She was angry that I was upset about a 'silly little kiss that meant nothing'. I knew it meant nothing, I saw him try to push her away, but there's always been this thing between Janis and her sister."

"Sibling rivalry?"

"Something like that. In the car she ... well, she just flipped. It was the drink, of course, but it sounded like the truth. She was livid, told me what a useless husband I was, how Tom was so much better, more handsome, more wealthy, more successful. Told me she wanted a new house with a big conservatory like her sister, that I should expand the garden centre, open another one, bring in more money. Why should her sister have everything when she didn't? Told me ... " He pulled a face again. "Told me she didn't love me, had never loved me, that she'd backed the wrong horse and was disappointed that I turned out to be such a poor provider."

"Harsh."

Mark gulped at his beer. "It's been driving me mad ever since, what she said. It blew everything up, this little life we had together, which apparently wasn't good enough for her. It was all a sham. This afternoon something just clicked in my head, maybe it was the rain, maybe my brain imploded. Went round there, told her we were over, even told her she could keep the house. She flipped again, not drunk this time, said she couldn't afford the house on her own and why didn't I just crawl off and die somewhere, or words to that effect. Made me laugh actually." He laughed now. "The fog in my head was gone and I just saw her for who she really is; envious, paranoid, riddled with jealousy and hate. Narcissist, my mates kept telling me, but you don't listen, do you, you think they're just jealous or trying to cause trouble. Then I saw it for myself in her face, ranting and raving because she couldn't have what she wanted. It was weird but in a good way, you know, to suddenly see who someone really is."

"An epiphany."

"Yeah."

"So, it's over then?"

"Yeah. I was angry at first, then upset, but I actually feel okay now." He laughed, raising his glass. "Probably the booze, but it feels like the right thing, just ending it, you know, not having to walk on eggshells all the time, wondering what she's going to demand next?"

"Always go with your gut instinct, I say, but ... don't rush into anything."

"You mean Olivia? She's married, Bri, I don't do married women. Besides, she's way out of my league. Lovely, though," he sighed, watching her, "Really, really lovely."

Faye and Olivia finally came over and flopped into seats. "Oh, I did enjoy that," Olivia said, "I think I have a knack for it."

"You should open up your own restaurant."

"I could call it Egg, Chips and Beans," she laughed.

"Did he pay you for your services?" Mark asked.

"Oh no, I wouldn't let him charge for the meals, it was an act of human kindness."

"I bet he loved that!"

"I'll give him some money for the food we used tomorrow."

"You will not!"

"No?"

"No, stingy git can afford a few plates of egg and chips."

Sophie said, "Your bag's been buzzing all night, Olivia."

"Probably Ri- ... *Dick*, keeping tabs on my whereabouts. Let him ring, I won't answer."

"I knew Bethany wanted to throw me out," Jim suddenly said, slumped in his seat and staring into his empty glass. "One of her mates told me, the same mate who told me what a low life I was and why didn't I stop leeching off her friend and bugger off."

"She has a point," Mark laughed.

"Shut up."

"So, to stop your wife throwing you out you take up with Julie?"

"Thought it would make her jealous, didn't I. Didn't,

though, she won't even speak to me now."

"You just used Julie then."

"She fancied me, I fancied her, where's the harm in that?"

"The harm is, she's probably lying in bed right now sobbing her little heart out. You're a callous little shit, Jim."

"I liked Julie, we had a good time, I needed a good time and so did she." He lowered his head again. "Loved Bethany though, gutted about that."

"Maybe it's time to grow up and take responsibility for yourself."

Jim huffed. Then he said, "I couldn't sleep in your caravan tonight, could I, Mark?"

"No, you couldn't."

Faye said to Mark, "Did you say Ant's got guest rooms upstairs?"

"Yeah, five I think. Something else he's let slide due to chronic lethargy."

"These people are going to need somewhere to sleep tonight, they can't go back to their tents in this weather."

Mark jumped up. "On it," he said, and they watched him approach the bar and say something to Ant, who cried, "What? For *free*?"

Mark went over to the crowd around the fire and asked which of them had wrecked tents they couldn't sleep in. About half of them raised their hands. He told them to follow Ant upstairs and they started gathering their things. "I'll bring the radiators," Mark said, unplugging them one by one and wrapping his jacket around the hot metal. A couple of the men did the same. There was much banging on the ceiling as people settled down in their rooms. The other half stayed by the fire, ordering drinks and talking. The atmosphere was warm and comfortable.

And then the door to the pub opened and Tel walked in, tall and handsome and clearly in despair. He looked straight across at Sophie and mouthed, 'I'm sorry'. She was on her feet in an instant, rushing over to him. They hugged tightly and kissed. The table cheered.

"Oh, isn't that lovely," Olivia sighed. "I can't remember the last time I was kissed like that."

Brian slapped a giant hand down on Mark's arm to stop him getting up.

"Tel!" Jim shouted over, "Welcome back, and mine's a pint."

Tel and Sophie were talking quietly, smiling and touching each other's faces by the door. The man in sunglasses openly stared at them.

"Whenever you're ready," Jim shouted, "It's not like we're parched or anything."

"Don't you think you've had enough?" Brian asked.

"I'll have had enough when it stops hurting."

"Better put the brewery on standby then."

Faye reached over and patted Jim's hand.

"Listen," Brian suddenly said, holding up a finger.

"What is it?"

"Can't you hear it?"

"Hear what? I can't hear anything."

"Exactly. It's *stopped raining*! Right, I think we'll call it a night."

"We?" said Faye, "I've just bloody sat down after feeding the starving dozens, I wish to partake of some alcohol and gossip before I go home and crash out."

"Oh, fair enough."

"And I'm a free woman," Olivia said, waving at Ant to bring over another round. "I can stay out all night if I want to, so I'm going to enjoy myself. Do you think they do cocktails here?"

"They barely do wine," said Faye.

Ant brought another tray of drinks over. "I'll come up in the morning to make breakfast for everybody," Olivia said to him, who quickly replied, "We're charging this time."

"She is too," Mark said, and Ant's face fell.

Jim at some point had wandered over to the group around the open fire, sitting with them a while before slowly sliding sideways until he lay prone on a padded bench. They left him there, at least he had somewhere to sleep.

The van clan, deciding they'd had enough to drink and enough excitement for one day, left with the last of the tenters. Outside the world was damp, with a battleship grey sky and a few spots of rain still falling, but the deluge had stopped. Huge puddles swamped the gravel driveway and they had to pick their way through them back to the caravans, Brian and Faye holding hands, Tel and Sophie with arms wrapped around each other's waists. Mark glanced at Olivia and started singing, "Lonely, I'm so lonely." She laughed and grabbed his hand, and they swung them like children.

The field beyond the entrance gates was a big lake of mud. Several of the tents were flattened and lay like discarded plastic wrappers. Campers struggled to haul them up again, salvaging what they could from inside. As they were surveying the devastation there was the crunching of quick footsteps behind them. Olivia jumped. They turned to see the man in sunglasses rushing up towards them. They stopped walking and waited for him to catch up, but he just marched straight pastfoll them.

"Everything okay with your tent down there?" Brian asked.

The man raised a thumb in the air but said nothing, continuing his quick, splashy walk onto the soggy field.

"There's a cooked breakfast in the pub in the morning, if you're interested," Olivia called after him, but he made no indication that he'd heard. They continued on and, outside their caravans, said goodnight to each other before heading in; except Mark and Olivia, who stood on the driveway between his caravan and her motorhome, no longer holding hands, smiling awkwardly at each other.

"I'll keep all my windows open tonight, if you need me just shout."

"Thank you, you're very kind."

"Not a problem. Do you want my mobile number in case of emergency?" Mark fished his phone out of his pocket and she pulled hers from her bag, noticing the multitude of missed calls and texts from Richard. "Ring this number," he said, reciting it. She dialed and his phone rang.

"Good. Honestly, if you feel nervous in the night just shout or call. Will you be okay on your own?"

"Yes, yes, I'm quite used to being alone, just not at night. Thank you, Mark."

"Well," he said, backing reluctantly towards his caravan, "You know where I am if you need me."

"I do. Thank you."

He nodded and went inside, immediately opening all his windows.

Olivia felt a warm fuzziness as she climbed into the motorhome and assumed it was the drinks she'd had, or maybe the lingering excitement of cooking for all those people, or perhaps it was just knowing that she was safe, surrounded by kind people who would keep an eye on her.

She pulled down all the blinds and got ready for bed. The phone kept ringing in her bag but she ignored it.

Mark didn't pull out his bed, he padded the cushions and blankets around him in a sitting position and got comfy on one of the sofas. He spent the night watching the motorhome through the big front window, dozing occasionally but determined to ensure that Olivia, with the high voice, the tinkly laugh and the cute overbite, would be safe on his watch.

CHAPTER 13

The screaming started just after 1 o'clock in the morning. "MARK! MAAARK!"

Mark leapt off the sofa and made it to the caravan door in one enormous stride. He threw open his door and came face to face with a man wearing strange, protruding glasses, like someone at a steampunk festival, who was just sneaking past his caravan. Without thinking, Mark leapt over the caravan steps, formed a fist in mid-air and brought it down hard, punching the bloke in the side of his face. The man gave a high-pitched howl of pain and fell to the ground, rolled instantly, jumped to his feet, and ran into the woods holding the side of his face. Mark ran to the motorhome.

"Olivia!"

"MARK!"

He tried the door but it was locked. Olivia screamed again.

"Open the door!"

Quick footsteps inside, then the door swung open and Olivia was wildly waving her hands, urging him in, jumping from foot to foot and whimpering, clearly in a state of panic.

"Was it the man?" he gasped, jumping up.

Olivia stared at him with eyes as wide as dinner plates. "WHAT MAN?"

"Mark?" someone called from outside.

He stepped over to a window and raised the blind. Brian was standing outside holding a spatula in one hand. Behind him he saw Tel running down the driveway carrying what looked like a carton of milk.

"What is it?" Mark asked Olivia, who was now standing on the sofa next to him, still hopping from foot to foot.

"In there!" she cried, *"It's in there!"*

"What is?"

"I don't know, but it's small and furry and it's *in there*." She was pointing towards the bedroom, the concertina door wide open. "It ... it ... it *ran across me in bed!*"

Mark moved towards the bedroom, wishing he'd brought a weapon with him, a carving knife or a mallet. He peered through the door. Darkness.

"Where's the light?"

"On the left."

Mark felt along the wall until he found a switch, then turned it on. The room lit up. It was very neat and tidy, except for the unmade bed. "Where abouts is – *oh my god!*"

Olivia screamed again. He was vaguely aware of Brian and Tel clambering into the motorhome but he didn't turn and look, his eyes were glued to a large thing scurrying about on the floor in the corner.

"Bloody hell!" Brian boomed right next to his ear, making him jump out of his own skin, "It's the size of a bloody cat!"

Olivia screamed again. Faye climbed into the motorhome and went straight to her, asking, "What is it, what's happening?"

"A rat!" Brian boomed, "Biggest rat I've ever seen in my life, and I'm from Yorkshire."

Now Faye was up on the sofa, screaming along with Olivia, both clinging onto each other, just as Sophie poked her head through the door. "What's – ?"

"Bloody big rat," Tel said, and Sophie immediately screeched down the driveway to the Airstream, slamming the door behind her.

"Rat phobia," Tel said to Brian.

"When you see the size of this thing you'll have a rat phobia too."

The two women on the sofa screamed again, clutching each other tighter.

"How big is it?" Tel asked.

Brian held out measured hands.

"No! Are you sure it's a rat?"

The women pummeled the sofa with their feet, with Olivia screaming, *"Get it out! Get it out!"*

"How did it get in?" Brian asked.

"The bigger question is, how are we going to get rid of it?"

"Do you have a broom?" Brian asked, turning to Olivia, who shook her trembling hand at a tall cupboard next to him. He opened it and took out a broom; it was a very good broom, felt expensive. "Will this do?" he asked, handing it to Mark.

Mark took it from him and stepped forward, broom in hand, poking it towards the rat.

"Don't antagonize it," Tel said, peering over his shoulder, "It looks capable of fighting back."

The rat tried to make a break for it and ran towards them. Three men leapt back from the doorway as one, crying out in unison like baritones in a choir, making the women scream a few octaves higher, until the motorhome became a giant box of noise.

"Sweep it towards the door!" cried Tel.

"Step on it!" cried Brian.

"I ain't stepping on that!" Mark gasped, as the rat raced from the bedroom into the living room. "There'll be blood everywhere!"

The women screamed and pummeled.

Tel was now outside, looking in. Mark was frantically sweeping the floor in the vain hope of hitting the now revved-up rodent, which scurried around the edges of the sofas and the kitchen units, back into the bedroom again.

"Why didn't you get it?" Brian roared.

"It was quicker than me, and I didn't see you stepping on the thing with your size 19 feet!"

"Size 12, thank you very much. I have very small feet for a man of my size."

"*Just get it*!" Faye screamed, in a pitch he'd never heard from his wife before.

He grabbed the broom off Mark and told Tel to step away from the open door, "Unless you particular enjoy rats launching themselves through the air into your waiting arms."

Tel quickly moved.

Brian held the broom like a soldier on manoeuvres as he stealthily stepped into the bedroom, his eyes like Action Man with a button in its neck. The rat was sat up casually in the corner, almost as if it was ready to roll up its furry sleeves for a good fight. Brian moved the broom in his hands until he was holding it like a snooker cue and took a shot at the rat with the bristly end. The rat squeaked and frantically ran back and forth in the small space between the bed and the wall. Brian took another poke and watched as the rat, seemingly in slow motion, forced its way through the broom bristles, between his legs and back into the living room. Brian spun round, chasing after it as the women on the sofa screamed and Mark hollered, "GET IT! GET IT!"

Brian pulled the concertina door closed behind him and waited for the rat to come running back towards him. He held the broom like a golf club now and, as the rat finished traversing the floor plan and headed back towards the bedroom, he raised the bristles a few inches above the floor, as high as he could get it, and swung in a hard arc. The rat gave a final squeal of disapproval as it sailed through the open door.

"The rodent," Brian gasped, leaning on the broom, "has left the building."

* * *

"Did you leave the door open at any point?" Tel was asking Olivia.

"No."

"Did you leave a window open?"

"I don't think rats clamber up the sides of caravans to get in open windows," Brian said.

Olivia shook her head.

"Then how did it get in?" said Mark.

They looked around. Tel spotted a cabinet door under the sink slightly ajar and opened it, moved aside a plethora of cleaning equipment. Underneath was a vent. The vent was broken in one corner.

"Oh," said Olivia, "I dropped a full bottle of bleach on it the other day, Richard was furious."

"Not furious enough to fix it though, eh?"

"Oh, you shop at Waitrose?" Faye said, noticing the labels and casually opening a top cupboard full of food.

"Yes, Richard's very fussy, won't tolerate any other brand, says he can tell the difference in quality."

"Have you tested that theory?"

"Tested it?"

"Yeah, Brian swears by Heinz baked beans, doesn't know I've been buying shop brand beans for weeks now."

"I do now!" he boomed, then he paused and said, "I've mentioned to you every time we have beans that Heinz don't taste as good as they used to."

"That'll be why then," Faye laughed.

"Do you think it got in here?" Tel asked Mark, both peering at the broken vent in the floor.

"Lured in by the smell of food. We need to put something heavy on it for now, stop it happening again."

"Oh, Richard has a heavy book in the bedroom, I'll get it." Olivia returned with quite a hefty tome entitled, Old Churches of the Cotswolds. Mark read the spine and frowned. "So, if there's already a book on old Cotswolds churches, why is Richard writing another?"

"His will be definitive, he says."

"This," Mark said, lifting the heavy book in his hands, "seems pretty definitive to me." He covered the vent, placing a few bottles of cleaning liquid on top for extra security. "You should be alright now."

"Oh, thank you, thank you all so much." Olivia held each of their hands in turn, her gratitude overwhelming.

"You're all so kind, I don't know what I would have done if you hadn't come to my rescue."

"All part of the service," Mark beamed, liking her holding his hand. They caught each other's eye and pulled away quickly.

"Right, woman, off to bed, in the vain hope that we'll get to sleep at least one full night before this holiday is over."

"I think I'll stay here," said Faye, "I'll sleep on the sofa, keep Olivia company."

"Oh, thank you!" Olivia was clutching her hand again, gasping with relief. "But not on the sofa, we have a Queen-size bed, we can pretend to be sisters or chums having a sleepover, won't that be fun. That's if Brian doesn't mind."

"No, no, go right ahead," he said, picking his spatula off a countertop and clambering out of the motorhome, "A night without the wife will be a treat."

"Thanks, Bri!"

"Whole bed to myself, spreadeagled like a starfish, snoring to my heart's content with no sharp elbow prodding me awake. Ah, to sleep," he muttered, lumbering off into the darkness, "perchance t'dream."

"I'd better check Sophie's okay," Tel said, picking up his carton of milk and also leaving.

"Catch you in the morning," said Mark, following Tel, "Have a good rest of the night, Olivia."

"Thanks, Mark. Goodnight."

He heard her close and lock the door behind him. As he walked back to his caravan he thought about the tall man in strange glasses he'd encountered earlier. He briefly wondered if it was the remnants of a dream he'd been having, but the impact of the punch was real, he could still feel it on his knuckles.

Odd.

It was only when he was lying on the sofa, about to doze off, that he thought, 'A spatula and a carton of milk?'

Day 6 – Wednesday

Brian slept like a rock.

Everyone else had fitful sleeps, woken with starts when Brian's snoring reached a crescendo loud enough to shake rocks from mountains.

Except Faye, who was used to it.

She woke the following morning and stretched luxuriously. The sheets felt wonderful against her skin, the pillows plump and soft. For a moment she wondered where she was, and then she remembered when Olivia came into the bedroom carrying a china cup and saucer of tea, which she placed on the bedside cabinet. "I wasn't sure what time to wake you," she whispered.

"What time is it?"

"It's 7 o'clock, but I'm going up to the pub to start breakfast for all the campers, that should give me enough time to nip to the shops for provisions first."

"I'll come with you." Faye sat up, groggy but remarkable refreshed, given the night's activities. The mild headache was, she assumed, from all the screaming and the two pints of lager she'd managed to gulp down last night.

"Drink your tea first."

Faye did, sitting up in a Queen-sized bed, on what could only be Egyptian cotton sheets, careful not to spill any. She watched Olivia through the open concertina door and thought about the chat they'd had before eventually falling asleep last night. It had been interesting, very, very interesting.

* * *

"Where you two off to?" Mark called over, coming out of his caravan with a mug of tea and his book under his arm, just as they were coming out of the motorhome.

"We're off to feed the hungry hoards."

"I'll pop up in a bit and lend a hand."

"Glutton for punishment, eh?" Faye laughed.

The women cut through the dead bushes towards the pub and could still hear Brian's snoring vibrating the air all around them.

"How do you ever sleep?" Olivia asked.

"You get used to it. It's when he stops snoring that I suddenly wake up and check he's still breathing."

They laughed as they approached the pub, and found the door locked. They tried banging on it for a while but nothing happened. Not sure what to do next, they sat at the lone wooden table outside, the other having been stolen and was currently residing outside Tel and Sophie's Airstream.

"Thanks for the chat last night," Olivia said, "It was very ... cathartic."

Faye, who wasn't exactly sure what cathartic meant, just said, "That's okay."

"It felt good to get it all out, like holding up a mirror to my own face, my own life. I could see myself through your eyes and ... well, I didn't really like what I saw."

"Oh no, Olivia, I think you're fabulous, everybody does."

"Do they?"

"Yes. You're an amazing woman, you should remember that. We think ... well, we all think you deserve a bit better."

"I've never really spoken about it to anyone before, you know, about Richard and how I feel. Well, there's nobody really to tell, I don't have any friends and mommy says I should consider myself lucky to have someone to look after me and I should just get on with it, but ... I get quite lonely sometimes."

"I can imagine." Faye held her hand across the table. "It's good to talk about your problems, get them out in the open. A problem shared is a problem halved, they say."

"Yes. It's nice to have a friend. You will stay in touch afterwards, won't you?"

"Oh Olivia, of course I will." Faye quickly pulled a small notebook and pen out of her bag and started scribbling on it. "This is my mobile number, my email address and my Facebook page." She handed it over. "We will stay in touch, I promise."

"Good." Olivia gave a huge smile. "Thank you."

They both took a deep breath. Faye puffed hers out and said, "We might as well go back if Ant's not getting up."

* * *

"S'up?" Mark asked, as they wandered back to the caravans.

"Can't get Ant to answer the door."

"He's a lazy bugger." Mark pulled out his phone and dialed a number, then yelled, "Get up, you idle git, there's women at the door wanting to come in! No, not those kind of women, women who cook." He hung up. "He's up now," he said, and the two women turned and wandered back. Ant opened the door to them this time, wearing only underpants, and baggy ones at that. They both averted their eyes, it was much too early to be coping with dangly bits.

Ant watched from the kitchen doorway, yawning and scratching his dangly bits as they checked cupboards and the stainless steel fridge. Faye nipped next door to check the stock in the shop and wrote out a list.

"Sainsbury's opens at seven in Witney," Ant said, before another yawn overtook him.

"Can you take us?" Olivia asked.

"Car don't work."

"Oh." Just as they were deciding to call a taxi, Olivia's phone rang. She almost pressed the cancel button, thinking it was Richard again, but the screen said 'Mark Mob'.

"Did you get in?" he asked.

"Yes, we're in," she giggled, "Just going to get a taxi to take us to Sainsbury's in..." She looked at Ant.

"Witney."

"...Witney."

"Oh, I'll come round and pick you up."

"That's very kind of you."

"No trouble at all."

"We'll need some cash," Faye said to Ant.

He pretended not to hear as he suddenly started moving pans around, and she repeated it. Flustered, he went into the bar and opened up the till, slowly pulling out a £20 note and reluctantly handing it over. Faye took it and held her hand out for more. Ant huffed loudly and gave her another 20 before firmly slamming the till shut again. "I want receipts," he said, "And the change, and I'd better make more than that selling breakfast."

Mark drove them in his flowery van to Sainsbury's and waited while they dashed down aisles and came running out with a trolley full of food. They returned to the pub just as the 'guests' from the upstairs bedrooms were getting up and wandering down, and the 'tent survivors' from the field were coming in. They noticed, as they walked through the bar area with the bags, that Jim was still asleep on a bench. They also noticed that Ant had put a cardboard box on the counter with a gouged out hole in the top; on the side, in uneven marker pen, he'd written 'Pay Here'. There was no sign of Ant.

Faye did tea and coffee while Olivia cooked and plated up breakfast, which was a bit like the meal she'd done the night before but with added bacon, sausage, fried tomatoes, mushrooms and black pudding. Faye took them out to the tables in the bar area, to the sound of much gratitude and famishment, then started washing up. They had a good system going and they yakked throughout about nothing in particular. There was still no sign of Ant, but Jim had woken up and was sitting at a small table behind a wooden column, just staring into space. When Faye placed a cup of tea in front of him he didn't move or speak. She poked him and he rolled his eyes towards her.

"Tea?" she said.

"Thanks," he croaked.

"You okay?"

He shook his head and returned to staring off into space. He said nothing when she placed a breakfast plate in front of him a few minutes later. He didn't touch it and, when it was cold, Faye took it away again.

"Summat's up with Jim," she told Olivia.

"What?"

"He's either sulking or ... thinking."

"Thinking?"

"Yeah."

Sophie and Tel, closely followed by Mark, came in and wolfed down their breakfasts at the big table, chattering away and laughing. Faye rang Brian. When he finally answered, muttering incoherently, she said, "Your breakfast's getting cold."

"What breakfast? I see no breakfast."

"It's at the pub."

"I have to walk to get food!"

"You sure do, now shake a leg, husband, before it's all gone."

"Gone? I'm on my way."

He burst into the pub three minutes later wearing only his dressing gown, and sat at the big table, yawning. Tel glanced over and down, saying, "I see you remembered to put pants on this time."

Brian crossed his legs, carefully.

Mark went over to Jim, who was still staring at nothing, and tried talking to him, but Jim's only response was slight movements of his head. He seemed to be in a complete daze.

"You don't think he's had a stroke, do you?" he asked Brian, coming back.

"Brain implosion?" Tel suggested.

"Let me try," said Brian, and went over.

"You okay, lad?"

Nothing.

"We just want to know if you need medical attention or if you're just ... thinking."

"Thinking," Jim said.

"About?"

"Bethany."

"Ah. Do you want some old man advice?"

Jim finally turned his head and focused his eyes on Brian. Brian proceeded to give him guidance on recovering from a broken heart, how to possibly win Bethany back, and how to cope with it if he didn't.

"Anyone got a pen?" Tel asked, as Brian's baritone voice echoed round the room, "I feel I should be writing this stuff down."

Brian eventually patted Jim on the back and returned to the table. "Lad's got it bad," he said, "I think it's only just hit him."

They all stared at Jim, who stared off into nothingness.

"Let me try," Sophie said. She sat with Jim for a while and he nodded and shook his head a little, but he didn't look at her and eventually she gave up and came back.

"Heartbroken," she said.

"I thought you had to have a heart before it could be broken," Mark laughed.

"This is a serious matter," Brian said. "We'll need to keep an eye on him."

The man in black from the bottom of the field wandered in and sat at the bar, furtively looking over his shoulder at them. He was wearing the sunglasses and his hoodie pulled low over his face. Faye immediately placed a mug of tea and a breakfast plate in front of him, and he again looked surprised but didn't speak. Mark stood up and went over to him. "Er," he said, "Were you wandering around the caravans last night, by any chance?"

The man shook his head and ate his breakfast.

"Looked remarkably similar to you," Mark persisted, wrinkling his eyes suspiciously, "Same height, same build, wearing strange glasses that stuck out like goggles."

Again, the man shook his head and continued eating.

"I think it was you."

Another shake of the head.

"It was you, wasn't it."

The man stopped eating and slowly turned his head towards Mark, who could feel the glare of his eyes though the sunglasses.

"Can I see your face?" Mark asked. When the man didn't respond, just kept staring at him, Mark reached towards his hoodie. He instantly threw up the palm of his hand and held it in front of Mark's face.

"I'm watching you," Mark said, backing away. "I definitely think he's the one who's been lurking round our caravans at night," he said to Brian.

"But you can't prove it."

"No."

"We'll just keep an eye on him."

"Eyeballs everywhere!"

"Sometimes, grasshopper, a person needs to be acutely aware of those around him."

"Old proverb?"

"No, it's on this tablemat."

The campers started getting up and gathering their things together, and Ant suddenly reappeared behind the bar. "Pay as you go!" he yelled. "Food and lodgings out of the goodness of my own heart, but donations welcome. Oi!" he shouted out to a family heading straight for the door, "Donations welcome!"

"Donation implies a voluntary payment," the man said.

Ant pointed pointedly at the box and said, "I'm not running a charity, y'know."

The man stomped up to the bar and thrust a couple of notes in.

"I thank you," said Ant.

The other campers passed the box on their way out, depositing various sums of money. Ant watched them like a hawk, saying either, "Much appreciated," or, "More than that, this is a country pub, not McDonald's!" When they'd gone he counted out the contents of the box on the counter and smiled. Mark approached the bar, just as Olivia and Faye came out of the kitchen. "Girls get half," he said.

Ant snapped his head up and cried, "Half?"

"Oh," said Olivia, "We don't need – "

"Half," Mark said again.

Ant reluctantly counted it out and handed a wad of notes to Olivia, who counted it out and handed half to Faye.

"Buy me something!" Brian bellowed from the table.

"*You* can buy me lunch later," Faye said. "I've done enough cooking for one day. Are you wearing underpants under that dressing gown?"

"Aye."

"Good, I've seen enough sausages for one day."

"What time does your cleaner come in?" Olivia asked Ant, "Only I could start stripping the beds upstairs if you want?"

"Stripping them?"

"Yes, put clean sheets on."

"But they've only been slept in one night."

"You ... you have to change them even if they've only been slept in for one night."

"Really?"

"Yes, really."

"Your parents will be turning on their sun loungers," Mark tutted.

"Okay," Ant shrugged. "There's a laundry chute at the end of the hall, takes it down to the basement where the washing machine and dryer are."

"It's £15 an hour," Mark said, winking at Olivia.

"An hour!"

"Pay it, Ant, you know you'll be too lazy to do it yourself."

"I'll give you £30 for two hours," Ant said, addressing Olivia directly, "But get everything done in that time."

As Olivia nodded her head, excited at the challenge, Mark said, "That's not how it works. You pay her for the work she does, and if it isn't finished you pay her some more."

Ant sighed heavily and, overwhelmed with it all, walked away.

"Cleaning and cooking," Olivia said, "They're the things I'm good at."

"Just don't let him take advantage of your kind nature."

"That's what Richard's always says," she giggled, and Mark cringed.

Faye walked with Sophie on the way back to the caravans. The men walked behind them, chatting animatedly about the previous night's events and mentioning the strange behaviour of the man in sunglasses, their ideas becoming more and more outlandish; Faye heard the words 'CIA' and 'spy for the British government' being bandied about.

"Olivia isn't quite what we thought," Faye said.

"How do you mean?"

"We had a very interesting chat in bed last night."

"Did you now?"

"No, not like that. She told me – "

"Faye!" Brian cried, "Fancy going for a walk later with Tel and Sophie to test out their new boots?"

"Oh yes," Sophie said, "Weather's supposed to be better today, we're walking to the village and back if you want to come?"

"I think I actually want to put my feet up after all the running around I've done in the pub."

"Fair enough."

"But about Olivia – "

"Faye!" Brian yelled.

"WHAT?"

"Did you buy Heinz beans for breakfast?"

"I did."

"So, complete strangers get Heinz but I just get the cheap supermarket brand?"

"Yes, Bri."

"How is that fair?"

"Life is cruel."

"My wife is cruel. I demand Heinz from now on."

"Okay." She turned back to Sophie. "So, about last night – "

"Sophie," Tel cried, "How far is it to this village?"

"I don't know, a couple of miles?"

"Is that far enough to break in our walking boots?"

"I don't know, I've never owned a pair of walking boots before."

"So, about Olivia – "

"I'm off to my garden centre," Mark said, "If anyone's interested in tagging along and spending vast amounts of money?"

"Ooh," said Faye, a keen gardener, "That might be interesting."

And Olivia was forgotten.

For now.

* * *

They were just about to set off, Tel and Sophie on their walk, the other three to Mark's garden centre, when Sophie glanced off down the field and said, "Is that Jim?"

They all looked. Jim was walking with his head down from one side of the field to the other.

"What's he doing?"

"Exercising?"

"He's thinking," Brian said.

"He wants to be careful," said Mark, "His brain's not used to it."

"Well, if he likes walking so much maybe he'll want to come with us, Tel?"

"I'd leave him be," said Tel, who just wanted to be alone with Sophie. "Seems like a man who wants to spend some time on his own."

They all watched Jim reach the trees on the left-hand side of the field, turn, pause for a moment as he rubbed his face, and then stoically walk towards the other side again, disappearing behind what remained of the tents.

"Right, we're off," said Tel, and marched down the gravel driveway.

"You'll wear yourself out at that pace," Sophie laughed, and ran to catch up with him.

* * *

Inside the pub, in one of the five upstairs guest rooms, Olivia busily stripped off the beds and had quite a lot of fun pushing them down the laundry chute. When she eventually found the basement, she began loading up the large washing machine. Above it was a shelf, and on the shelf were books, cookery books. Olivia picked one out, Gordon Ramsey, and began flicking through the pages.

It was then that she had the spark of a very brilliant idea.

Excited, she raced back to the motorhome to fetch the sheets off the bed and a notebook. She had a lot of notes to make.

CHAPTER 14

Along a narrow country lane two people were battling against the constant onslaught of traffic.

"I thought the Cotswolds was supposed to be quiet and peaceful?"

"They still have to get places."

"In such numbers?" Tel stepped up onto the grass verge to avoid an oncoming lorry. "Is this rush hour or something?"

"Chill your boots," Sophie laughed.

"I wish they were chill, my feet are on fire and they're starting to rub at the back, is that normal?"

"It's just a little walk, Tel."

"Little? We've been walking for *hours*!"

"25 minutes."

"We've covered *miles*."

Sophie looked at the map on her phone. "0.4," she said.

"And how far to the village?"

"Another 1.8."

"I'm not going to make it."

"Can you *please* stop moaning!"

"I can't help it, I'm in pain. I can feel a blister forming and my legs hurt, my feet too. I think they gave me the wrong sized boots. Why are we walking when we have a perfectly good sports car back at camp?"

"Because it's fun."

"No, it isn't."

"It might be if you stop complaining."

"No, it won't."

Sophie quickened her pace to get ahead of him.

"Wait for me!" he cried.

"Less whining, more walking, Tel."

Faye was in heaven. Mark's garden centre was small but it was crammed full of pretty things. She wandered around the aisles and the giant trays of plants, touching everything, marveling at the lushness of it all.

"I can spot a satisfied customer a mile off," Mark said. "My wallet is already trembling in anticipation."

"I'm just popping to the office to check on things, but don't forget," he said, laughing, "I have a very big van to deliver all your purchases, so don't feel you have to hold back at all." He wandered off, still laughing. Brian slowly and nervously followed Faye around the display areas, shaking his head every time she said, "Do you like this?" and hoping she wouldn't spot the outdoor space.

She did.

* * *

Olivia pulled a load of bed linen out of the giant washing machine and pushed half into the dryer, then set another load on to wash. She was enjoying herself, doing something useful and something she was good at. She was also excited by an idea that had popped into her head and was growing with each cookbook she pulled down from the shelf.

Her phone rang on top of the dryer. She didn't answer it, she was far too busy, so she just let it ring. It stopped and immediately started again. And again.

With a heavy sigh she glanced at Richard's name on the screen. He seemed really determined that she answer it. She didn't want to, he would be furious that she hadn't taken any of his calls, but then she couldn't put him off indefinitely, she would have to face his wrath at some point.

"Good morning," she said brightly.

"Where the bloody hell have you been?" he raged instantly. "I was calling you all night and you didn't – "

Her thumb seemed to move of its own accord to press the red button. Silence. She put the phone back on the dryer, pulling a face, feeling nervous and excited at the same time. She'd never hung up on anyone before in her life, not even telesales people. As she expected, the phone rang again. With her heart pounding in her chest she picked it up and pressed the green button. Without even putting it to her ear she could hear Richard shouting furiously. She hung up again and gave an anxious laugh, covering her mouth with a hand before realising she was smiling. Smiling? What kind of horrid, rude person would find it amusing to hang up on someone, let alone their husband?

The phone rang again. She answered, putting it to her ear when she didn't hear him yelling. "Hello."

"Olivia!"

"Yes?"

"What do you mean, yes? I was trying to ring you all last night and you didn't answer! What's gotten into you?"

"Oh, I think the volume's broken on my phone, I didn't hear it." Now she was a liar too! She felt a thrill run through her. She thought she was possibly going a little mad.

"Didn't hear it? For god's sake, Olivia, didn't you think I'd be calling to check on you?"

Check on me, she thought, not check to make sure I was okay but check to make sure I wasn't doing something I shouldn't be doing, like having fun or cooking for starving people in a pub buzzing with hungry excitement

Olivia glanced at her watch. It was gone 11 o'clock. She felt a twinge of something but couldn't identify what it was; indignation, maybe, or perhaps annoyance. "I'd have thought, Richard, that if you were so worried about me you'd have made the effort to come back this morning, or at least call earlier than 11 o'clock to make sure I was still alive. Roads are clear now, aren't they? Where are you?"

"I'm somewhere near Malmesbury. I made an appointment with the vicar to open the church especially for my visit and it's magnificent."

"I meant, why aren't you here with your abandoned wife, who had to chase a rat out of the motorhome last night?"

"A rat?"

She waited, saying nothing, wondering what his reaction would be.

"Did it make a mess?"

And there it was, his only concern was for himself and his germ phobia. She could have been bitten, contracted rabies, but no, all Richard cared about was the mess it might have left. She felt terribly disappointed in him.

"Did you clean everything thoroughly, and I mean *thoroughly*, using double-strength disinfectant? Rats are filthy vermin, they caused the bubonic plague, you know."

Olivia sighed. "I have to go, Richard, I'm extraordinarily busy."

"Busy doing what, cleaning the motorhome?"

"Cleaning guest rooms, actually, and this morning I cooked a full English breakfast for 22 people and they all thought it was lovely."

"What? What are you talking about? I told you to stay near the motorhome for your own safety, not get yourself a job as a cook and cleaner! What on earth's gotten into you?"

She wasn't sure. It was something. Nervous breakdown? Early midlife crisis? Bored to sobs with her life?

"Anyway," he continued, "I'll be back around 5 this afternoon, if I can figure out this ridiculous bus timetable, or else I'll take a taxi. I quite fancy a roast beef dinner tonight, so get some – "

"I'm sorry, Richard, but you're breaking up, I can't hear you. I'll see you when I see you," she said, and hung up.

Determined not to let him spoil her fun, Olivia turned down the sound on her ringing phone until she could no longer hear it, and concentrated on her list.

Her idea was expanding, and she felt very excited.

* * *

"How exactly," said Brian, gruffly, "are we supposed to get that home?"

Faye was walking round a three-foot concrete statue of a naked woman leaning against a pillar, cooing excitedly. "I've been wanting something like this for the garden for ages. It'll fit in the caravan."

"You know there's a weight limit for towing? That's if it doesn't fall through the floor on the M40."

"You don't even know how heavy it is. Try lifting it up."

"With my back?"

"Or they might deliver."

"Cotswolds to Birmingham, 70 miles, should only cost a small fortune."

"You're not being very helpful, Bri."

"I'm being practical, Faye."

"You don't like it, do you."

"I can't envisage a naked woman in our garden, at least not one made out of concrete."

"Well, how about this lifelike gorilla then?"

Brian made a noise at the back of his throat.

* * *

"Are you crying?"

Tel was making a strange sound as he limped, aided by a supporting hand against walls and shop windows, down the main street of the village. "No," he said, "I'm just holding back my screams of pain."

"And that helps, does it?"

"No, not really, nothing can help me now except a soft pair of moccasins or death brought about by severe blood loss. I can actually hear squelching inside my boots!"

"My boots are fine."

"I'm very happy for you."

"Have yours not loosened up at all?"

"If anything, they seem tighter around my swollen, shredded feet."

"Here, sit down, I'll nip inside and get us both a coffee."

Tel fell into a metal chair outside a café and slowly untied his laces, pulling off a boot and peeling off a sticky, painful sock. His foot looked like a mangled piece of meat and it felt twice its normal size. It also hurt, a lot, particular the raw bits where the boots had worn away any semblance of skin.

Sophie came back carrying two coffee cups. "Oh," she said, noticing his empty boot on the ground, "you shouldn't have taken it off."

"Why not?"

"It'll be so much harder to get it back on again."

"I'm not putting it back on again."

"Then how will you get back to the campsite?"

"By taxi. I can't take another step, Soph. Look at the state of my foot, and the other one feels worse, I'm almost too afraid to look at it."

"Don't be such a baby."

Tel dropped his mouth and indicated his raw foot with both hands.

"You'll be fine." She put the coffee cups on the table and sat down. "Just put your boot back on before it swells too much."

"No, I'll order a taxi."

"I thought you didn't give up easily," she grinned.

"I don't, but you can't expect me to carry on when I'm in such agony."

"Wimp." Her grin broadened into a smile behind her coffee cup. Tel glared at her, and she added, "*Quitter*."

"I am not a quitter!"

She took another sip of coffee, trying not to laugh at the indignation on his face. He huffed loudly, then started putting on his sock back on, wincing and gasping, then wincing and gasping even more when he pulled on his boot.

"Not so bad, was it," she said.

"Chopping my feet off with a blunt axe would hurt less."

"Poor baby."

"Shut up."

"I tell you what," she said, "If you walk back to the campsite with me I'll take you for a spa day tomorrow at that hotel we found to help you recover, how does that sound?"

Tel looked up at her, a smile playing in the corner of his mouth. "Sauna and a full body massage?"

"Of course."

He put his newly booted foot on the ground and grimaced.

"Be brave, Tel, challenge yourself."

"Okay," he said, "I'll do it."

Sophie raised an eyebrow and grinned.

* * *

Mark came out of his office when he'd finished checking his books and talking to his staff. Both were fine and he felt proud of the people he had working for him, but also slightly disappointed that they'd managed perfectly well without him. He definitely felt he was ready to come back to work full time now and resume his life again, and then he'd sort out the house; if Janis was going to stay he'd have to find alternative accommodation. He felt positive for the first time in ages.

As if sensing his positivity, or perhaps because he'd been thinking about her, his phone rang as he walked down the succulent section. He'd been ignoring her calls after the fight they'd had yesterday, but now he felt ready to answer it.

"Mark!" came her high-pitched voice, "I've been trying to reach you!"

"I've been trying to avoid you."

"We need to talk!"

"No, we don't." He felt surprisingly calm. "A decision has been made."

"*You* made the decision, I had no say in the matter."

"You've said plenty, Janis, more than enough. I wish you all the best in finding someone better."

"Mark, don't be like this, all relationships have their ups and downs."

"I don't want this relationship any more, Janis, it's died a death, stabbed through the heart by my apparent shortcomings and your raving demands. You don't have to endure it any more, and neither do I."

"Come home and we'll talk about it, properly this time."

"No."

"If you don't come right this minute I'll – "

"You'll what, throw a strop, go into a sulk, cry? Go ahead, makes no difference to me."

"Mark, you're being totally unreasonable. Come home immediately so we can sort this out."

"Oh no, no, no," he said, and he realised he was smiling; no bowling ball of anxiety in the pit of his stomach, no impending sense of doom, no being careful with his words so as not to upset her, "You don't get to tell me what to do any more, Janis. It's over. We're done. I told you this yesterday, you throwing insults at me the whole time doesn't change anything. Just let me know if you're staying in the house or moving on."

"You know I can't afford this house on my own!"

"Then find your own place."

"I'm entitled to half of all your assets! You'll have to sell the house *and* your business to pay me off."

"What, after a whole year of marriage? Not gonna happen. Get your solicitor to call my solicitor."

"Mark!"

"Janis, I'm busy, I have to go."

He could still hear her screeching when he ended the call. He felt nothing except relief. The argument they'd had yesterday had been terrible, recriminations flew like fireworks, but it was over and done with now, just like their relationship.

He found Faye and Brian at the tills and started laughing. Brian remained poker faced as the checkout operator struggled to ring up a four-foot cheese plant.

"You went for the Monstera Deliciosa then?" Mark sniggered. "Grows to about 10 to 15 feet indoors."

"What?"

"Taller if the pot's big enough and you feed it regularly."

Brian glared at the checkout operator, still wrangling with the plant, and was just about to call a halt to the purchase when it rang up.

"Congratulations, Bri, you are now the proud owner of a Triffid."

Mark helped load the rest of Faye's collection of plants, fertilisers and shiny things to hang in the garden onto the trolley and pulled it to his van, loading it all up. Faye looked very happy as she clambered in, Brian just looked resigned. "Garden centres and book shops," he muttered, "The woman has no control in garden centres and book shops."

"What's your vice then, Brian?"

"Beer," said Faye.

"I have no vices, I'm practically perfect in almost every way."

Faye snorted. "Western films, war films, Roman history books, air gun pellets, who'd have thought there were so many different types of pellets, eating, growling and yelling 'What?' because he won't wear his hearing aids. And Charlize Theron, he's obsessed with Charlize Theron, he's seen all her films."

"Finished?" Brian sighed.

"I'd say they were in the top 10."

Mark laughed, pulling out of the parking space. Unable to resist, he said, "The van feels really heavy to drive now."

"Shut up," said Brian.

* * *

Sophie went into the café for another coffee and came out carrying two chocolate muffins as well, "To keep your strength up," she said, sitting down. "I was talking to the woman behind the counter about where we're staying and she says there's a shortcut to the campsite."

"Music to my ears!"

"It's just at the top of that hill over there."

Tel turned in his seat to look. "A hill? Looks more like the side of a mountain."

"Steep Hill, it's called, isn't that ingenious."

"Is there one called Gentle Slope we can use instead, or, better still, Down Hill?"

Sophie laughed. "You see the trees at the top, that's the same wood that runs next to our campsite. It *halves* the walking distance, Tel."

"Fantastic."

"I thought you'd be pleased."

* * *

When Olivia could hear movement in the bar area she went to talk to Ant. "I've almost finished putting clean linen on the beds," she said.

He immediately looked at his watch. "Oh good."

"You don't have to pay me."

Ant's face split with a smile.

"But I'd like something in return."

His smile disappeared.

"I'd like to – "

"ANT!" Jim cried, bursting through the entrance door, "Need a word. I've been giving it some serious thought, and I mean *serious* thought, my head is *buzzing*, and I think I know what to do to win Bethany back. I need to turn my life around and prove myself to her, so I'd like to rent one of your guest rooms on a weekly basis. What's your best deal?"

"I usually charge 90 quid a night."

Jim pulled a horrified face, then said, "Yeah, but you haven't had any guests in a while and I'm offering a regular income, so what's the best rate you can offer me?"

Ant pulled a calculator out from under the bar and prodded at it. "Seven nights at 90 quid a night comes to ... 720 for the week."

"You're having a laugh! I could rent a house for that much!"

"Feel free," Ant shrugged, "Makes no odds to me."

"How does 100 quid a week sound to you?"

"It sounds like you want to stay homeless, but I'm just guessing."

Jim groaned, rubbing his lower back. "I need a proper bed, all this sleeping on the floor lark is killing me. Come on,

Ant, hit me with your best mate's rate."

"You're not a mate."

"I'm Mark's mate, and he's your mate, so your best mate-of-a-mate's rate?"

Ant rubbed his chin. Olivia, who was standing at the end of the bar waiting to finish her talk with Ant, said, "It *is* a regular income."

"There you go," Jim grinned, "You'd be a fool to turn down steady money, and those rooms are just going to sit empty otherwise, going to waste, not earning you anything at all, and I'm offering *actual cash.*"

"300 quid a week."

"Halve it and you've got yourself a deal."

Ant hesitated. Jim held his hand out across the counter. Ant said, "200 quid."

"£175, with evening meal thrown in."

"Don't do meals."

"Breakfast then."

"Don't do breakfasts."

"Okay, 160 is my final offer."

"170."

"You drive a hard bargain."

They shook and the deal was done. Jim headed towards the door, saying, "I'll just bring my things in, can't turn up for work with a van full of stuff."

"Paid two weeks in advance!" Ant hollered after him.

"I'll pay you Friday."

"Ant," said Olivia, when he was gone, "I'd like to use your kitchen tomorrow."

"I'm not forking out for any more free food."

"Well, technically it wasn't free, was it," she giggled, "You made them pay."

"Voluntary contribution, and I gave you and the other one half, barely made even."

"Yes, well, I'll finish the rooms upstairs in exchange for using your kitchen tomorrow and the use of the bar tomorrow night."

Ant shrugged. "As long as I don't have to pay for anything, help yourself."

Olivia was so excited she clapped her hands together, smiling broadly.

It was *so* exciting.

***

The outside of Brian and Faye's caravan looked like a boot sale for plants, there were so many of them, including a giant cheese plant and an enormous fern. Windchimes sparkled the sun, and a couple of coloured things hung from the poles in the awning. She set about watering them immediately, while Brian flopped into his chair and picked up a book.

Further down, Mark was also reading his book and nearing the end. It had been a very good book and he was quite sad to finish it. He kept glancing over at the motorhome, wondering if Olivia had nearly finished her book, but it was silent and empty. He guessed Olivia was still at the pub but resisted the urge to walk up there to see how she was getting on and to make sure Ant wasn't working her too hard. Instead, he stared out over the tent field, thinking of the book that he didn't want to finish, of Janis, and thoughts of Olivia kept creeping in too, her tinkly laugh and her cute smile. He shook his head clear and focused on his surroundings: Faye, still fussing over her plants; Brian, dragging his chair outside the awning to read in the sun; the eight or so tents at the top of the field on the right; and the white bell tent at the far left corner. As he looked the man, still wearing sunglasses and a dark hoodie despite the heat of the day, emerged from the tent carrying a large sports bag and a fold-up chair. Intrigued, and glad of the distraction, Mark watched the man walk up the left side of the field. The bag he was carrying over his shoulder seemed heavy.

He suddenly disappeared through the broken wire fence that ran around the campsite. Mark watched his shadow move along the perimeter until he was almost opposite Tel and Sophie's shiny Airstream, and then he ducked down out of sight.

Mark put his book down on the table and slowly stood up, searching for the man in the trees. He'd disappeared. He hadn't wandered off into the distance and out of sight, he'd just vanished behind a mound of bushes.

He ambled over to Brian. "Just seen something weird," he said.

"A man brought to his financial knees at a garden centre?"

"No, the man at the bottom of the field."

"Creepy guy?"

"Is that what we're calling him?"

"Girls do."

Neither of them saw the man poke his head up from behind the bushes, looking offended.

"He walked up the field and disappeared into the trees. I think he's still there, hiding, right next to Tel and Sophie's van."

"What's strange about that?" Brian asked, looking over at the trees behind the shiny tin can and seeing nothing.

"Dunno, just seems ... odd."

"Maybe he's taking a dump."

"Same distance to the toilet block."

"Maybe he has a shy colon."

"A what?"

"You know, when you can't 'evacuate' when other people are around, your sphincter just – "

"I get the picture, but he was carrying a fold-up chair."

"Camping commode?"

Mark shrugged.

"What are you looking at?" Olivia asked, appearing next to them with a notebook and pen on top of a pile of crisp sheets.

"The man from the bottom of the field."

"Oh, Creepy Guy?"

No head popped up from behind the hedges this time.

"I think he's hiding in the woods, watching us," Mark continued, "I think he's the one that's been creeping around the caravans at night, the one I punched."

"Oh dear," said Olivia.

"What's this?" Faye asked, leaving her precious plants to join them.

"Mark has some conspiracy theories about Creepy Guy."

"Not conspiracies," Mark said, "He's just acting a bit ... weird."

"Weirder than normal?" Faye laughed, "Is he wearing jumpers and ski boots now?"

"He's probably from the Inland Revenue," said Brian, "You've all paid your tax and national insurance this year, haven't you?"

They all laughed, except Mark, who tried to remember if he'd heard from his accountant recently.

"Maybe he just has a caravan fetish and can't afford his own, that's why he's so interested in ours," Olivia offered.

"Ooh, Olivia," said Brian in mock horror, "I'm surprised you even know what a fetish is."

Olivia blushed profusely and Faye said, "Leave her alone, she can't help being sweetly innocent."

"No, she can't," Mark said, staring at her, then, realising he was staring at her, abruptly stopped staring and coughed awkwardly when he caught Brian and Faye staring at him and grinning. "So, what do you think we should do, Bri?"

"About?"

"About the Creepy Guy."

"About a man taking a dump in the woods? Nothing."

"He could be dangerous."

"Throws his shit around, you mean?"

"Come on, I'm being serious. What's he doing hanging around here at night? He could be a psychopathic murderer looking for his next victim, it could be one of us he's stalking."

Olivia gasped out loud. Faye put an arm around her

shoulders and said, "Take no notice, love, we're not in any danger, not with Brian around."

Brian winked at his wife, who winked back, and then he said, "What book is it you're reading, Mark?"

"It's a crime thriller, very good actually."

"It is," Olivia agreed.

"Crime thriller, eh?"

"Yeah, you can borrow it when I've finished if you ... Oh, I see where you're going with this, but I'm not paranoid just because I've read a crime thriller. I have a gut feeling about that guy, and you did tell me to follow my gut instinct."

"He's just different."

"Yeah, different in a serial killer kind of way."

"We'll just keep an eye on him."

"Like we were supposed to keep an eye on Jim, who's nowhere to be seen? Where is he?"

"Oh, he's renting one of the guest rooms off Ant," Olivia said. "He said he's going to put his life back on track and win Bethany back by showing her that he's worthy of her love, and he's gone back to work."

"Blimey," Mark laughed, "Talk about setting impossible goals."

"Good luck to him, I say," said Faye.

Brian suddenly jumped up out of his chair, staring off into the trees. "What's that?" he gasped.

"Oh, now you're just taking the – "

"Shhhhh! I hear something."

"What?" Faye asked, and Mark suddenly realised that Brian was being serious.

"What do you hear?"

"There's something in the woods."

"What is it?"

"It's getting closer."

"What is it, Bri?"

"There's ... there's someone there, coming towards us."

"I hear it," Mark said, "Is it Creepy Guy?"

They all stepped forward onto the gravel driveway, peering into the shadows of the trees behind the Airstream.

* * *

"How much further, Soph?"

"Not far."

"You said that 15 miles back."

"I've told you a million times not to exaggerate," she laughed. "There should be a path leading to the campsite down here somewhere." She peered through the trees, looking for sight of a caravan or a tent.

"My feet are killing me."

"So you keep saying."

"And I'll keep saying it until the pain goes away, if it ever does." He grimaced as he slowly plodded one foot in front of the other, occasionally gasping out loud and leaning against a tree. "Do your feet not hurt at all?"

"A bit, but doesn't it make you feel good?"

"No."

"All this exercise and fresh air, and it's so beautiful here."

"I can't see the beauty for the tears of agony in my eyes."

"We're nearly there."

"You don't know … Oh, is that a caravan?"

Sophie looked through the trees at a bright light on the right. "That's our Airstream!"

"Oh, thank god!"

"Honey, we're home. Look, here's the path to the campsite."

"We've just got to run the gauntlet of stinging nettles and brambles, and of course we're wearing shorts."

"Come on, Tel, just a bit further."

"Argh!" he cried, raising his arms in the air as he wriggled his way through the prickly, stingy plants. "ARGH!"

They emerged on the other side of the brambles a short distance from the fence that ran around the campsite. There was a man sitting on a log, surrounded by a barrier of strategically placed branches and holding up what looked like a very small umbrella. He was wearing a large pair of headphones and snatched a pair of binoculars from his eyes when he heard them approaching. The man quickly pushed sunglasses onto his face and they realised it was the man from the bottom of the field.

"Morning," Sophie said, walking past, followed by a limping, gasping Tel, who just nodded in a pained way.

The man was stiff and motionless on his log, staring straight ahead, not looking at them or acknowledging them in any way. They walked passed, glancing back a couple of times. The man didn't move, he was like a statue in the woods.

"Strange," said Tel.

"Very."

They clambered over a bit of fallen wire fence onto the campsite, Sophie pleased to have made it and feeling very proud of herself, Tel whimpering with relief. "I didn't think we were going to make it," he gasped, "I thought I was doomed to walk in these bloody boots until the end of time."

"Drama queen." Sophie put an arm through his and helped him walk the last few steps from the trees onto their gravel pitch. "Oh," she cried, "Hello."

CHAPTER 15

Sophie deposited Tel on the wooden picnic bench outside their Airstream and looked at the group standing on the gravel driveway, seemingly staring at them. "Are you just glad to see us or did we miss something?" she asked.

"Did you see anything in there?" Brian asked, "Anything ... unusual?"

"Saw Creepy Guy squatting on a log."

"I told you!" said Mark.

"Why, what's going on?"

"We think Creepy Guy is the one who's been hanging around the caravans at night, the one I punched."

"Not 'we'," Brian said, "*You* think that."

"How certain are you?" Sophie asked.

"90 percent certain it was him. Maybe 85. Or a bit less, but not much less, maybe 82 percent, 82 and a half."

"You can't accuse someone of something if you're only 82 and a half percent sure it was them," said Sophie, "You need proof."

"My gut tells me it's him."

"Your gut won't stand up in a court of law if he sues you for defamation of character or grievous bodily harm."

"Innocent until proven guilty," Tel said, lifting his feet up onto the seat of the bench with some effort. "Soph, give me a hand with these boots."

She knelt on the ground next to him to undo the laces.

"What you been up to, lad? You seem in some pain. You only went for a walk, didn't you?"

"Pain doesn't begin to describe the agony, Bri. We've walked *miles*."

"Four."

"We've climbed *mountains*."

"A hill."

"It was a 45-degree incline, that's a mountain."

"Not a fan of the great outdoors then?" Brian laughed.

"Never again. I swear to god I will never put on a pair of walking boots as long as I live."

"Oh," Sophie suddenly said, holding the boot she'd just pulled from his foot and looking inside it.

"What?" Tel gasped, "Have all my toes fallen off?"

"No. What shoe size do you take?"

"Ten."

"Oh," she said again. "They've given you the wrong size, this is a size ... nine."

"I knew it!" he cried, "I thought they were tight when I put them on, I thought they were meant to be like that until you wore them in and loosened them up. Size 9! I'm crippled for life, I'll never walk again! I'll sue the shop for gross negligence! Look at my foot!"

They all looked. It wasn't a pretty sight.

"I'll get the First Aid kit," Faye said, as Sophie began removing his other boot, "You're going to have to soak those in antiseptic if you want to keep them."

"Keep them?" He looked horrified.

Faye dashed back to their caravan and filled a spare washing up bowl she kept under the sofa with warm water. She splashed in some antiseptic and pulled the First Aid kit from a cupboard. By the time she got back to Tel he was biting on his hand as Sophie carefully peeled off a sock dark with blood. "Are all my toes there, Soph? Tell me the truth, are they all there?"

"Yes, Tel, they're all there."

"Here, stick them in this." Faye put the bowl on the ground in front of him and Tel gingerly dipped his heels in. "ARGH!" he cried, immediately yanking them out again.

"Too hot?" Faye asked.

"What's in it, acid?"

"Antiseptic."

"Do you need a stick to bite down on?" Brian asked.

"No, I'll be okay. Right, I'm going in!" His face scrunched up as he thrust his feet into the water with a strangled cry.

"You're so brave," Sophie said, squeezing his hand.

"Patronising much?" Tel asked through gritted teeth.

"Tiny bit."

As they all stood there watching Tel soak his feet, Olivia suddenly said, "I'm glad you're all here, I … I've had an idea." They all looked at her and she squirmed awkwardly. "Tomorrow's our last full day together – "

"Oh yeah," Mark said quietly.

" – and I'd like to do something special as a kind of thank you for being so lovely. I'm arranging something for tomorrow night, if you're not doing anything else."

"Sounds intriguing," Brian said, giving Olivia a sideways hug.

"Don't break her," Faye said, adding, "You don't have to do anything for us, Olivia."

"Oh no, I want to!"

"Silence, lass, I suspect there may be food involved."

Olivia giggled. "There might be."

"We'll be there!"

"Lovely."

"Our last day," Sophie said. "It's gone so quickly."

"It has."

"I actually feel a bit sad."

"Me too."

"I've learned so much."

"How to mingle with the commoners?" Brian laughed.

"Oh god, was I that bad?"

"No, no," Faye said, giving Brian the evil eye. "You just looked a bit like a deer caught in the headlights of an oncoming car when you first turned up."

Brian asked, "What are you going to do, Mark, stay on

here for a bit?"

"Not sure yet. Need to sort out the house and finances with the soon-to-be-ex-wife, and just try not to go bankrupt, that sort of thing."

"Oh, I'm so sorry to hear that," Olivia said, touching his arm.

"I'll be having reconstructive surgery on my feet and some intensive physiotherapy," Tel winced. "Hopefully I'll be able to walk again, but I suspect my jogging days are over."

"You've never jogged a step in your life!" Sophie laughed. "I think I'm just going to make a few lifestyle changes, you know, slow down a bit, ease the stress a little."

"Will this new lifestyle include me?" Tel asked.

She smiled. "Of course."

He smiled back. "How about you, Bri, what are you two going to do?"

"Just carry on as normal, I suppose. Go back to work, try not to piss the wife off too much, and stay married for as long as possible."

"You don't piss me off," Faye said.

"WHAT?" he boomed, and everybody laughed. "What about you, Olivia, what are your plans after this seriously weird holiday that's clearly sent us all a bit bonkers?"

"I ... I'm not sure yet. I've been giving it some thought but ... " She shook her head, glancing back at the motorhome. Mark pursed his lips together so he wouldn't blurt 'Leave the bugger' or 'Divorce the git'. "I'm not sure. Anyway, I'm just going to tell the other campers about tomorrow night."

"Are they involved in this mystery plan of yours too?"

"Yes," she giggled, and headed off towards the field.

"So, what's happening tomorrow night then, Olivia?" Brian called after her.

She turned as she walked and tapped the side of her nose.

"We'll torture her for information later," he laughed.

* * *

Brian discovered he'd dozed off reading his book under the awning. When he opened his eyes he saw that Faye was asleep in her chair too, her book on her lap, her head back and mouth wide open. He looked around. All was quiet. He could see Tel and Sophie opposite, sitting at the wooden picnic table and talking softly, touching hands. Tel's feet were still up on the seat in front of him but were now wrapped in bandages.

Brian glanced at his watch, then pulled the coolbox close to him and reached in for a can. He tried to do it quietly, but the hissing of the ring pull made Faye's eyes flutter. He kept dead still, holding his breath. She didn't wake, and he took a deep, satisfying gulp.

In front of him Olivia had dragged the bistro set to the front of the motorhome, where the sun was, and was busily flicking through what looked like cookbooks and scribbling furiously in a notebook. Brian smiled, whatever she had planned for tomorrow definitely included food. Opposite her, Mark sat in his chair under his gazebo, ostensibly reading his book but, Brian noticed, constantly glancing over at Olivia. "Be careful there, lad," he muttered.

Faye stirred at the sound of his voice. "I fell asleep!" she croaked.

"We both did."

"What time is it?"

"5.30, and I'm *starving*."

"You're always starving."

"I'm more starvinger than normal. I fancy a curry."

"Oooh," said Faye, "I think there's an Indian restaurant in the village."

"I'm too lazy to eat out. MARK!" he suddenly bellowed, making Faye jump.

"WHAT?"

"DO THEY DELIVER TAKEAWAYS TO THE CAMPSITE?"

"YEAH, IN THE SAME AMOUNT OF TIME IT WOULD TAKE TO RAISE YOUR OWN CHICKEN AND GROW YOUR OWN RICE. WHICH TAKEAWAY WERE YOU THINKING?"

"INDIAN."

"OH YES."

"Oooh," said Olivia, raising her head, "I haven't had a curry in ages."

"DID SOMEONE SAY CURRY?" Tel shouted across.

"Curry it is then," he said to Faye.

Tel tapped on his phone for few seconds and said, "I'VE GOT THE MENU FOR THE NEAREST ONE."

"Send us a link."

There followed much shouting of numbers as Tel created a WhatsApp group called Campers and invited them all to it, then sent a link to the menu. They drooled over it for a while before shouting their orders out to Olivia, who wrote it all down in her notebook.

Tel, hearing the rustle of leaves from the trees behind them, turned his head and yelled, "HEY, MAN IN SUNGLASSES WHO LIVES IN A TENT AT THE BOTTOM OF THE FIELD, DO YOU WANT ANYTHING FROM THE INDIAN TAKEAWAY?"

There was no reply.

Sophie ran across the driveway and threw herself down on the grass in front of Olivia, coiling her long legs beneath her. "What about Richard, will he want anything?"

"Yeah, where is Dickie-boy?" Mark asked.

"Oh, I'm being punished," Olivia said with a giggle. "At least, he thinks it's punishment, but I'm quite enjoying myself."

"Punished for what?"

"I hung up on him when he called this morning."

"You didn't!" Sophie gasped in mock horror, putting her hands on the side of her face like Munch's The Scream.

"I did," Olivia giggled, "And he sent me two texts this afternoon, one asking if I'd thoroughly cleaned the motorhome after the rat incident, the other to ask if I'd got a nice piece of beef for dinner. I didn't answer them either."

"You little rebel!"

"I know! He'll be furious, but I don't care. He doesn't

like curry anyway, much to spicy for his delicate palate."

"Add a chicken masala to the list," Sophie said, "That's nice and mild, just in case. Shall I order?"

"Yes, but – " Olivia jumped up and raced into the motorhome, rushing back with a plastic card and handing it to Sophie, along with the list from her notebook. "My treat," she said.

Mark bounded over. "You've treated us enough already," he said, taking out his wallet and handing Sophie another card, "Let me."

"I should pay really," Sophie said, "I haven't contributed anything to this little gang of ours yet."

"No, honestly, it's on me," said Mark, trying to get her to take his card. "I'll take care of this."

"As much as I hate to pull rank," Sophie said, "I'm a senior partner at a prestigious law firm where my dad is the CEO, and I earn a six figure salary, plus expenses."

Mark stared at Sophie for a moment, then pulled back his card and quickly pushed it into his wallet. "Thanks very much," he said, "Very kind of you."

"Just order!" Brian boomed, "My stomach's throwing a strop."

"Tell them we'll come and pick it up," Mark said, "It'll be quicker that way."

Sophie tapped her phone and started to read out the list. Everyone suddenly stopped talking about how hungry they were and how long it had been since they'd last had an Indian takeaway to listen to her, enthralled by her enunciation and her velvety voice. Tel nodded proudly and said, "She can make anything sound like a pornographic M&S advert."

"What?" said Sophie, ending the call and noticing they were all staring at her.

"You have a beautiful voice," Brian said.

"Yeah, you'd have said 'Send curries and send lots'," Faye laughed.

* * *

They were all under Brian and Faye's open awning, chatting and laughing. Tel, unable to walk on his bandaged feet, had been carried over by Brian and Mark, who also carried over the wooden picnic table. That, and Brian's camping table, were lined with a paper tablecloth, down the middle of which stood various curry containers and accompaniments piled high on paper plates. There was much swapping of curries and passing of naan breads as they bantered and laughed together.

"Whoa!" Mark cried, his eyes watering, "Who ordered the vindaloo?"

"Me," Tel laughed, forking it up from his plate, "but they sent two by mistake, so dig in." After a moment of chewing he opened his mouth and gasped, "Oh, it is a bit hot, isn't it."

"Hot?" Brian winced. "You could light a fire off it."

"It could strip wallpaper," Faye said, fanning her mouth.

Olivia took a spoonful from the container to taste. "Nice," she said, spooning more onto her plate of rice. She offered it to Sophie, who held up her hand and said, "I don't do hot."

"Oh, I think you do hot very well," Tel smirked.

She pushed an onion bhaji into his mouth.

In the midst of a heated debate about spices, Mark's eye was suddenly drawn by a movement at the entrance gate to the campsite. A figure moved swiftly towards the caravan pitches. He stiffened, thinking it was Creepy Guy lurking around again, but it wasn't.

"Your charming husband's back," he said to Olivia, who nonchalantly sat back on her bistro chair and rubbed her stomach. "Is he?"

They all turned at the tables to watch as Richard marched straight over to the motorhome and disappeared. Moments later he was out again, scouring the area, quickly spotting them all sitting under the awning staring at him. He stormed over.

"Uh-oh," Tel said, "Man don't look happy."

"God, when does he ever?" Olivia huffed.

"OLIVIA!"

"Yes, Richard?"

"What the hell do you – ?"

"Can I just stop you there?" she said, holding up a hand and sounding quite calm. "I'm enjoying an Indian takeaway with my friends and you're more than welcome to join us." They all nodded. "There's a masala staying warm in the oven if you want it."

"And there's plenty of naan breads and giant crisps left," said Faye, holding up a poppadom.

Brian pulled a can out of his coolbox and offered it up. "Take a seat, lad, we promise not to bite."

Richard looked apoplectic, his face was puce and his eyes were wide as they darted from one to another. Mark, sensing the oncoming eruption, slowly clenched his fists on the table. Next to him Brian straightened in his chair. Tension hung heavy in the air as Richard struggled to speak through his rage.

"GET BACK ... TO THE MOTORHOME ... THIS INSTANT!" he spat.

"No." Olivia stared straight back at him, unblinking. "Join us or leave."

"OLIVIA!"

"She said she wants to stay, mate." Mark stood up.

"It's okay." Olivia reached out to touch his arm. "I can handle this."

"Get back to the motorhome, Olivia. Do it now and stop embarrassing me in front of *these people*!"

"These people?" Sophie laughed, "*These people*?"

"I think he means the lower-classes," Faye said.

"Scum of the earth," said Mark.

"The plebs, the philistines, the *unsophisticated*," Brian boomed.

"Good one, Bri."

"Thanks, it just popped into my head."

"We're lawyers from London," Sophie said, casually

wagging a finger between herself and Tel as she bit into an onion bhaji. "This lovely couple are from Birmingham, not sure what they do but they're what's known as 'salt of the earth folk', give you the shirts off their backs, they would."

"Ah thanks, Sophie."

"You're welcome, Faye. And this man here," she said, pointing over at Mark, "He runs a very successful business. So what exactly do you mean when you say 'these people', Richard?"

Richard's face was a twisted mass of indignation. He took a deep breath and finally spluttered, "This is a private matter between my wife and I, and I don't appreciate your interference. Olivia, I'd like a word in the motorhome *right this minute*."

"Have as many words as you like, Richard, but I'm certainly not going to listen to them, why would I? You've been gone every day since we got here and," she glanced at her watch, "absent for the last 48 hours. You've enquired about the cleanliness of the motorhome and the menu for your evening meal, but you've not asked about *me*. So I've taken care of myself and I've made friends and I've had fun. Yes, I've had fun, it's been bloody marvelous!" Faye reached over and patted her hand. "I'll come back to the motorhome when I'm good and ready, Richard. I'm staying here to finish my very lovely curry with my very lovely friends. What you do is entirely up to you, you can stay or you can go, I really don't care."

There was a long gap of open-mouthed silence. Tel broke it by saying, "Can we clap? I feel like that deserves a round of applause."

Richard glared at Olivia and spat, "*How dare you speak to me like that*? You will get up this instant and follow me back to the – "

Brian stood up. He was a big man, wide of shoulder, not fat but broad in all directions. Richard instantly stopped speaking and looked up at him, then at Mark, standing up beside him. "I don't wish t'be rude," Brian said, "But you're spoiling our meal. I'm going to have to ask you to leave our pitch."

"Oh, I'm leaving," Richard snarled, "And so is my wife."

"Am I?" Olivia looked at Sophie. "Did he not hear a single word I just said?"

"Don't speak about me as if I'm not here, Olivia!"

"I think it's selective hearing," Sophie said, "He's choosing not to hear you so he doesn't have to deal with what you're saying."

"Or maybe," Faye said, leaning towards them, "he's just a bit *slow*."

"*Excuse me*!" Richard snapped.

"Yes," said Brian, "You may be excused, you're starting to get on my nerves now."

They all glared at Richard. He glanced from one to the other, coming to rest on Olivia. "You want to spend time with people like *this*?" he growled.

"I do, more than I want to spend time with you."

"Fine! Finish your curry!" He spun around and stomped off. "I'll expect you in the motorhome shortly."

"Don't wait up," she called after him, "There's rather a lot of food and I may be some time."

"You have 10 minutes!"

"Oooh," she said, tearing off a piece of naan bread and dipping it into a jalfrezi, "10 minutes. There's at least another 30 minutes eating time left."

They went back to chatting and laughing around the table, passing food to each other. They deliberately didn't talk about Richard but they could sense him watching them. A window of the motorhome suddenly snapped open up and Richard bent his head at an awkward angle to shout, "Olivia!" through the gap.

"Yes, darling?"

"I'm waiting."

"Are you, darling?"

"Yes. Haven't you finished yet?"

"Another bhaji?" Sophie asked, holding up the plate.

"How lovely. They are nice."

"Olivia!"

"Yes, darling?"

"How much longer are you going to be?"

"I don't know. As long as it takes. As long as I like."

"What am I supposed to do in here all on my own?"

Olivia lifted her head and threw such a look towards the motorhome that even Faye, sitting next to her, felt the force of it. "Do what I do, Richard. Clean. Cook. Await the return of your spouse. Oh, you might want to remember where you put all that loose change I'm meant to find when I clean, that should keep you busy for a bit."

The motorhome window slammed shut, then almost immediately opened again. "Olivia?" he yelled.

"What, Richard?"

"Have you washed the bedsheets? Are they clean? There's not rat piddle all over them, is there?"

"I boiled them in the pub washing machine, Richard."

"Good. And the floor and surfaces, did you give them a thorough wipe down with double-strength disinfectant?"

"Yes, you're perfectly safe in there, I've cleaned everything.

The window slammed shut and the blind was pulled down.

"That's okay, darling," she said quietly, "You don't have to thank me or anything."

The three air vents in the motorhome roof were open and they could hear Richard stomping up and down, muttering furiously to himself.

"He's really got a cob on, hasn't he," Faye said.

"A cob on?" Sophie laughed. "Oh, I'm so using that next time I have a furious client in my office."

"Take it, it's yours."

"CAN YOU *PLEASE* KEEP THE NOISE DOWN!" Richard bellowed.

"He's a miserable git," Mark said quietly, "How do you stand him?"

"He's my husband," Olivia said, "It's my duty as a wife to put up with him, at least that's what mummy says and she's put up with my father for decades. She says I have it easy with Richard."

"You know you *don't* have to put up with it though, don't you?" Faye said carefully.

"I hope," Brian said, casting a firm eye at his wife, "That our casual banter is not encouraging you to do something you might later regret."

"No." Olivia dabbed at her curry with a fork, keeping her voice low. "You're not saying anything I don't already know. I haven't been happy for a long time, not since … " She put her fork down. "He had an affair," she said, "Well, kind of an affair, about six months ago. He left me for another woman and, by all accounts, the other woman was quite surprised about it. I called her when I found out, got her number from his phone when he was in the shower; very naughty, I know, but I needed to know what had happened and Richard wouldn't tell me. Angela, her name was, she sounded really lovely and a little bit horrified, said he'd flirted furiously with her at the golf club Christmas party and the next thing she knew he turned up on her doorstep saying, 'I've left my wife for you'."

"Poor woman," Mark said.

"Poor you," Sophie said, rubbing Olivia's hand. Faye put her arm across her shoulders.

"No, it was nice. He was gone for three days. Angela said she couldn't get rid of him and eventually had to call her brother round to chase him off. They didn't sleep together or anything, she said she found him a bit repulsive. When he came back I felt quite … disappointed. Isn't that terrible? He promised to change, said things would be different from now on, and they were for a bit, but then it just went back to the way it was before. Worse. I told mummy and she just said it's what men do, they can't help themselves, but I didn't …"

She scrunched up her face, staring at the motorhome. "I felt differently about him after that."

"I'm so sorry," Sophie said.

"Why didn't you leave him?" Mark asked.

"I thought about it, a lot, but daddy would have been furious. He picked him, you see. He says Richard looks after me, takes care of me, and I should just be grateful to have him."

Mark stiffened on the other side of the table.

"There are places you can go," Sophie said softly, "Women's refuges, safe houses."

"Oh, he doesn't hit me or anything," Olivia gasped, "He's not physical. Daddy would kill him."

"No, but if you want to leave him and don't have the money to – "

"I have money."

"That's what I was trying to tell you this morning," Faye said to Sophie. "It's not what we think."

"What did you think?" Olivia asked.

"We thought you didn't have the money to leave him, didn't have anywhere to go."

"Oh." She looked at their concerned faces and smiled her cute, overbite smile. "You're all so lovely to worry about me like that, but I have money, quite a lot actually. Richard keeps a tight rein to stop me squandering it all, that's why daddy chose him, to look after me and the dreaded finances, but it's my money, mine and mummy's, all of it. Daddy gives us a monthly allowance and tells us when we can use the family account to pay for big things, like my car." Her face suddenly lit up. "I have a Mini, it's cream with a Union Jack on the roof. I love it, I call her Minnie Mouse."

"What car does Richard drive?" Mark asked.

"A Mercedes Benz."

"Of course he does."

"And he has a Harley Davidson in the garage too, but he never uses it, I think it's too big for him. Everything's in my name because I paid for them, so technically I guess they're mine, but I never say that to Richard, he gets all huffy, and I don't really want to drive a big car or a motorbike. The house is mine too, daddy insisted it was just in my name because I paid for it. I pay for everything."

There was a long moment of silence while they all digested this new, unexpected information. "So you're not trapped in a loveless marriage with no way out?" Sophie asked.

"Well, it is loveless I suppose in that there's no hugging or kissing or, you know, anything like that, but I'm not trapped, not financially anyway. I guess I'm trapped by Richard, under daddy's strict instructions."

"Control by proxy," Mark breathed.

"They've taken away your autonomy," Tel said. "Restricted your access to funds to keep control of you."

"Yes. Funny, I hadn't thought of it like that before."

"So Richard isn't looking after you, he's looking after the family fortune. Your father too."

Olivia stared at Tel, deep in thought. "Yes, I suppose they are."

"What does Richard do for a living?" Brian asked.

"He used to be an accountant, but now he takes care of our finances."

"Full-time?"

Olivia gave a little laugh. "Yes, there's a lot to take care of. Daddy does most of it and Richard just deals with the investment side and ..." She rolled her eyes. "It's all very complicated and I'm not very good with numbers."

"Where does all this money come from?" Sophie asked.

"Mummy's side of the family." She looked at them, all staring at her and frowning. "She's the only daughter of a very wealthy family, just like me. They made their fortune in limestone, owned a lot of quarries."

There was another long silence.

"At the risk of overstepping the boundaries," Mark finally said, "You don't need him, Olivia. Pay an accountant or an investor or whatever it is he does and get rid. He's no good for you. You deserve a lot better."

"Steady, lad."

Olivia had a strange, faraway look in her eyes. "It never occurred to me until just now that Richard was chosen to protect the family wealth, not me. I ... I must be very stupid."

"You're not stupid," said Faye.

"Far from it," Sophie added, "Maybe a little gullible, understandably, given your background, but you're very erudite and caring and ... just a lovely woman."

"And your cooking is *amazing*," Brian added.

"Brian!"

"What?"

"You're always thinking of your stomach!"

"Sounds to me," Mark said, "that the husbands need the wives more than the wives need the husbands. Sounds to me," he said, with an edge to his voice, "that the husbands are exactly the type of people they're supposedly protecting you from."

Olivia was staring at the motorhome in front of them. As if sensing a change in atmosphere, or perhaps sensing his wife's intense gaze, Richard suddenly shouted, "Are you coming, Olivia?"

She didn't answer, just kept staring. Sophie quietly said, "You do whatever you feel is right for you, Olivia. Don't rush into anything. He might genuinely love you, he might – "

"He doesn't, he never has. He says he's *fond* of me, and he's only ever said that a couple of times. I don't think I even like him very much."

"Then find a good solicitor and get some legal advice."

"Oh, we have a lawyer."

"Is it daddy's lawyer?" Mark asked.

"Yes. We had a family lawyer but daddy didn't like them, said they were useless, so he got ... he got his own lawyer."

"Find another one, a good one," Sophie said. "Get independent advice. You can be whoever or whatever you want to be, Olivia, with or without Richard. Set yourself free, be the real you."

"I don't know who the real me is, I've never had the chance to find out." She tore her eyes away from the motorhome and placed them on Sophie's beautiful, olive-skinned face. "I'd quite like to be you, actually."

"Me?"

"Yes. Not the gorgeous bit, obviously, I'm not talking miracles, but confident and capable."

"Haughty and high maintenance," Tel laughed.

"Shut up, Tel, I'm being admired. Olivia," she said, hugging her, "You can be anything you want to be."

"I don't know who I want to be. I don't know who I am."

"Find out."

"How?"

"Try everything." Sophie's eyes sparkled. "Try *anything*. Hand-gliding, rock climbing. Travel the world, go places, meet people. Open a tea shop, anything, *everything*."

Olivia's eyes were wide now. "It does sound rather exciting."

"It is. I'm jealous. I may have to try a bit of hand-gliding myself."

"You're afraid of heights," Tel said.

"Potholing then."

"Claustrophobic."

"Swimming with dolphins."

"You can't swim."

"Are you trying to hold me back, Tel?"

"Wouldn't dare," he laughed, holding up his hands, "Wouldn't know how."

"OLIVIA!" Richard yelled, "I THINK IT'S TIME TO COME BACK NOW, DON'T YOU?"

"Oh," Olivia said, looking at the curry strewn table, "I've talked so much everything's gone cold."

"We've eaten most of it."

"I'm stuffed," Brian said.

"For at least 10 minutes," Faye laughed.

"I'm full as an egg," said Sophie.

"I'm never eating again," groaned Tel.

"I'll help clear the tables." Olivia stood up and started picking up plates and metal containers.

"Worry not, I have al fresco dining down to a fine art," said Faye, "Observe." She pulled the camping table away from the picnic table and pushed a kitchen bin lined with a bin bag between them. Producing a dustpan, she laid it at one end of a table and cried, "Everybody duck!" She pushed all the takeaway containers, the paper plates and the plastic cutlery into the bin. She did the same with the other table while they all bent sideways clutching onto their plastic glasses, and in no time the remnants of their meal had been cleared away. Faye looked well pleased with herself.

"I'm stealing that too," Sophie said.

"It's my gift to the people of the south."

"And the south thanks you."

"I suppose I'd better go," Olivia said. "It's been a lovely evening, I've really enjoyed myself. Sorry if I talked you all to death."

"You didn't," Faye said. "I think you need to talk more often with people who genuinely care about you."

"Are you going to be alright?" Sophie stood up to give her a hug. Faye did the same. Mark stood up too, but then wasn't sure what to do and sat down again.

"Yes, don't worry about me, I'll be fine," Olivia said, hugging them back. "He'll just ignore me as a punishment, turn his back on me in bed in a huffy way and go to sleep. He won't be happy in the morning though when I tell him what I've got planned."

"Why, what have you got planned?" Brian asked innocently.

Olivia tapped her nose and laughed.

She went back to the motorhome and they all listened for a while, pretending not to, brushing crumbs off the tables and swirling their drinks in the plastic glasses, but there were no raised voices.

"I think I'd like to lie down," Tel said, as he rested his head on the picnic table. "It's been a long and arduous day. Would you gentlemen kindly carry me to my bed?"

They did. Sophie followed.

Mark went to his caravan. Brian took the binbag to the rubbish bins by the toilet block, and Faye tidied up the awning and pulled down the sides.

"Good night, wasn't it," she said, as they snuggled up together under the duvet, the sofa beneath them creaking.

"Certainly an eye-opener."

"It was. Poor Olivia, what a life she must have had with two dominating men controlling her every move."

They both stared at the ceiling.

"You're a good husband, Brian."

"You're a good wife, wife."

The night passed peacefully, filled only with the gentle sounds of distant flatulence.

Until...

CHAPTER 16

Day 7 – Thursday

Brian slowly opened his eyes. He sensed straight away that something was not right. He sat up in bed and listened. All was silent, except for the sound of someone farting somewhere outside. Besides him, Faye stirred. He sniffed and said, "What's that smell?" Faye was immediately awake and sitting bolt upright next to him, hissing, "What? What smell? Is it gas? Is it burning? What? Answer me, Brian! What is it?"

He sniffed again. "Something's ... burning."

"What kind of burning?" Faye, unable to smell herself, was furiously shaking Brian and already on the verge of a hysterical panic. "Is it fire? *Are we on fire*?"

Brian reached up and turned on the ceiling light. It was only then they could see that their caravan was filled with languid grey smoke. They both leapt out of bed. "What is it, Bri? Where's it coming from?"

Brian opened the oven door and thick smoke drifted out.

"Oh my god," Faye cried, "It's the chicken masala and rice we were keeping warm for Richard."

Brian grabbed a tea towel and pulled the two foil trays off the shelf. Holding them precariously in one hand, one on top of the other, he opened the caravan door with the other and, howling at his burning fingers, threw them both out. The containers broke open and black goo smouldered on the grass outside. Faye stood behind him, wafting a hand towel around. "What time is it?"

He looked at his watch and groaned. "Five thirty."

"Oh." Faye was still wafting. She suddenly stopped

wafting and said, "OH!" again, this time with more vigour.

"What?"

She looked at him, wide eyed, threw down the towel and disappeared into the toilet. "Save yourself," she hissed, "Get out now while you still can."

Brian left the caravan, closing the door behind him and smiling with amusement. His smile vanished as his tummy grumbled, and then grumbled again. He sensed an urgency building up inside him, growing stronger. He gasped at the sudden cramp in his abdomen.

"Are you going to be long, Faye?"

"As long as it takes!"

"Is it a 'world falls out your bottom in an instant' type evacuation, or a more leisurely – "

"Leave me alone, Brian, I'm trying to poo!"

There was no question about it now, he had to find a toilet and find it fast. Without thinking, he bolted towards the toilet block taking tiny steps as fast as he could whilst tightly clenching his buttocks and holding a bunched-up tea towel in front of his naked, swinging manhood.

Tel, wearing some very shiny, possibly silk, pajamas, sprinted past him on his bandaged toes, crying "Ouch!" with every step he took and hissing, "Our bloody toilet's full again!" Behind him Brian heard a caravan door being flung open with some force and crashing against a caravan side. Glancing over his shoulder as he minced his way to sanctuary, he saw Mark tiny-stepping in his direction wearing a pair of lime green underpants. Brian briefly wondered how many cubicles there were in the men's toilets. There were three, he was sure there were three, there *had* to be three.

Tel threw himself into the men's toilet like the hounds of hell were chasing him and disappeared inside. Brian charged in seconds afterwards. One door was already closed, but, thank god, two remained open. He shuffled into one, just as Mark came bursting in. "I didn't think the caravan toilet could handle this!" he cried, slamming his cubicle door shut.

"Mine's full," Tel yelled.

"Oh my god," Brian gasped, "I can barely breathe in here for the *stench*."

"It's not me, mine smells of flowers and lollipops."

"Mine smells like a decomposed body mixed with – "

"Stop, I'm seriously going to puke."

"Safe to say nobody suffers from a shy colon then," Tel laughed.

"This is no laughing matter."

"I was just trying to drown out the sound with casual conversation, Bri?"

"A brass band couldn't do that."

"Er," said Mark, "There's no toilet paper in mine, can you pass me some, Bri."

"There's none in here, either. Tel?"

"I've got ... six sheets."

"Two sheets each isn't going to cut it."

"Who thinks they have time to dash out in search of loo roll?"

"Not me."

"I'm not risking it."

"Then what are we going to do?"

Sophie was just waking up, wondering why Tel wasn't lying next to her in bed and what the smell in the caravan was. It was then she heard it. It was distant and partially lost in the gentle breeze wafting through the surrounding trees, but if she held her breath she could just about make out the sound of her name being called from far, far away. She got up and went outside, standing still on the gravel pitch and listening intently. There it was again, "Sophie!"

"Hello? Is there anyone there?"

"Sophie!"

She took a step forward, and another one, turning her head to try and locate the distant voice calling out her name. And then, very softly, she heard the voice cry, "There's no toilet roll in the men's loos!"

* * *

"Tel?" Sophie called out as she entered the men's toilet. The curious tone of her voice changed significantly when she hit a pungent wall. *"Oh my god!"* she gasped, "It smells like something died in here!"

"We're aware," said Brian.

"Did you bring toilet rolls?" Tel asked.

"Rolls, as in plural? No, I just have the one I grabbed out of our tin can of a toilet."

"Tell me it's a full roll."

"No," she said, looking at it and pinching her nose closed with her fingers, "Maybe half."

There was a trio of groaning.

"Throw it over," Tel said, "And look around, see if you can find any more."

"There's one on the window ledge."

"Me!" squeaked Brian.

"Share!" squeaked Mark.

"Is there anything else you boys need?" she asked, and they could all hear the amusement in her nasally voice.

"Would you be so kind as to retrieve my dressing gown from my caravan?" Brian asked.

"Your dressing gown?"

"Yes, if you wouldn't mind."

"Why, what are you wearing now?"

"Nothing."

"Nothing at all?"

"He's absolutely bollock naked," Tel laughed, and then he stopped laughing and cried, "Get out, Sophie, get out now!"

She hurried gratefully from the men's toilet and, even through the closed door, heard three men relax at her departure.

* * *

Sophie tapped on the caravan door. "Faye! Faye!"

"Little busy, Soph."

"Brian wants his dressing gown."

"What? Where is he?"

"In the men's toilets."

"Is he? I've been talking to him for the last five minutes. I wondered why he didn't answer, I just assumed he didn't have his hearing aids in or was practicing selective hearing again. What's he want his dressing gown for?"

"To cover his nakedness."

"He's naked in the men's toilets?"

"Apparently so."

"I hope nobody saw him, they'll need counselling."

There was a moving sound and the caravan rocked slightly. Faye shouted, "Okay, open the door."

Sophie did, then stepped back as a pungent odour seemed to physically hit her in the face. The toilet door in front of her opened outwards a crack and a dark blue dressing gown was pushed through.

"Couple of toilet rolls too, Faye, just in case?"

One oval toilet roll was squeezed through the gap, followed by another. Sophie turned her head, sucked in a deep breath, and reached in for them.

* * *

Quite some time later the men walked out of the toilet block together, waving their hands in front of their noses. "Bloody hell!" Tel grimaced, hobbling, "Nearly suffocated in there. Should we leave a warning sign or an apology note or something?"

"People will know," Brian said, "They'll know."

"This is all your fault, Tel, you ordered the vindaloo."

"It was certainly hotter than I'm used to."

"Hot?" Mark winced, "I can't feel my posterior, any of it, it's all just ... numb."

"My intestines are on fire."

"Talking of fire," said Tel, "I caught a brief glimpse of something smouldering on the grass outside your caravan as I leapt over it, Bri."

"Scorched masala from last night. It was like lava in a

tin."

"Good job your howl of pain woke me up," Mark said, "You don't consider the dangerousness of a fart when you're asleep."

Tel suddenly stopped walking. "Oh no," he said, wide-eyed. "This isn't over yet, lads." He turned and hobbled quickly back to the toilet block.

Mark was about to laugh, and then stopped and said "Oh," instead.

"OH!" cried Brian.

They hurriedly minced after Tel, wedging the entrance door open with a hastily kicked mop bucket so that a single spark wouldn't obliterate them and the block, if not the entire campsite, with it.

* * *

Brian, freshly showered and no longer breakdancing from stomach cramps, had just finished scraping the black goo off the grass when Faye, still ensconced in the toilet, hissed, "Shut the caravan door, Bri."

"But it stinks in there."

"Does it?"

"Yes, it does."

"But everyone will hear me, shut the door."

Brian took a deep breath and stepped inside, closing it after him. "They'll still hear you through the ceiling vent." He heard the sound of the ceiling vent being slammed shut. Reaching inside a top cupboard, he pulled out an aerosol can and began liberally spraying it around the caravan, opening windows as he went and waving across at Sophie, who was also opening the windows in the Airstream. He hurried back outside, into the fresh air under the awning, closing the caravan door behind him. Mark was sitting outside his caravan and they raised a hand at each other.

"How you feeling?" asked Brian.

"It's easing off. You?"

"I'm starting to believe I might live. Faye's still suffering though."

"I wonder how Olivia is?"

"I'm fine," came a voice.

Inside the motorhome Richard looked up from writing at the table and huffed, "Do you have to shout like that? It's very unladylike, Olivia. Who are you talking to anyway?"

"Mark and Brian."

"Please cease immediately."

"Don't be silly, I'm just – "

"Stop talking to them."

There was a moment of heavy silence, and then Olivia, who was poring over cookbooks and making notes of her own, looked across the table at him and said, "Are you looking at churches today?"

"No."

"No?"

"No, I thought ... I thought I'd spend the day with you instead."

"Oh, but I've got plans for today."

"Plans? What kind of plans? Nothing to do with *them*, I hope."

"It has everything to do with them, actually."

"I forbid it."

"Forbid?" Olivia gave a little laugh. "I'm not a child."

"Then stop acting like one. This nonsense ends now, and I'm staying here to make sure it does."

"It's not nonsense, Richard, you're just annoyed because you feel left out, you always feel left out because you don't make the effort with people."

"I don't wish to feel a part of it."

"Well I do. They're nice people and they're my friends."

"They're not your friends, Olivia, they just want to take advantage of you, everybody wants to take advantage of you, you're just lucky you have me to take care of you."

"I don't need taking care of, Richard."

"Don't you? You've been galivanting about with these

complete strangers since we got here, and I insist that it stops right this instant."

"Stop? I'm not stopping." She gave him a serious look, no smiles, no tinkling laughter. "I'm just starting."

"Right, that's it." He slammed his notebook shut. "I've had just about all I can take. They've clearly led you astray with their heathen habits and I'm not putting up with it any longer." He snatched up his phone and said, ominously, "I'm calling your father."

"Oh, say hello from me." Olivia's phone pinged with a message and she picked it up. "My taxi's here."

"Taxi? What taxi? Where on earth do you think you're going?"

Olivia picked up her bag and went to kiss Richard on the side of his face, but he pursed his lips and turned away.

"I'm going shopping."

"Ah, good. I was thinking maybe a steak dinner tonight, with some beef fat chips and some – "

"Oh, not for you," she said, "For … well, everybody."

"You're shopping for everybody?" His face was a mass of confusion that slowly morphed into volcanic rage. "Olivia, this has gone too far, I won't tolerate it a – "

"Must dash, don't want to keep the driver waiting. See you later."

She left the caravan, just as Mark was saying, "I wonder how Olivia is?"

"I'm fine," she called over.

"No sudden … no feelings of … "

"NO REVENGE OF THE VINDALOO?" Brian hollered.

"No." She gave a tinkle of laughter. "Mummy says I have a cast iron stomach. I thought it was rather nice actually, the vindaloo, very flavourful."

"Olivia!"

She ignored Richard, who was now following her like an indignant shadow, so close she could feel his breath on her neck.

"Will you please stop talking to them," he hissed.

"I'll talk to whomever I please."

"I'm definitely calling your father, you appear to be in the midst of an emotional crisis of some sort."

"Do whatever you want, Richard. I have to go, I have a very busy day ahead."

"Olivia!"

"Anyone want anything from Sainsbury's?" she called out.

"Toilet rolls," Brian and Mark said in unison.

"IMODIUM," shouted Faye from inside the caravan.

* * *

Olivia enjoyed herself at the supermarket. She'd allowed herself plenty of time and could peruse the aisles at her leisure, ticking off items from the list in her notebook and picking up random things that caught her eye. She could feel the almost constant vibration of her phone in her bag but she didn't pay it any attention and certainly had no intention of answering it – it could only be Richard or her father, and she didn't want to speak to either of them, she was having far too much fun and she wasn't going to let them spoil it.

At the till it felt nice and a bit naughty to use her bank card without Richard's permission – he'd have thrown a fit at the amount she'd spent. She looked briefly at the noticeboard full of handwritten postcards as she was walking out and spotted one for a DJ. Excited, she pulled out her phone and called the number.

"Yes, he's available," a woman's voice said, "But we'll have to pick him up at 9 o'clock 'cos it's a school night."

In the background a boy's voice cried, "Mom!"

"How old is he?"

"15, but he's good with music, he's done a bit of DJing for family and friends and stuff. Daniel, will you please get your uniform on, you're going to be late. So, is 9 o'clock okay for you?"

"That's no problem," Olivia said. "Can he be at The

Woodsman pub for 5?"

"Daniel, can you be there for 5 o'clock."

"Yes, tell them yes. What music do they want?"

"What music do you want?"

"Oh, I hadn't thought of that. Anything, I suppose. Nothing too young, we're not young," she giggled, "And no reggae, I don't like reggae. Just something ... upbeat and familiar."

"She says upbeat and familiar."

"Got it covered."

"He says he's got it covered. He's got everything on that iPhone of his."

"Iphone? Oh, I thought the advertisement said DJ. It's quite a big room to play music on an iPhone."

"He plays it through speakers using blue teeth or summat, makes a hell of a noise when he plays it in his room, drives us mad, but he's good at it."

"Thanks, mom."

"We'll bring him at 5 and collect him at 9."

"Stay and have something to eat," Olivia said. "There'll be plenty of food, you'll just have to pay for your own drinks. Saves you travelling all the way there and back again, twice."

"Oh," said the woman, "We've got two other children and won't be able to find a babysitter at short notice."

"Bring them, there'll be other children there.

"Oh okay. Thank you, we will."

"Good. I'll see you then."

When she got outside and the taxi still hadn't arrived she started to worry about her frozen food. She flicked through Google on her phone, looking for a particular name and phone number. When she found it, she called it. She recognised the voice that answered straight away, and smiled.

Luckily Ant had unlocked the pub door early, as they'd agreed, although there was no sign of him anywhere. The driver was kind enough to help her unload the bags into The Woodsman and through to the kitchen, where they sat piled on the counters. Olivia felt very happy and excited.

As she was unpacking the shopping a young man poked his head through the kitchen door and said, "Are you making breakfast this morning?"

Olivia hesitated for just the briefest moment, opening the fridge door and glancing inside, before smiling and nodding. He turned and said, "She's doing breakfast again!" To her amazement there came a small cheer from the bar. When she went out to look three tables were already full of hungry campers and another family was coming through the unlocked door.

Ant suddenly appeared at her side, startling her. "You doing breakfast again?" he asked.

"Yes."

"Good, I'm charging a set price this time. Table for four, is it?" he asked yet another family coming in, "Right this way."

"You're making the hot drinks," Olivia said, when Ant came into the kitchen with orders scribbled on the back of a pork scratchings card.

"Where's that other woman who helped you last time?"

"Oh," she cried, snatching up a small blue box, "You've just reminded me."

She tried to ring Faye on the WhatsApp group but couldn't figure out how to do it. She wandered into the bar, still pressing the buttons on her phone. "Ant," she said, "Do you know how to ring a person in a WhatsApp group?"

"WhatsApp?" Ant pulled a face.

A small child of about seven wandered over and held his hand out towards her with an 'adults know nothing' face. She tentatively gave him her phone. He tapped on the screen and said, "Who do you want to call?"

"Ghostbusters," Ant laughed.

She told him and he tapped some more, then handed the phone back. It was already ringing. "Thank you," she said, as the child wandered back to his table to play with a toy car.

"Miss Olivia, how lovely to hear from you," came Brian's

deep voice. "I'm afraid Madam Faye is slightly indisposed at the moment, would you like to leave a message?"

"That's why I'm calling, I have the medication she wanted. Is she still feeling poorly?"

"Well enough to tell me to put my hearing aids in or she'll kill me with a single fart," Brian said, "So definitely on the mend."

"Oh good. Can you come up to the pub to collect it? I'm doing breakfast if you're interested."

"I'm always interested in breakfast. I'll let the others know." He hung up, stood up in the awning and bellowed, "CAMPERS, THERE'S BREAKFAST AT THE PUB!"

Considering the morning had started incredibly early with a furious dash to the toilets, everyone seemed remarkably hungry. Even Faye said a full English breakfast would do her the world of good as she combed her hair and handed Brian his hearing aids.

"They irritate my ears," he complained, pushing them in.

"Not half as irritating as my hands around your neck if you say, 'What, love?' one more time."

"You think you can get your dainty hands round my enormous neck," he laughed.

"I'd give it a bloody good try."

"Quite aggressive for so early in the morning."

"It's been a long morning."

"For me too, but I only ooze with love for you, my love."

Faye laughed and threw a cushion at him.

"Where are you all going?" Richard asked Mark, who was hurrying through the dead bushes to catch up with the others.

"Olivia's making breakfast at the pub," he said.

"Olivia?"

"Yes." Mark quickened his pace, but Richard stepped down from the motorhome and called after him, "My Olivia?"

"Not that many Olivia's round here, mate, believe it or

not."

Richard slammed the motorhome door shut behind him and stomped after the group.

* * *

"Olivia!"

"Richard."

"What are you doing in a pub kitchen?"

"I'd have thought it was obvious, I'm cooking."

"I can see that."

"Then why did you ask?"

"Because I couldn't quite believe my eyes."

"Maybe you need glasses. It might help you to actually *see* me."

"What on earth has gotten into you lately?"

"Life, Richard, life's gotten into me."

Richard, standing by the open doorway of the kitchen watching her plate up meals with his mouth agape, said, "*Why* are you cooking in a pub kitchen?"

"Did you see all those people out there in the bar area?"

"Yes."

"They're hungry. I'm feeding them."

"Again, why?"

"Because I want to. Because I enjoy it. Because it makes me feel useful."

"You're useful back at the motorhome, Olivia."

"Am I? Am I really?"

Faye, who was making tea and coffee over by the sink and starting to feel a little awkward in the midst of a domestic spat, brushed past Richard with a tray of mugs and said, "You're in the way there, Dick. Help out or get out, but don't get in the way."

"Did you *hear* the way she just spoke to me?"

"I did."

"And?"

"And, get out of the way."

Richard exited the kitchen in a huff. Two minutes later

he was back again, coming to stand next to Olivia and holding his phone out to her. "It's your father," he said.

"Hello daddy," Olivia shouted at the phone, turning bacon in a frying pan and giving the baked beans a stir, "Can't talk now, I'm incredibly busy."

Richard pulled the phone back to his ear. "No, Harry, she won't take your call."

"I'll call you later, daddy." She rushed to pull a tray of sausages from the oven.

"No, she's having some kind of nervous breakdown. She's been cavorting with *strangers*, she claims they're her *friends*. I know, absurd. I've told her but she won't listen to me. Okay, I'll try. Olivia, your dad wants a word." She brushed passed him and the outstretched phone on her way to the eggs cooking in a pan of boiling water, dishing them up onto plates just as Faye came back with an empty tray. "Those ready to go out, Liv?"

Olivia stopped serving and straightened up. "Liv?"

"Oh, sorry, I meant Olivia."

"No, no, I like Liv. I've never been called Liv before."

"No, Harry, she positively refuses to talk to you. She's behaving very strangely. I don't like it, I'm worried."

"Richard!" Olivia cried, as she reached over for the pan of bacon, "You're *in the way*! Just get out, go on, get out."

"Can you hear the way she's talking to me, Harry? She's *pushing* me! Yes, physically *pushing* me, can you believe it?"

"I'll hit you with a frying pan if you don't get out from under my feet."

"Did you hear that, Harry? Did you hear what she said? She's threatening to turn violent!"

* * *

"Our last day," Sophie sighed, sitting back from her almost empty breakfast plate.

"I know," Mark said. "What are you doing with your last day?"

"Well, I was going to treat Tel to a spa day but his feet

still look like flayed pork."

"Please don't say that when I'm eating sausages."

"So we're going to go cruising round the Cotswolds instead and have lunch at the cutest pub we can find. I'm driving to give his poor feet a rest."

Tel stopped eating. "You're driving?"

Sophie nodded, smiling sweetly.

"I didn't know you could drive."

"Yes, I'm a very good driver."

Tel seemed to lose his appetite and pushed his plate away. Jim appeared at that moment and threw himself into a chair at their table. "Not eating that?" he asked Tel, and swiped up a sausage.

"Look what the cat dragged in," Mark tutted. "On the scrounge as usual."

"Not scrounging, just waiting for my breakfast."

"Breakfast," said Faye, putting it down in front of him and hurrying back to the kitchen, pushing her way past Richard, who was still lingering by the doorway.

"You're still here then," Mark said.

"I am indeed." Jim tucked into his meal. "Renting a room upstairs and sorting my life out."

Mark laughed. "Course you are."

"No, seriously, I've had a think."

"Painful, was it, this *thinking*?"

"I'm going to win Bethany back. She's the love of my life."

"And how do you intend to do that?"

"Already started. Sent her a bouquet of flowers yesterday."

"Wilted blooms from a petrol station isn't going to – "

"Interflora, mate. Cost an arm and a leg, but she's worth it. Roses, they were. She sent me a text saying thank you. Here, want to see?"

Before Mark could answer, Jim thrust his phone into his face. Mark just about made out the words on the screen, inches from his eyeballs. They read, 'Thank you for the flowers. Don't send any more, waste of money you don't have.'

"Clearly overwhelmed," he snorted.

"Give me some credit, mate. At least it's a start."

"Where'd you get the money from?"

"Asked the boss for a sub till Friday."

"You still have a job then?"

"Yeah, boss has been great, been married three times himself so he knows what it's like, given me some pointers."

"As did we all," said Brian.

"Yeah, and it really helped. Got me thinking, made me see the error of my ways."

"It won't last," said Mark.

"It will," Jim said, brimming with confidence as he pushed bacon into his mouth.

"So how come you're not at work then at – " Mark glanced at his watch. " – 9 o'clock on a Thursday morning?"

"Worked till late last night, overtime, need the dosh to woo the woman I love. Boss said I could come in a bit later." He picked up a mug and took a huge gulp of tea. Brian expressed surprise as it was his mug. "Gotta dash, catch you later."

"Oh, Jim!" Olivia called, as she came through from the kitchen with two plates, deftly avoiding Richard, "Can you be here at 5 o'clock tonight?"

"Said I'd work overtime."

"I'd really like you to be there?"

"Okay, I'll see what I can do." And then he was gone.

"What's happening at 5 o'clock tonight then?" Brian asked, leaning back in his chair to peer at her.

"You'll see," she laughed. She moved to deliver the plates to a famished table but Richard stood in her way. She tutted and wriggled past him. He looked forlorn, like a lost child who wasn't quite sure what to do.

"What are you and Faye up to today?" Sophie asked.

"Well, first thing this morning the plan was to visit the nearest A&E department, but I think the revenge of the vindaloo has thankfully passed. We may head back to Blenheim Palace to look at the gardens."

"The amount of plants outside your caravan you don't need to visit any gardens," Tel laughed.

"I'm going back to work," said Mark, looking at his phone. "And maybe find a good solicitor."

"But you'll be back for five though, won't you?" Olivia called over as she rushed back into the kitchen.

"Absolutely."

"Olivia, I – "

"I'm busy, Richard. Sit down and I'll bring you some breakfast."

"Here? You expect me to eat *here*, with all these people *breathing their germs*?"

"Stay and eat, or leave and starve."

He sat at the bar, away from everybody else, next to a man wearing a hoodie and sunglasses. Olivia came back out and gave them both breakfast.

"You're more than welcome to join us later," she said to Creepy Guy. He turned his head to look at her and nodded curtly. "Lovely," she said.

* * *

Olivia cooked all day and loved every single minute of it. Richard kept wandering in looking miserable, looking angry, machine-gunning her with questions or just standing there, saying nothing, glaring at her from the doorway with a mixture of outrage and disgust. "I don't know why you're doing all this for people you don't even know," he growled.

"I'm not doing it for them, I'm doing it for me."

"Your father's coming."

"Oh? Is he bringing mummy?"

"He didn't say, he's coming straight from the golf course."

"Lovely."

"He'll sort you out."

"I don't need sorting out, Richard, I need to be left alone

to get on with my cooking."

"Ridiculous!"

"Fun," she said, smiling and stirring sauces.

He eventually wandered off.

At 4 o'clock she checked her lists. Everything was going exactly to plan and she was pleased with herself and what she'd achieved. Ant helped her set up the bar area and carried things through from the kitchen. She quickly showered in one of the guest rooms and then, after a final check on everything, hurried back to the motorhome with some special bags of shopping.

Richard was sitting slumped on the sofa with his head leaning on one hand. "Oh, so you've decided to come back, have you?" he snapped as she came in.

"To get changed." She hurried into the bedroom. He leapt up and followed.

"You've *embarrassed* me in front of people."

"You've embarrassed yourself, Richard."

"I've told your father everything and he's furious."

"Nothing new there then." She took off her jeans and jumper.

"I hope he gives you a good telling off for your appalling behaviour."

"He can try, but I'll probably be too busy to listen."

"Can you hear yourself? This is not how I expect my wife to behave!"

"Then get a new wife."

"What?"

"If you're so disappointed in me – "

"Oh, I am, *I am*."

" – find a more obedient wife."

"I have an … I have a wife."

"No, you have a cook and a cleaner."

"What are you blithering on about now?"

Olivia tutted and pulled a dress out of a Sainsbury's carrier bag. It was very floaty and summery, much brighter and nicer than her other clothes.

"Is that new?" he asked.

"Yes, I got it this morning."

"From *Sainsbury's*?" he rasped, spotting the bag, "You're wearing a dress from a *supermarket*?"

"Yes, do you like it?"

"No, I do not."

"Good job I didn't buy it for you then."

"Who did you buy it for?"

"Myself."

"It's ... it's *inappropriate*, Olivia, you're displaying far too much cleavage."

"Don't be silly, Richard." She pulled new shoes out of a bag and slipped them on. A spray of perfume from a drawer, Chanel No.5, her favourite, and then she pulled out her makeup bag and a mirror. She didn't see him take the caravan keys from her bag.

"I forbid you to go back to that pub," Richard snapped, watching her every move. "You will *not* leave this motorhome, you will wait here until your father arrives, do you hear me?"

Olivia deftly applied eyeliner, a touch of shadow and mascara, until her naturally large eyes popped. She dabbed on the new lipstick she'd bought, not the 'natural' colour that Richard preferred but a muted red that really seemed to really match her skin tone. She smiled at herself in the mirror, then checked her curly hair piled up on her head and adjusted it a little. She chose earrings and a necklace out of the drawer and put them on.

"Olivia!" Richard snarled, "Are you listening to me?"

"I am." She stood up, wishing there was a full-length mirror in the motorhome. She felt lovely in her new things, very elegant, very ... feminine. She hadn't dressed up like this in ages.

"Olivia!"

"It's Liv," she said.

"What?"

"I want to be called Liv from now on."

"Have you completely lost your mind?"

"If I have," she said, picking up her handbag, "I'm really enjoying it."

She moved towards the door, ready to leave. Richard stepped in her way. "You're not going anywhere," he said.

"Get out of my way, Richard."

"I will not. You're staying here."

"I have guests arriving shortly."

"*Scroungers*," he spat, "Imbeciles. *Commoners*!"

Olivia looked at him, at his twisted features and frothing mouth. She was quite surprised at how she felt inside; calm, happy, pretty. She hadn't felt happy or pretty in a very long time and she wasn't going to give it up easily.

"Richard," she said, "I have food in the oven, on the oven and around the oven. I have things to do, to prepare. Now please, move out of the way."

He pressed his hands against the sides of the door, physically barring her way. He lifted his chin defiantly.

Olivia lifted her knee.

Olivia stepped over him, writhing and whining on the floor as he clutched at his manhood, and went back to the pub.

She could barely contain the electric fizz of her excitement.

CHAPTER 17

Brian was just driving back from Blenheim Palace, passed the pub, when he suddenly slammed on his brakes.

"What's up?" Faye asked.

Brian threw the car into reverse and backed up until he was level with the open pub doors. "Oh my god," he breathed.

"What?" Faye looked. She couldn't see anything. "*What?*"

"The smell."

"Of?"

"Food, lots and lots of food."

Faye glanced at her watch. "It's almost 5 o'clock."

"Let's get back to the caravan and change into something more elasticky."

A few minutes later Mark did the same, driving passed the pub in his van and then coming to an abrupt halt for a good, deep sniff of the air. He smiled and patted the long bag next to him on the passenger seat, and glanced at what he had in the back.

Shortly after, Sophie and Tel's red sports car pulled up outside. "I think," said Tel, looking at the open doors and hearing music playing, "This is going to be a good night."

"Aren't you glad you didn't have that massive lunch now?"

"I am."

"Let's quickly get changed and come back."

* * *

The group arrived en masse, scrubbed and brushed and carrying gifts. They walked into the pub to find it already half full of campers sitting excitedly at tables. Music came from what appeared to be a young boy sitting in the corner, hunched over a phone, with two enormous speakers either side of him. The atmosphere was buzzing, the air filled with the delicious smell of food. Olivia was waiting for them near a small crowd at the bar.

"Olivia!" Brian gasped as she approached them, a vision in a floaty yellow and orange dress. She was wearing makeup and an enormous smile. "You look beautiful!"

"Thank you," she said with a tinkly giggle, "I scrub up quite well."

"You do," said Mark.

"You look quite smart yourself." They all turned to once again observe Mark, who had been the subject of much ribbing as they'd walked up from the caravans. He was wearing a three piece-suit in a very nice shade of brown, complete with a matching dickie bow.

"Nipped home for a change of clothes and this was all I could find," he said, "Is it too much?"

"No," Brian said, "You look very fine and handsome."

"Dickie bow too much?"

"A tad."

Mark whipped it off.

"It's lovely that you've all made such an effort," Olivia cried, delighted.

"I've even pulled proper shoes over my blistered, raw feet," Tel winced, lifting one.

"Here," said Sophie, stepping forward with an enormous bunch of flowers, "We got you these."

"Oh, they're *lovely*!"

"And we found these," Sophie added, opening a small box containing silver, star-shaped earrings that sparkled in the light, "at a craft shop in Evesham."

"Oh, they're beautiful! You shouldn't have!"

"We saw them and immediately thought of you," Tel said, "Our little star."

Olivia hugged them both over the top of her enormous flowers, then put them carefully on the bar counter, touching the colourful petals.

"I, er, brought you this," Mark said, holding out a plant. "It's a very rare flying duck orchid. Look, the flowers look like flying ducks."

"Oh, they do!" she cried, "How splendid!"

"And there's a gift card for the garden centre if you're ever, you know, in the area again. I'm not much of a shopper."

"Thank you, Mark." She kissed the side of his face and Mark's cheeks burned.

"And these are from us," Faye said, holding up two bottles of champagne from her stash. "I wish I'd thought to buy flowers now, but these are cold, they've been in the fridge all day."

"Oh thank you! You didn't have to bring anything, any of you. I feel rather emotional, you're all so lovely."

"Don't cry," boomed Brian, "I can't stand to see women cry."

"We just wanted to show our appreciation for everything you've done," Sophie said.

"But I haven't done anything."

"You've cooked," Brian hollered, "Saved us from starvation with some exceptional fine dining."

Faye peered up at him. "Have you got your hearing aids in? You're very loud."

"I'm always loud, and yes, I'm wearing them and can hear everything that family in the far corner are saying, it's very distracting."

"I've saved a table for you," Olivia said, pointing at a reserved sign. "Our table."

They all looked at it and there was a moment of silence as they all recalled the fun and fights they'd had around it. Olivia caught her breath and said, "I'll just put this champagne in the fridge, we can have them later. Help yourselves to food. I've not made anything too spicy after last night, you poor things. Oh, except the kedgeree, that has a bit of a kick to it so you might want to avoid that if you're still feeling a bit queasy."

They all stood, open mouthed and wide eyed, surveying the mounds of food spread out along three buffet tables covered in pretty paper tablecloths that lined the whole of one wall. There were sandwiches, filled bread rolls, home-made sausage rolls and mini pasties, colourful salads, a spectacular bowl of coleslaw, spare ribs and flavoured chicken pieces, crusty bread and baguettes, nibbly things, cheesy things, tangy pasta, meat and vegetable rice salads, frittatas and quiches.

"No desserts, I'm afraid," Olivia said, "I hope the children aren't too disappointed, but I don't bake much, Richard says he doesn't want a fat wife. He might not have a wife at all, fat or not, the way he's been carrying on." She laughed but her eyes looked sad, or was it anger? She quickly rallied and pointed at the end of the tables where two Bain Maries stood steaming. "There's steak and ale stew, kedgeree, chicken in white wine sauce, rice, and, for the children, hand-cut chips, breaded chicken pieces, battered cod fingers and beefburgers, all made from scratch, of course."

"My god!" gasped Brian, putting a hand on his chest.

"You did all this by yourself?"

"It looks amazing!"

"It smells delicious. Looks delicious too."

"I've died and gone to heaven," Tel said.

"Olivia, this is unbelievable!"

"Liv," she said, smiling at Faye. "I like to be called Liv."

"Liv, this is incredible!"

"Extraordinary!"

Olivia giggled, smiling her cute overbite smile and modestly waving away their compliments. "Look," she said, picking a plate from a pile of plates at the bar, "The pub has real plates and cutlery."

"Real plates!" Tel said, holding one to his chest and stroking it, "I'd almost forgotten what they looked like."

"How have you done all this on your own?" Sophie asked.

"Oh, it was just a matter of timing, and Ant helped lay

everything out. You have a very well stocked kitchen, Ant."

"Yeah, Ant, you should do this more often," Mark said, "Really bring the punters in."

"I can't," Ant shrugged. "I'm ... "

"Too lazy, I know."

"Go and help yourselves," Olivia said, "There's plenty for everyone. I'll ask Ant to bring some drinks over."

They didn't need telling twice. Grabbing a plate each they shuffled slowly down the buffet table, piling them up and chatting about the gorgeousness of it all. Families came up from the tables and through the door, all excited and astounded by the buffet. The atmosphere was warm and cosy, electric with excitement, as people helped themselves to food and ordered drinks - Ant was doing a roaring trade at the bar and looked very happy about it.

Tel came over to where Mark was standing at the bar, surreptitiously watching Olivia chatting to everybody. "You don't know anyone who wants to buy an 88 inch TV set, do you?"

"You selling it then?"

"I can hardly take it back to London in a sports car."

"I might be interested."

"Really?"

"Yeah, my wife pretty much emptied the house when she left this morning, took everything she could carry, smashed everything she couldn't, and left my clothes smoking in an incinerator bin in the garden, hence the suit, only thing left in the wardrobe."

"I'm sorry to hear that."

"Well, I guess it was time for a new look, now that I'm single."

"I am sorry, Mark."

"Don't be, saves me the trouble of having to go through solicitors to get my house back, empty and wrecked though it may be, so yeah, I'm interested in the TV."

"I've been thinking about getting a TV for the bar," Ant

suddenly said, sidling up. "How much do you want for it?"

Tel told him. Ant whistled and pulled a face. "Too much," he said.

"Take off 20% for general wear and tear and you've got yourself a deal," said Mark.

"But it's only a couple of days old."

"Been sitting in a damp awning though, hasn't it, and it's been used."

"Yes, *you* watched it."

"There were other eyeballs on it too, it all adds up."

"Take off 15% and I'll have it," Ant said.

"10%," said Mark, glaring at Ant, "Final offer."

Ant shrugged and walked away to serve a throng of customers. Tel and Mark shook hands.

Jim came through the pub door wearing his work clothes. "Brilliant!" he cried, and headed straight for the food.

"Oi!" Olivia shouted over, and they all turned, surprised at her high-pitched loudness. "Don't you touch my lovely food with your dirty hands, go and wash them first."

"Yes, mom," Jim laughed, and hurried upstairs. When he came down again he'd changed too. He snatched a plate off the bar and went directly to the hot food, then threw himself down at the table, knocking the beer glass Mark was holding. "What's this funny rice stuff?" he asked, shoving it into his mouth.

"Kedgeree," said Faye.

"Bit spicy."

"Don't eat it then."

"No, it's nice. And what's this?" he asked, poking at the steaming stew.

"Just eat," Brian boomed, "It's all delicious."

"It's a skill, that," Mark said, wiping the beer off his suit.

"What is?" Jim was now attacking the chicken in white wine sauce.

"Irritating people."

Jim looked around the table. The women were smiling

benevolently at him, Mark and Brian had raised eyebrows. Tel was too busy tucking into his food to have any expression other than joyous indulgence.

"I've never eaten so much or so well in my life," he said.

"I know," Sophie said, "I'm trying not to think about it too much, I just hope my suit still fits me when I get back."

"Back," Tel sighed.

"I know."

"How was your Cotswold car cruise?" Brian asked them.

"We didn't crash!" Tel said. "Although careering round bends on two wheels was a whole new experience for me."

"Hey, cheeky. It was lovely, Bri, the Cotswolds is just so beautiful. How was Blenheim the second time round?"

"Expensive," Brian cried. "There was a shop that sold blankets, and we all know Faye has a problem with blankets."

They all laughed, except Faye, who rolled her eyes.

"How are things with you?" Brian quietly asked Mark, as the women indulged in a conversation about blankets, and Jim and Tel were, oddly, discussing spices.

"Good," Mark said. "Better than expected. I imagined months of legal wrangling over the house, but she went off on her own, probably in a huff."

"She's gone for good then?"

"Yeah, practically emptied the house, wrecked what was left, and burnt all my clothes, but worth it, I think. She sent me a text, very emotional it was." He laughed, pulling his phone out of his suit pocket and reading from it. "'Mark, it's over. Keep your crappy house and your crappy plant shop, I hate them and I hate you. You'll never see me again.'"

"Short and to the point."

"Yeah, a bit like our relationship."

"You're taking it very well."

"I've brooded, I've accepted, it's time to move on now."

"I'll drink to that," Brian said, raising his glass.

Olivia came over and threw herself down in a chair, puffing.

"Where've you been?" Faye asked.

"Talking! I've never talked so much in my life. Such lovely people. I should do this more often."

"You should."

"I'd definitely come again," Jim declared, scraping at his now empty plate.

"Free food," said Mark, "Of course you would."

"No, this is so good I'd pay for it."

"There's a compliment for you, Liv, Jim's willing to pay."

"Thank you, Jim."

He stood up with his plate and looked around. "There's baskets under the buffet tables for the used plates," Olivia said, "Just help yourself to another."

"Brilliant." And off he went.

Olivia held Faye's hand across the table and reached out for Sophie's. "You will stay in touch, won't you? You've both been so nice to me, I'd hate to lose you."

"Of course we will, Liv."

"Definitely." Sophie squeezed her hand. "We're best buddies now."

"We'll have to find a middle point between Birmingham, Bath and London where we can meet up," Faye suggested.

"Ladies who lunch *out of town*!" Sophie said, tapping on her phone.

"Oh, I like the sound of that"

"Oxford is roughly in the middle of us all, we could find a nice restaurant there."

"Or a hotel," Olivia breathed.

"Are you thinking what I'm thinking?" said Faye.

"I'm thinking ... *sleepover*!"

"Perfect!"

"What dastardly deeds are you women planning now?" Brian boomed.

Before they could answer, the door to the pub opened and Richard came storming in.

Closely followed by Olivia's father.

They both looked livid.

Olivia's father was tall and bore an uncanny resemblance to Richard, just older. He had a long face, neatly cut grey hair and a small goatee beard. His eyes were ice blue and penetrating. Richard stood behind him like a child who's tittle-tattled and wants to see what happens next. They both approached the table and stood there, looming over them all.

"Daddy!" Olivia cried. "Richard said you were coming. How lovely to see you! Is mummy here?"

"Olivia."

"Liv," she giggled, "I want to be called Liv from – "

"I'd like a word." He turned and walked out of the pub, with Richard following and glancing back nervously.

Olivia stayed in her seat, looking confused. "Has he gone out to *look* for a word?" she said with a tiny giggle.

"I hope you haven't had too much to drink," Sophie said softly, glancing at Olivia's wine glass. "I have a feeling you're going to need your wits about you."

"No, this is Ribena. I don't really like alcohol very much, but carrying a wine glass around makes a great prop."

"I don't understand the concept of not liking alcohol," Faye said, frowning.

"You wouldn't, you lush," Brian said.

The pub door opened and the man in black, still wearing sunglasses, scuttled in and sat at the bar, raising a finger at Ant, who hurried over to serve him.

"It's like," Faye continued, "when you read about freezing left over wine, and I think – "

"Left over wine?" Sophie cackled.

The pub door opened again and Olivia's father marched towards them once more, looking a lot more agitated than before. A small child running around the room bumped into him and his agitation increased to the point where his goatee beard scrunched up into a tiny furball on his face. As he approached the table the small toddler ran into him again and fell backwards onto the floor, sucking in air in preparation for a good cry. Olivia reached out and helped the child to its feet.

"You'll need to wash your hands, Olivia," Richard snapped, as the child ran off wailing to its parents. "Children are filthy animals, covered in germs and bacteria. You need to wash your hands."

"I would like a word," her father said sternly.

"Yes, you said, and then you left before I could think of one."

"Are you being facetious?"

"No, daddy, I was just making a ... joke."

"This is no laughing matter, Olivia."

Olivia stifled a giggle and said, "It is a little bit."

"Outside at once!"

"I can't leave," Olivia said, halting her father in mid turn. "This is my party. I'm the hostess. I've been planning it for two days."

Her father, Harry, glanced back at Richard, who was motioning hand washing at Olivia. "Are these the people you told me about?" he asked.

"Yes, these are the ones."

"From what I've been told," he said, addressing them all now, "You've led my rather gullible daughter astray and caused me to drive all the way down here?"

"Up," said Sophie, "The Cotswolds is *up* from Bath and a bit ... right."

Harry pierced her with a look that she was familiar with from many of her clients. She shrugged nonchalantly.

"We haven't led Olivia astray," Mark said, swirling the last of his beer in his glass. "We've all had a very nice time together."

"They're my friends," Olivia said.

Harry huffed nastily. "These aren't your *friends*."

"We are," said Faye.

"I would like a *private* word with my *daughter*, if you don't mind." He tried to silence Faye with a look, but she said, "You're in the middle of a busy pub, mate, not much privacy here."

"Which is *why* I asked to speak to her *outside*. And I am most certainly not your *mate*."

"I don't want to go outside," Olivia said, "I'm staying here, with my friends."

Mark sighed heavily and stood up. "'Nother pint, Bri?"

"Don't mind if I do."

"Tel?"

"Very kind."

Sophie coughed.

"Ladies?"

"I'm fine," Olivia said, snatching up her wine glass.

"Drinking now, too, are you?" Harry sneered.

"No, daddy, it's Ribena, but I might have a drink later if I feel like it."

"Outside!"

"You might want to wash your hands first," Richard said anxiously.

Mark watched from the bar as Ant flustered over the orders for several people at once. Faye held Olivia's hand under the table. Tel picked at his plate with a fork, irritably glancing up at the man looming over their table.

"Olivia, you will stand up and follow me outside."

"No, daddy."

"You will do as you're told this instant."

"I will not."

"How dare you disobey me!"

"I'm not a child, daddy, no matter how much you treat me like one. I'm a grown woman. I'm not being disobedient, I'm exercising my autonomy and my right to say no."

Anger bloomed on Harry's face. "Did they become your friends the instant they found out you had money, Olivia?"

"Excuse me?" Sophie snapped. "Are you suggesting – ?"

"Be quiet, I'm addressing my daughter!"

Tel dropped his fork on his plate and looked up. "Don't talk to my girlfriend like that again."

"I'll talk to her however I want."

Tel stood up. Sophie stood up to get Tel to sit down again, saying, "He's trying to get a reaction from you, don't let him."

"We're not interested in her money," Faye said, horrified, "We like Olivia for who she is. She's lovely and we don't think she's being – "

"Stop talking, this has *nothing* to do with you!"

Brian loomed up out of his chair and bellowed, "TALK TO MY WIFE LIKE THAT *ONE MORE TIME*!"

At the sound of his deep, powerful voice the whole pub fell quiet. Even the teenager with the iPhone paused the music.

Harry looked up at Brian in surprise. Richard was slightly behind them, his eyes darting between them both. Faye gasped out loud.

Brian said, "I suggest you leave now, we don't tolerate arrogant, jumped up bullies here."

"Not ..." Harry gulped and lifted his chin. "Not without my daughter."

"Liv," said Brian, not moving his eyes from Harry's face, "Do you want to go outside with your father and husband?"

"Not really, Bri."

"There," he said, "She doesn't want to."

"What she thinks she wants and what she needs are two very different things."

"That may be true, but right now we're in the middle of a party that Liv has been preparing for all day."

"For *you* people!"

"Daddy!"

Brian bent forward and put his face in Harry's face until their beards almost touched. "You're spoiling our fun," he said, quiet and sinister. "You've disrespected my wife, upset Liv, snapped at a leading partner of a ... what is it?" he asked, turning to Sophie.

"Senior Partner at a prestigious law firm in London,

where my dad is the CEO," she said.

"Ditto," said Tel, raising a hand. "Well, apart from the dad bit. We're the litigators, so watch your mouth, *pal*."

Harry seemed lost for words and glanced from one to the other. Richard was still wringing his hands and mouthing 'wash your hands' at Olivia, who was looking both embarrassed and infuriated. The pub was still silent, all eyes upon them.

Mark came back with the tray of drinks and pushed his way past Harry to get to the table. Harry looked enraged and stepped back, glaring at them all with his horrified mouth hanging open. Brian sat down and picked up his pint.

Harry said, "I'm only going to say this once more, Olivia. Follow me outside."

"I'm staying, and that's my final answer. I don't wish to discuss it anymore, daddy."

Mark was passing out drinks. Olivia spotted Tel's double whisky in a tumbler and stood up, snatched it up and gulped it down in one.

"Olivia!" Harry reprimanded.

She held up a finger and took a deep breath, concentrating, waiting. She suddenly exhaled and said, "Oh, that's better. Horrible taste though."

"You're welcome," Tel grinned, "It's a single malt."

"It's not," said Mark, "Stingy barman doesn't run to single malt, it's some blended crap in a screw-top bottle."

"Is the blended crap still good for Dutch courage?" Olivia asked.

"I guess we'll just have to wait and see."

"*Olivia!*"

"Daddy."

"If you're not out that door within the next 10 seconds Richard will be driving the motorhome back without you and you'll be stranded here, alone. Do you understand?"

"Yes, daddy, except … well, there's five guest bedrooms upstairs that I can stay in for as long as I want, can't I, Ant?"

"Absolutely, Liv."

"Big word for Ant," Mark said.

"And she won't be alone," Faye said.

"She'll have us," said Sophie.

"How touching, and how will you pay for your room, Olivia?" Harry sneered.

"We will," said Faye and Sophie together.

"No payment, glad to have her around," shouted Ant.

"Oh, thanks, Ant."

"No problem, Liv."

"I'll be paying, daddy, with my own money."

"You will not, I forbid it. You want to be careful, Olivia," he said, pointing a finger at her and screwing up his eyes, "I might be forced to disown you if you carry on behaving like this."

"No, daddy, you want to be careful I don't disown *you*. And you, Richard."

"Harry?" Richard whined.

"She's bluffing."

"Am I?"

Harry lowered his hand slowly.

"It's my money, mine and mummy's, and I think you should stop telling us what to do all the time. I've spoken with our old family solicitors – "

"You've done *what*?"

"Spoken with our old family solicitors, who you sacked for incompetency but actually they'd been doing a very good job for a very long time. They're happy to have me and mummy back."

"Lawyer, at your service," Tel grinned, raising a hand again.

"It's not quite our area of expertise," Sophie whispered.

"I would make it my area of expertise."

"I'm not going to be bullied anymore," Olivia said to her father and to Richard. "I've had enough of being treated like a naughty child all the time, I'm an *adult*. I've finally found some happiness and I want to keep it. I want to live a different life, a better one. Oh," she cried, glancing at Tel, "I think the Dutch courage just kicked in."

"Excellent," said Mark, looking up at Harry and adding, "You don't want to mess with Liv when she's had a drink, she's right feisty. Isn't that right, Dick?"

Harry turned to look at Richard, who lowered his head and said, "There was a slight altercation with a frittata the other night."

"Is that right? You're slacking in your duty, Richard, I'm very disappointed in you."

Richard's head fell lower.

"Daddy, why don't you stay and have some food? I made it all myself and you must be hungry after driving all the way up here from the golf course? There's kedgeree, your favourite, and I used mummy's recipe."

Harry glared at her, beyond outraged now. His face was maroon behind his grey goatee. Seemingly at a loss for words in the face of such insubordination, he turned and shouted, "10 seconds, Olivia!"

Olivia sat down. "He thinks it's a threat," she said, "but it would be quite nice to have some time to myself."

"We'll look after you," Faye said, patting her hand.

"Oh, I don't need looking after, not anymore, but thank you, thank you all so much for being here with me."

"Wouldn't want to be anywhere else," Tel said, raising his empty glass.

"To Liv," boomed Brian, raising his.

"To Liv," they all said, and Olivia blushed and dabbed at her eyes with a paper napkin.

"Are you okay?" Sophie asked.

"Yes, I'm fine. Better than fine, actually. It feels like a huge weight's been lifted off my shoulders. I've never spoken to my father like that before, I feel quite giddy."

"That'll be the cheap whisky," Mark laughed.

The man in black, sitting at the bar, slowly slipped

off his stool and stood in front of everyone, taking off his sunglasses and squinting at the light. "I don't mean to interrupt your evening," he said, in a thick American accent.

"He speaks!" Mark cried.

"But I thought, while it's quiet, I'd take the opportunity to make an announcement."

"CIA," Mark said, "I knew it!"

Brian shook his head. "Definitely FBI."

The teenager with the iPhone suddenly started playing the theme music from the X-Files. The man without sunglasses patted his hands down and the music stopped, to be instantly replaced with Will Smith rapping about men in black.

"Yes, thank you." The music stopped. "My name," he said, slowly pushing back his hoodie, "Is Iain Flemmingway."

Olivia gasped. Mark sat up straight in his chair. "It can't be! Is it?" He twisted round to Olivia. "Is it?"

Olivia's mouth was a perfect O-shape. Her eyes were as wide as the dinner plates on the bar.

Everyone else looked at each other, shrugging, curious as to what the announcement might be. The tenters thought it might be the winners of a raffle they hadn't had a chance to take part in.

"I'm a writer."

"It is!" Mark squeaked at Olivia, "It's him!"

"I usually write thrillers and I was working on my next novel, set in England, and researching what living off the grid would be like for my character, Paul McGuire."

"Paul McGuire," Mark clapped, "Brilliant name."

"Unfortunately, I got distracted from my research by a group of people in caravans."

"Oh my god," Olivia cried, "He means us, we distracted Ian Flemmingway!"

"Who is he?" Sophie whispered to Tel.

"No idea."

"Somebody had an Amazon parcel delivered here, a

book," Iain continued.

"That was me," Mark told everyone, "It was me."

"I became curious as to what the book might be, if it was one of mine."

"It was, it was! The Cincinnati one where Christian Christianson had to find the bomb."

"And how did you like it?" Iain grinned.

"It was brilliant." Mark nodded at everyone. "A masterpiece."

"Well, I didn't know that then," Iain continued. "I became obsessed with finding out what book it was, the same book that this young lady here was also reading. Rather shamefully I took to peering at them through the trees and peeking through their windows in the middle of the night to see if I could catch a glimpse of their books."

"So it *was* you!" Mark gasped. "I knew it! Totally forgive you, Iain, love your books."

"You certainly pack a punch," Iain laughed, rubbing his face.

"I do! Sorry," Mark said, raising a placatory hand, then staring at the hand and gasping, "I touched the face of Iain Flemmingway!"

'Who is he?' Faye mouthed at Brian, who shrugged and shook his head.

"I apologise for any alarm I caused. I couldn't speak because I thought, once you heard my American accent, my cover would be blown."

"The Cotswolds is full of Americans," Jim said, "All rummaging around in antique shops and saying how quaint everything is. You can barely move for the buggers round here."

"I take your point," Iain said, "But I couldn't risk it, not even when you offered me Indian food."

"You were there then," Tel laughed.

"I was, and I was sorely tempted, I love Indian curries, but I was hooked on my new story. I'm ashamed to say I even resorted to using listening devices, trying to catch you talking about the book."

"Ah, the tiny umbrella," Sophie said. "Wait, have you been recording us without our permission?"

"Not recording, no, just listening and making notes when you were outside, never inside. It's the same as overhearing a conversation on a street, or on a *buzz*," he grinned, looking at Faye, who returned a fake smile. "There was no infringement of privacy. The book isn't about you, per se, it's about your stories. The middle-aged couple who seem really happy together."

"We are," Brian said, raising his glass at Faye, who winked back.

"The young couple, very much in love."

Tel lifted Sophie's hand and kissed it.

"The lonely man in the corner."

"Well, I was until you lot came, and I had your book to keep me company, Iain."

"The drunken women in the campervans, and the sad woman in the motorhome."

"Oh," gasped Olivia.

"All their stories played out in front of me, real lives, and my writing changed. I started writing a different story, I started writing ... your stories."

"Erm," said Sophie, raising her hand, "Not using real names, of course."

"Of course."

"That's good then. Litigation can be very protracted and nasty."

"I wrote a quick draft," Iain continued, clearly comfortable with public speaking as he started pacing up and down, gesticulating with his hands. "I sent it to my agent, who loved it and sent it to someone they know in Hollywood, who also loved it. In short," he said, and one of the people at the back, "If you wouldn't mind, bloody parched back here."

Iain paused for effect, staring at the group at the table,

before saying, "They're going to make a film, about you."

Olivia gasped. Faye gasped. Mark looked like he was about to expire with joy. "Us? A film about us?"

"You'll run it past our lawyers first though," Tel said.

"Absolutely. Nothing will be done without your say-so. We will, of course, pay a fee for your participation in the project."

"Ooh," said Faye, looking at Brian and mouthing, 'New caravan'.

"Here's my card," Iain said, placing several on the table. "Get in touch with my secretary and we'll work out the details. Sadly, I have to disclose and run, I have a plane to catch, but we'll be in touch soon."

And he nodded once and left.

There was a moment of stunned silence in the pub, and then the teenager with his phone played When Will I Be Famous, and everyone started talking at once.

"Do you think I'm in it?" Jim said excitedly.

"Better hope you're not," Mark said, "Not sure Bethany would appreciate it."

"Yeah, you're right. Sacrificing fame and fortune for the love of my life."

"And you're not interesting enough," Mark added.

"You okay, Liv?" Sophie asked, "You look a bit pale."

"I'm ... was that ... ?" She shook her head. "Does cheap whisky cause hallucinations?"

"It was real, Liv," said Mark, "It was really Iain Flemmingway."

"And he's making a film about us?"

"Seems so."

"And I just disobeyed a direct order from my father?"

"You were bloody marvelous."

"Oh, I really do need a drink now."

"Shall I bring the champers over, Liv?" Ant shouted from the bar.

"Perfect timing."

CHAPTER 18

They were all slumped around their table, full and tired. Jim had rested his head on the back of his seat and promptly fallen asleep with his arms hanging limp at his sides. It had been a great night.

The teenager with the iPhone had left at precisely 9 o'clock and was pleased with the money Olivia handed to him.

"Straight into your savings account for university," his mother told him.

The boy pulled a face. Olivia slipped him another note while his mother wasn't looking and his face lit up.

The pub was quiet now except for the gentle murmur of voices from those that hadn't left to put their fractious children to bed. Olivia was swamped with compliments, a barrage of thank yous and quite a few glasses of wine, which she shared with the others, preferring to stick with her Ribena. She wouldn't let anyone leave without taking something with them.

"There's plenty of food left," she insisted, "It would be a shame to waste it, so help yourselves, take anything you can carry."

"Hey!" Ant shouted at a punter at the far end, "Put that chair down! And you, take your eyes off my Ban Murrays!"

As Olivia spooned leftovers into the plastic tubs she'd bought from Sainsbury's, she began clearing away the buffet tables. Faye and Sophie got up to help, but suddenly a group of women merged at the tables and took over, getting their men to carry the crates of dirty plates through to the kitchen. "You sit down, love," one said to Olivia, "You've done enough."

The dishwasher was loaded, the plates piled up for another load. Ant dragged the Bain Maries back into the kitchen and the containers were washed by a gaggle of very merry individuals at the sink. A man sang Elvis songs as he wiped down the bar tables, another tried to figure out how the vacuum cleaner worked, and a small child who'd overlooked bedtime did his best to finish off the sausage rolls by popping them one by one into his mouth.

In a burst of furious activity, the detritus of the buffet was cleared away.

"Saves me a job in the morning," Olivia beamed.

"And where will you be in the morning, Liv?" asked Brian.

She sighed heavily. "I don't know, I haven't really had time to think about it. I could go back to the motorhome and face the wrath of Richard, if he's still there, or I could stay here."

"Welcome to stay, Liv," Ant said, as he passed on his way to take down an empty buffet table.

"Thank you, Ant."

"No charge."

"You're so kind."

"Money in the till is a great ... " He paused, staring off into space.

"Way to repay the marvelous hostess who put it there?" Mark suggested.

"No. Well yes, but that ain't what I was thinking."

"You want to be careful with that thinking," Mark grinned, "Your brain could explode."

"Could it?"

"No, Ant."

"Money in the till makes you appreciate your fellow man?" said Brian.

"No, that ain't it."

"Brings out your more caring, generous side?" Tel tried, and Mark laughed.

Ant shook his head, screwing up his face with deep concentration.

"Motivator?" said Sophie, "Money in the till is a great motivator."

"Yeah, that's it."

"Knew it," Mark laughed, "Somebody else does all the work and he reaps the benefits, it's the perfect scenario for lazy people."

"I ain't that lazy, you know," Ant said, walking past with a folded buffet table under his arm, "I'm just ... sad, you know, since Chelsea left."

"Oh Ant!" the women cooed.

"Don't be taken in, he's always been a lazy bugger even before his girlfriend left him."

"Don't be so heartless!" Faye cried.

Ant, sensing sympathy, put down the table and arranged his face into a sad expression. "Yes," he sniffed, "I was a lonely child, a sensitive boy."

Mark cackled.

"Nobody ever really liked me."

"Yeah, because you were either fighting the other kids, stealing their lunch, or slobbering over the girls."

"Mark, don't be so harsh, can't you see he's upset?"

"He's not upset, he doesn't have the capacity for emotions, just ask his girlfriend. Oh wait, she's not here."

"And where's your wife then, Mark?" Ant asked.

Mark shrugged. "Out of my house, I care not where."

"You can join our gang, if you want?" Faye said softly.

"Nah," Ant said, picking up the table again, "You'll expect things from me, people always do, and I can't be arsed." He wandered off.

"Oh," said Olivia. "Odd."

"You don't know the half of it," Mark said, "I've seen sloths with more vitality."

"What are you going to do about Richard?" Faye asked gently. "Do you know yet?"

"I've not had enough time to process everything, such a lot has happened. I just know that, after seeing how normal relationships work, mine isn't normal, will probably never be normal. I want normal," she said with conviction, "I want to have what you all have. I want the freedom to be myself for possibly the first time in my life, whoever I am, whoever I want to be." She smiled at Sophie. "I want to be happy."

"It's a goal we all strive for," Mark said.

"Yes, but you're a lot closer to it than I am, I can just see it in the distance, waving at me."

"'Olivia, we're here, come get us'," Tel said in a small voice.

"'I'm coming'," Olivia laughed. "'Wait for me'."

"'We will, we will'." Sophie was looking at him strangely, so, briskly changing the subject, Tel said, "What do we think about this film deal then?"

"Amazing," Mark beamed.

"This time next year we could be millionaires," said Faye, half-joking.

"Probably come to nothing," Sophie said, "A lot of them do."

"How do you know?"

"Women's magazines mostly, films and documentaries too. Hollywood's notoriously cruel and fickle, I wouldn't hold your breaths."

"It might pan out," Mark said. "He's a big-time author."

"Maybe."

"I'll believe it when I see it with my own eyes at an IMAX screening. Until then," Brian said, with a quick glance at Faye, "We're keeping the caravan we've got."

"Spoilsport."

"Realist."

"I guess we'll just have to wait and see," said Tel.

"I'll be looking at beach houses in the Caribbean first thing in the morning," Mark laughed.

They were all quiet for a moment, thinking of caravans and beach houses, fame and fortune, and then, like the dream that it was, it was pushed aside and forgotten.

"I can't believe this is our last night together," Faye said. "I've had a really good time. Well, apart from the sleepless nights and the drunken yummy-mummies."

"Creepy guy scaring us all half to death," said Sophie.

"The overt displays of debauchery," Brian said, staring at a now snoring Jim.

"Brian getting stuck between the sofas and having to haul him out, naked" said Mark, "That will stay with me for a long time."

"And a naked giant streaking across the grass towards the men's toilets, that's a memory not easily forgotten," said Tel. "I may need therapy."

"The line dancing," Faye sighed.

"Film night."

"Curry night."

"Swiftly followed by evacuation morning."

"The rain flattening the tents."

"The sense of camaraderie in the pub afterwards."

"The walk," Tel gasped, "Oh my god, the bloody walk."

"The food."

"The friendships."

"I'm going to cry," Olivia sniffed.

"Me too," said Faye.

"I don't want it to end," Sophie said, her voice breaking.

Tel dramatically threw his head into his arms on the table and began to howl. Mark, struggling to keep a straight face, gently patted his back. Brian said, "It's okay, lad, we'll get through this."

Mark covered his eyes, his shoulders shaking with laughter, and whimpered, "I can't take it, Bri, I just can't take it."

Tel let out another howl.

"Oh stop it," said Sophie.

"Time for bed," Brian said, standing up and adding, "As Zebedee said to Florence."

"Who?" said Tel, lifting his head.

"Too young," Faye said, "A generation untraumatized by The Magic Roundabout."

"Our last sleep as a group," said Sophie, and Tel threw himself across the table and started howling again.

"Well, technically speaking I'll be sleeping upstairs," Olivia said, "But I know what you mean."

"You be okay?" Mark asked her.

"Yes, I've got Ant and Jim." They all looked at Jim, snoring with his head flopped back at a 45 degree angle, and Ant, standing like a zombie behind the bar.

"Call if you need us," Mark said. "We're only in the field outside, crying ourselves to sleep in our caravans."

"Stop it!"

"Night, Liv."

"Night, friends."

They hugged and parted, leaving Jim fast asleep at the table.

* * *

"It's still here, they didn't drive off and leave her stranded," Faye gasped, approaching the darkened motorhome. "Is he in there? I can't see anything."

"The blinds are down," Brian said, "Probably to stop nosy neighbours peering in, this campsite is apparently notorious for it, especially this week."

"I think he's gone."

"Good," said Mark. "They've probably raced back to put their affairs in order before Liv unleashes the shit-hot lawyers on them."

"Did I hear 'shit-hot lawyers' being mentioned?" Tel smirked, as he and Sophie sauntered up arm in arm.

"Is Dick in there?" Sophie asked.

"I don't think so, it's all quiet inside."

"He could be asleep," said Brian, "Or lying there wondering what all the whispering is about outside."

"Harry could be watching us right this minute."

"Ooh, creepy."

"So stop peering through the window then, Faye."

"I want to know if they just left her here on her own."

"Gits," said Mark.

"They may be patiently and quietly waiting for her to come home," Brian suggested.

"In the dark?"

"All the better to watch for meddlesome campers."

"Ooh!"

"I'm off to bed," Mark said, striding off in his suit. "See you in the morning. Our last morning," he cried, covering his eyes with his hand.

"Night, Mark."

"We're off too," said Tel. "It's quite exhausting, this camping lark, isn't it."

"Not always," Brian said, "Sometimes there's only fire and pestilence. Come on, Faye, prise yourself away from that window."

"I think they've gone and left her."

"Let's get some sleep before we start lobbing eggs and flour at their motorhome, eh?"

"We're out of eggs, Bri."

"Fortuitous. Come on, woman, come snuggle up to your husband instead of fretting about someone else's."

* * *

"Brian."

"Yes?"

"I've had a lovely time."

"So have I."

"Do you think we'll all stay in touch?"

"Hope so. Only time will tell."

"Such a nice bunch of people, and we all hit it off right away."

"Yes, it's not often a group of people gel like that."

"We've been lucky."

"We have. Faye?"

"Yes, Brian?"

"Are you crying?"

"I can't help it."

"Come here, you big softie."

* * *

"Tel."

"Yes?"

"Can we do it again?" She was snuggled up on his warm, hairy chest.

"I may need a few more minutes."

"No," she laughed, poking him, "I meant camping."

"I thought you hated it."

"I did, but I'm allowed to change my mind if I want to."

"Woman's prerogative."

"So, can we?"

"Yes, of course."

"Maybe in a larger caravan next time?"

"Definitely, biggest one I can find. We're gonna need a bigger car though."

"We can hire one."

She was silent for a moment, and then, "I feel really sad about leaving tomorrow."

He scooped her off his chest and onto her back. "I may have something to cheer you up."

* * *

Mark lay in his bed, clutching Iain Flemmingway's book to his chest and staring at the back of his outstretched hand, smiling. He'd punched Iain Flemmingway with that hand, he had actually touched his living flesh.

He slowly lowered his hand to the table, where another book sat, the book that he and Olivia had chosen in the supermarket together. He picked it up and hugged that to his chest too.

Day 8 – Friday

"GOOD MORNING, CAMPERS!"

"Brian!"

"What?"

"They might want a lie-in."

"It's 9 o'clock, woman, how much sleep do they need? I've done everything I can apart from take down the awning, and we have to be off site by 11."

"I don't think Ant's too strict about that," Mark shouted.

"Well, we can't pack up until SOMEBODY MOVES THIS TV SET!"

"Oh, I'll take that," said Mark, coming over.

"You're taking it?"

"Yeah, paid Tel by bank transfer last night."

"I wasn't checking, I just thought you meant you were taking it back to London for them."

"Nah, taking it straight to the house and plugging the PlayStation in it, where it will sit, undisturbed, as shall I."

"Then help yourself."

"Do you want the box?" Tel asked, coming out of the blinding Airstream in his underpants.

"You still have it?"

"Yeah, somewhere, if I can remember where I put it."

"Shouldn't take too long to search your caravan for eight feet of cardboard," Brian laughed.

Tel grinned as he bent down and pulled the TV box out from underneath the Airstream. "It's a bit damp but it's better than nothing."

"Cheers."

"I don't know how we're going to fit all this in the car," Sophie said, coming down the steps with a huge pile of camping clothes. "Anyone in the market for a blood-soaked pair of walking boots, size 9, only worn once?"

"Pass," Mark laughed, and Sophie threw them down on the ground next to a bin liner.

"What time are they coming to pick up the Airstream?" Brian asked.

"Midday. They've asked that we remove all personal

belongings."

"And put them where?" Sophie huffed. "Oh Faye, I have your blankets and sheets and cushions, and a blood stained washing up bowl if you want it back?"

Faye hurried over as Sophie deposited the pile of clothes on the back seat of the sportscar, crying. "We're never going to fit it all in!"

"You're aware that you'll have to turn off the gas cylinder, unplug the electric hookup, tip away the grey water, that's that plastic thing at the front, empty the Aquaroll, that's your water at the side, and, horror of horrors, empty the toilet cartridge and the toilet flushing system first, yeah?"

Tel's face fell. "Won't they do that?"

"They might, but they'll probably charge you an arm and a leg for it."

"I'll pay," Tel said, brightening. "Unless Faye fancies – ?"

"No!" she said, walking back to the caravan with a huge pile of home furnishings.

"Morning!" Olivia waved at them from the front of her motorhome, still wearing her summery party dress. "Just come to get changed and face the wrath," she giggled, pulling a face.

"Sleep well?"

"Oh, it was lovely, I had the whole bed to myself and slept like a log."

"No breakfast this morning then?" Brian laughed.

"No, I think I've cooked enough for a while."

She disappeared behind the motorhome and they heard her banging on the door. "Richard! Richard, it's me, let me in. Richard?"

"I don't think he's there, Liv," Faye called over.

Olivia reappeared on the gravel driveway. "He's gone?"

"We haven't heard anything all morning."

"But all my clothes are in there and I can't find the key."

"Here," Sophie said, rushing over with the retrieved pile of camping clothes, "You can have these. They're not washed,

I'm afraid, but I promise you I have a very strict personal hygiene regimen."

"He just left? They left me?"

Sophie put her arm around her shoulders. "Sorry, Liv."

"The buggers!"

"Don't hold back, Liv, just let it out, allow your feelings to – "

"The selfish, thoughtless, misogynistic *buggers*!"

Faye came rushing over. "We could break the lock on the door." She turned to Brian, "Could we break the lock on the door?"

"Only if we want to be charged with breaking and entering."

"We could *instruct* Liv on how to do it," Tel said. "Technically that's not breaking and entering since it belongs to her. It's a motorhome, how hard can it be to break the door lock?"

* * *

"Push it in a bit harder," said Faye.

"Turn it left a smidgen," Tel said.

"No," said Mark, "It should be the other way, lefty-loosey, righty-tighty."

"Will you stop saying that," Brian snapped, "We're not drilling in screws, we're trying to break a lock."

"Sorry for breathing."

"Sorry, I'm just a bit hot and sweaty and we still have to pack the awning up." Brian glanced over at Mark's caravan. His flowery van was parked besides it and the gazebo was down. "You packing up too?"

"I thought I might as well go home, take my few remaining clothes and start afresh."

"It's not moving," Olivia said, standing on top of the steps in front of the door.

"Turn it le-... jab it, Liv, give it a good, hard jab."

Olivia started hacking at the lock with the screwdriver like a serial killer with a knife. Scratches raked down the door and the three men winced.

"A hammer," she said, "I need a hammer."

"That'll damage it," Tel said.

"I don't care, I just want to get inside."

"Okay, out the way," Brian said, turning to them all and saying, "You never saw this, okay?" They all nodded.

Sophie stepped down. Brian didn't need to step up, he was tall enough. With a grunt of exertion, he plunged the screwdriver into the lock and gave it a hefty twist. The door crunched and swung open.

"Oh well done!" Olivia cried, jumping inside. Faye and Sophie followed. Olivia ran up and down the motorhome lifting up the blinds.

"Well," said Sophie, looking around, "At least he didn't wreck the place."

"He couldn't," Olivia said, "It's against his OCD and germ phobia to be reckless, or spontaneous, or have any fun at all." She threw open the wardrobe in the bedroom and found it half empty. "He's taken all his stuff!"

"Trash took itself out," Mark called from outside.

Olivia opened a drawer and gasped. "He's taken my jewellery! And my makeup! And the spare keys for the motorhome! Right," she snarled furiously, "This is war." She pulled her phone out of her bag and dialed a number. "Hello, yes, I'd like to report a stolen bank and credit card, please." To Faye and Sophie she said, "I'll show him who's in charge around here. I don't know why I never thought of it before." She laughed. "He'll be furious when he find out, but serves him right."

"We'll leave you to it," Sophie said, sidling out, followed by Faye.

* * *

Brian and Faye were rolling up the canvas awning, Sophie and Tel were dragging heavy bin bags to the bins, and Mark was finishing loading up his van, when they heard Olivia shouting from inside the motorhome. "What do you mean, have I learnt my lesson? Stop treating me like a child, Richard! I don't care what daddy says, start treating me like a wife or you might find you don't have a wife at all! Yes, I'm serious, I am very, *very* serious. Don't call me again unless you can speak to me with some respect."

She came out of the motorhome, still holding her phone.

"Everything alright?" Mark asked.

"Yes, everything's fine. It's quite nice taking back control, I feel like Superwoman."

"You are Superwoman," Faye shouted over.

"Go, Liv," Sophie cheered.

"Ey up, what's this?" Brian said. He stood up straight and watched two cars coming through the entrance gates.

"New campers?" Faye asked.

He glanced at his watch, "Bit early, we've still got an hour left."

"Keen campers."

"I bet they won't have as much fun as we've had," Sophie sighed.

"Don't start me off," Tel cried, throwing himself against the Airstream with a howl.

The cars crunched slowly along the gravel driveway, one turning off into the field and one turning into the caravan area. It wasn't towing. It came to a stop in the middle and a woman climbed out, a woman they all recognised.

"Hi there," Candice-Marie bellowed in her horsey voice.

"Good grief," Sophie said, "I think we've had a lucky escape, getting out before she arrived."

"How are you all?"

"Good," said Brian, "And you?"

"Much better, thank god." Candice-Marie opened the back door of her car and pulled out a hefty bunch of flowers. She hurried over to Faye and gave them to her. "Just to say thank you for taking care of my children the other day." She dashed back to her car and pulled out another bouquet, running over to Sophie with them. "Just a tiny token of my appreciation," she said. "Sorry if I was such a bore, I was a bit pissed off with the husband, to be honest, but we've made it up now." She hurried back to her car and opened the driver's door. "Thank you," she cried, and got in, started up the engine. They all watched as she performed a torturous 18-point turn, and drove off in a puff of gravel dust. As they watched her disappear through the entrance gates they noticed a crowd forming on the field opposite and a group of people came walking towards them.

"It's the zombie apocalypse," Mark breathed, "Brace yourselves for battle."

"Zombies bearing what look suspiciously like gifts," said Brian, turning to Olivia, who went, "Oh!"

The group crunched their way down the driveway, passed the first two caravans, and headed straight towards Olivia, who was so alarmed she took a couple of steps back. "We've all clubbed together," said the man at the front, holding out a big bouquet, while another held out a giant box of chocolates and yet another held out a smaller bunch of flowers. "I know it's not much, but we just wanted to say thank you, thank you very much for helping us in our hour of need, and for the fabulous party last night. It's been the best camping trip we've ever had."

"Here, here," a couple of people in the group said.

"Oh," said Olivia, struggling to keep hold of all the flowers and the box of chocolates, "You're all very welcome."

"Can we ask your name? We don't even know your name."

"It's Liv," she said, straightening up and lifting her chin. "My name is Liv."

"Well, thank you, Liv." The group turned as one and plodded off again, nodding at the others as they walked passed.

"Ah," breathed Mark, "I feel right at home surrounded by all these beautiful flowers, of the plant variety and the human kind."

"Charmer," Sophie laughed.

"What on earth am I going to do with all these flowers?" Olivia said. "Yours are still at the pub. I'll have to bring them down."

"You'll have plenty of room in the motorhome without Richard taking up all your space," Tel said.

"Yes, I suppose I will."

"You're staying then?" Mark asked.

"Yes, I think I might, have a bit of peace and quiet while I do some thinking and make some phonecalls."

"Me too," Mark grinned.

"I thought you were going home?" Brian said.

"No, no, just moving a few things around. Might stick around for a few more days." He smiled across at Olivia, and she smiled back from behind a forestry of petals.

* * *

"Hello, mummy, how are you? I was just wondering if you fancy taking a little break from all the housework and looking after daddy. Yes, I'm in the Cotwolds, it's beautiful here and the campsite is lovely. Yes, you could stay with me in the motorhome, you probably know Richard's not here, or we could go mad and stay at the on-site pub for a few days, or however long we want. It would be nice for us to spend some time alone together for a change without the men constantly interrupting, we haven't done it in ages, and I want to talk to you about something, something important. It doesn't matter if daddy likes it or not, come if you want to, you deserve a bit of time off and it'll be such fun, just you and me. What do you mean, daddy's taken your car keys? Don't worry, mummy, just pack a bag and call a taxi. I know he'll go mad, but honestly, mummy, does it matter? Well, he may not have the means to punish you afterwards, that's what I want to talk to you about. Just come, mummy, please, be brave."

* * *

"So, this is it then," Sophie said.

They were standing in the middle of the gravel

driveway, looking sadly from one to the other.

"I hate goodbyes," Olivia said.

"Then let's not do it," said Faye.

"We're not taking them home," Brian bawled, "We've only got a three-bedroom semi."

"No, let's say 'See you soon' instead."

"I like that better."

Faye hugged Sophie and said, "See you soon, oh beautiful one."

"See you soon, oh kind one."

"See you soon, Liv," she said, hugging her tightly. Sophie moved in for a group hug, which they held for a very long time.

The men coughed awkwardly.

"Well, see ya, Bri," Mark said, stepping forward to shake hands. Brian grabbed him in a huge bear hug and said, "See ya, Mark. It's been a real pleasure."

"Same here."

"Tel."

"Mark. Brian."

Brian pounded Tel heartily on the back and he almost lost his balance. "Gonna miss you," he laughed at the huge bear of a man.

"Don't," Brian said in a high-pitched voice, waving his giant hand in front of his hairy face, "You'll make me cry."

"Tel," Faye said, hugging him and planting a kiss on the side of his smooth face. "See ya, handsome."

"See ya, Faye. Look after yourselves."

She did the same with Mark, who returned the hug warmly and said, "Stay happy."

"You too."

"Right," Brian bellowed, "Let's get this show on the road. WAGONS, ROLL!"

He got into his car, already hitched to the caravan, which was full of foliage in pots, and started up the car. Faye got into the passenger side and started waving through the window with one hand and wiping tears from her face with the other. Brian slowly pulled forward, turning, the caravan following, exposing a pile of empty cans underneath.

"Oh Brian!" cried Faye, moving to open her door.

"It's okay," Olivia said, "I'll sort it."

"Thank you, you're a star."

Olivia touched the sparkling stars at her ears and smiled.

Brian pulled away.

Tel and Sophie slipped elegantly into the open-topped sportscar, the back seat piled with the memories of their camping trip, held down by the suitcases of inappropriate clothing they'd brought with them what seemed like a lifetime ago.

Olivia and Mark stood side by side on the driveway, in the middle of the empty caravan pitches, watching them and waving frantically as the red car and the towed caravan pulled away.

"You two be good," Brian shouted back as they crunched towards the entrance gates.

"We will. Safe journey."

"Bye," shouted Faye, waving furiously. "Bye."

"Don't do anything I wouldn't do," Tel laughed. Next to him Sophie raised an arm in the air and yelled, "Superwoman! Be anything, do anything! Bye both!"

"Bye," shouted Mark.

"Bye," waved Olivia, her voice breaking as tears slipped down her cheeks.

And then they were gone, leaving Olivia and her motorhome and Mark and his caravan all alone. The empty spaces looked sad, the sudden silence deafening; even the birds seemed to have stopped singing.

Their phones beeped at the same time. They both looked. A WhatsApp message to the camping group from Faye, reading, "Miss you already xx." They laughed, then came another message, this time from Sophie: "We can still see you, B&F, and still miss you. Also, Tel says can you pull over and let us pass, bloody caravanners lol xx."

Olivia replied, "Love you all. Thank you for everything xxx."

"Fancy a cup of tea?" Mark asked, putting a comforting arm across her shoulders.

Olivia smiled and nodded and walked with him back to his caravan.

"Maybe," he added, "We can start reading that book we bought together in the supermarket in funny voices, what was it called?"

"Tipping Point," she said, giggling, "Thuthanne hath a job she lovth, for a both she loathes."

EPILOGUE

Almost One Year Later

Their phones beeped at the same time. Brian didn't look at his, he was in the midst of reading a spectacular gladiatorial battle.

"Bri," Faye said, coming through from the kitchen and staring down at her phone.

"Yes, light of my life?"

"I've just had a message from Sophie on WhatsApp."

"How's she doing?"

"Fine, they're both fine. She says, 'Have you checked your email?'"

"Why?"

"She doesn't say."

Brian heaved himself out of his reclining chair and lumbered towards the computer table in the corner of the room. He turned on the laptop and waited for it to start up, then he clicked on the email icon. Faye came and stood behind him.

"This one?" he said, hovering the cursor over one with the heading: Free Camping Holiday. "Looks like spam."

"Open it and see."

Dear Brian and Faye.

I hope this finds you both well.

We would like to invite you, as our special guests, to stay at our new, improved campsite, The Woodsman Caravan and Camping Park. The site has changed hands since your last visit and has undergone extensive renovations. We would like to offer you one full week's stay on a hardstanding pitch to test out our new facilities, completely free of charge, including meals at our vastly improved pub, The Woodsman.

We hope that we have provided sufficient notice for you to attend our grand reopening on the 19th of July. Please call the number below to confirm.

We very much look forward to seeing you again.

Regards.

The Manager

The Woodsman Campsite

"Ooh," said Faye.

"Could be a con."

"Ring them."

"Now?"

"Yes, why not?" She handed him her phone and he dialed the number on the email.

"Hello," he boomed, "My name is Brian Bennett and I've just read your email inviting us to a free stay on your campsite in July. Brian and Faye Bennett. Yes, I'll hold."

He looked up at Faye, who was starting to get a bit excited, and said, "She's just checking the – Yes, it says here that the pitch will be free, as will the meals in the pub, is that correct? Oh."

"Oh?" said Faye, her excitement dipping.

"That's good, that's very good. Yes, we'd like to confirm our booking." He gave Faye a thumbs up and she gave a little squeal of delight. "Oh really? I didn't know that."

"What?"

"Splendid! We'll see you then. Thanks very much indeed."

"What?" Faye said again, when he ended the call.

"She said that all the people from the hardstanding pitches that were with us last year have also been invited."

"Oh! Olivia? Sophie and Tel? Mark?"

"And Jim too, apparently."

"Oh, that's brilliant!"

"Be nice to see them all again."

"Well, I've seen Olivia and Sophie a few times in Oxford. Oh, I must call them." She toddled back to the kitchen with the phone at her ear, saying, "Yes, we've just read it, are you going? Oh brilliant!"

Brian went back to his book with a big smile beneath his beard.

BOOKS BY THIS AUTHOR

Pitching Up Again! (Book 2)

Sequel to the much-acclaimed and very funny Pitching Up! The Woodsman pub and campsite is under new management, with new staff and improved facilities. The old gang, plus some new characters, return by invitation to 'check it out', and the adventures begin.

Pitching Up In Style! (Book 3)

The camping gang are back together and someone's getting married, in a big house, with lots of guests and lots of chaos. Interfering mothers, a nervous breakdown, miniature meals, revolting guests in both senses of the word, a curry run with a difference, and sleeping in the great outdoors. Funny, emotional, and a whirlwind of delightful celebration.

Tipping Point

Life, work, and all that jazz. It'll make you laugh (a lot). It'll make you cry (a bit). It'll make you go "Ooh" and "Ahh" and "Oh my God!" Emotional drama blitzed with huge dollops of humour.

GET IN TOUCH!

If you enjoyed PITCHING UP! please do leave a rating or a review (for extra brownie points) on Amazon or Goodreads

I thank you.

I'd also be thrilled to hear from you about anything!

Email: deborahaubrey01@gmail.com
Facebook: AuthorDebbieAubrey
Amazon Author Page: Deborah Aubrey

Until next time, ta ta. D x